MISSISSIPPI

MISSISSIPPI
A Documentary History

BRADLEY G. BOND

University Press of Mississippi/*Jackson*

www.upress.state.ms.us

The University Press of Mississippi is a member of the
Association of American University Presses.

Print-on-Demand Edition
⊗

Library of Congress Cataloging-in-Publication Data
Bond, Bradley G., 1963–
Mississippi: a documentary history/Bradley G. Bond.
p. cm.
Includes bibliographical references and index.
ISBN 1-57806-541-0 (alk. paper)
1. Mississippi—History—Sources.
2. Mississippi—History—Chronology. I. Title.
F341.5 .B66 2003
976.2—dc21   2002012157

British Library Cataloging-in-Publication Data available

CONTENTS

INTRODUCTION AND ACKNOWLEDGMENTS

In 1995, I began teaching Mississippi history. I came quickly to understand that students would benefit from having access to documents about the various themes addressed in lectures and reading assignments. Among academic historians, classroom use of primary sources, or first-hand accounts, is a long-accepted practice. In the famous history laboratories of the late nineteenth and early twentieth centuries—the classrooms in which the first two generations of professional historians received their educations—German and German-trained historians used primary sources to develop students' critical thinking skills and to introduce students to the raw material of historical study. Even though the description "history laboratory" has passed out of existence, the concept of history as a hands-on way of knowing remains alive and well. Historians continue to use primary sources to teach myriad topics. Indeed, the National History Standards, which have been adopted by some states and public school districts, recognize that while study of the past teaches students facts, history also teaches students how to analyze primary sources, which is to say the often-competing facts of history. Because of the persisting understanding that students of history must examine primary sources to learn about the past, the interested researcher can locate published collections of primary sources about many topics suited to historical inquiry, including the history of various states. For example, Thomas A. Scott's 1995 book, *Cornerstone's of Georgia History: Documents that Formed the State*, is a model collection of documents illustrative of a state's history. Yet, surprisingly, until now, Mississippi, a place that for real and imagined reasons presents the great sweep of American and certainly southern history better than most other states, has not been the subject of a documentary history.

Teaching students to use primary sources is not the sole justification for publishing a book of documents. The absence of a single-volume history of Mississippi, at least one designed for college students and interested lay readers, also acts as a justification. However good Richard A. McLemore's now dated *History of Mississippi* might be, the two-volume work is too cumbersome and—exceeding 1,200 pages—too daunting to serve the general public and students. While *Mississippi: A Documentary History* is not intended as a substitute for a textbook, it is intended to function as an introduction to the variety of voices that resonate in the Mississippi past. By providing a platform from which some of those voices might be heard, the volume serves as an introduction to the broad outline and complexity of Mississippi history. Thus, the volume is designed to serve a pedagogical function and also to aid readers seeking a better understanding of Mississippi's past. The volume attempts to accomplish its dual mission by focusing on accounts written by individuals who expressed their thoughts and feelings about distinct phenomena or who described their actions at epochal moments in Mississippi's past. My hope is that readers outside the classroom setting will find the volume a useful introduction to Mississippi and its history.

Compiling and organizing the documents in the book was complicated by the quantity and quality of material available at archival repositories. Yet, throughout the research process, I strove to keep uppermost in mind a series of questions. The questions were suggested by a friend who once said that one's understanding of state history could be organized around a few related questions: Was Mississippi an open or closed society? Was it a land of opportunity or a land of oppression? Have people perceived the state as open or closed to individual advancement and the achievement of personal liberty? Those are straightforward questions that seem easy to answer. But, in fact, they are not easy to answer. Any answer that might be given is complicated by considerations of time and place, by the perspective of witnesses upon whose testimony historians rely, and by the perspective of the historian who seeks answers. Furthermore, they are questions that seek to measure the ambition of individuals, their aspirations, and the ways in which Mississippi (as a society, political entity, and culture) hindered or aided efforts to achieve personal goals. What emerges in the book then is a set of voices that describe Mississippi as people wanted it to exist, as people imagined that it existed, and perhaps even, as it actually existed. In short, it is a book in which observers of the state talk about their individual identity as Mississippians and ultimately, the collective, if contested, identities of Mississippi. Additionally, readers will find throughout the volume various themes that link chapters, epochs, and people. Those themes, among others, include: religion, violence, education, gender roles, and race. Readers should look for those themes, and they should explore the rhetoric, metaphors, and arguments that link documents in different chapters. For even though the voices evident in the documents are varied, the recurrent themes suggest certain peculiarities of the Mississippi past as played out in reality and in the popular imagination.

The type of documents included in the volume reflect a personal preference for certain varieties of primary sources. I did not include certain types of primary sources, like representations of Native American pottery and other artifacts of material culture, courthouse records, census records, selections from published memoirs and novels, and the list could go on. Rather, I have privileged a particular type of written documents: documents that are (for the most part) previously-unpublished, located in archives or out of the way places, and most importantly, documents that, I trust—because they "tell a story" in a familiar form—might be most easily understood and analyzed by the greatest number of people. While courthouse and census records, for example, can reveal much about the past, they often lack the narrative structure that makes them accessible; pragmatic considerations kept me from including twentieth-century fiction and memoirs. Finally, I also assigned a high priority to documents that could be linked in a cluster that became a chapter and documents that could be linked to selections in other chapters.

Throughout the volume, I have attempted to restrain my voice, offering editorial introductions to the documents only to contextualize the voices that matter. That statement is not intended to suggest that the documents speak "The Truth" or that they speak for themselves. It does not deny that the editor, by choosing particular texts, plays a significant role in shaping the conclusions that readers can draw based on their readings of the documents. Instead, it is simply to remind the reader that the editor has tried to emphasize the disperate voices that can be heard in Mississippi's past.

Spanish and French voices echo in the first two chapters; the voices of Native Americans appear in the second chapter as well. The promise of Mississippi and the fluid world of European-Native American relations function as the primary themes of the two chapters. The third chapter on antebellum white society, and the fourth chapter about slavery offer thoughtful readers much to consider about habits of mind and lifestyles in the two distinct, but intimately connected, communities. The fifth chapter, which focuses on unionists and secessionists in the late 1850s and early 1860s, points to the role of slavery in the secession movement; and the sixth chapter about violence and free labor in the Age of Reconstruction portrays the desperation of black and white Republicans as they fought to secure liberty for ex-slaves. The next three chapters are likewise related. One chapter focuses on efforts to reform late nineteenth-century Mississippi as it entered the mainstream

of American economic life while weighted down by its old notions of race, gender, and class. One chapter focuses on the most significant effort at reform undertaken in the period, the effort that resulted in the disfranchisement of most African Americans but that paved the way for suffrage for white women. The final chapter in the cluster of three focuses on the world of Jim Crow that resulted from the efforts to reform Mississippi. The eleventh chapter examines the condition of Mississippi during the Great Depression and the role of the federal government and others in aiding Mississippians. The twelfth and thirteen chapters focus on the era of the modern Civil Rights Movement: Chapter Twelve tracks black and white reactions to the U.S. Supreme Court's *Brown* decision; Chapter Thirteen focuses on events that occurred during Freedom Summer, the highwater mark of the Movement in Mississippi. The final two chapters are more contemporary. Chapter Fourteen describes efforts to diversify Mississippi's economy, and the final chapter captures voices heard during the recent debate over the state flag.

Finally, like all books, this one is designed to be read. Yet, unlike a John Grisham novel or a historical monograph, the volume can not be consumed in one mighty gulp. Instead, listening to the voices requires a different pace, an attentive student's pace. The documents should not be merely read but dissected.

As I worked on *Mississippi: A Documentary History*, I benefitted from the assistance of many people. For their aid and support, I am grateful. Through the office of the Provost at the University of Southern Mississippi, I received a Summer Grant for the Improvement of Instruction, which allowed me to begin collecting documents. One of my colleagues in the Department of History at the University of Southern Mississippi, Charles Bolton, provided many of the documents used in Chapter Twelve. Three former graduate assistants— Lawrence Keitt, Jennifer Ford, Chris Gilcrease—helped track down elusive primary sources, as did librarians at archival repositories. I also owe a debt of gratitude to my former students in Mississippi history.

As I gathered documents for inclusion in the volume, I asked them to read certain selections, analyze the documents, and comment on their usefulness. They allowed me to turn the classroom into an old-fashioned laboratory; in the process, I was able to "field test" many of the chapters in the volume. Brenda Eagles and James G. Hollandsworth read a large portion of a near final draft of the volume. Their comments were extraordinarily useful. Trent Watts read the entire manuscript. He saved me from committing several errors of fact and made countless suggestions for improving the book. I incorporated most of his suggestions and undoubtedly erred by ignoring others. Brenda, Jim, and Trent helped shape the book in important ways. I will long remain in their debt and forever grateful for their criticism.

Near the end of the publication process, Kristy T. Wittman tracked down certain elusive information. Like most historians, she's a fabulous detective—patient, persistent, and able to deduce quickly where to find information and how to make sense of the sources.

As always, Deborah has been supportive of the project and for that I am appreciative.

Kenneth G. McCarty provided a starting point for this project; indeed, the idea of a documentary history was one that Ken, himself a dogged researcher and intrepid collector of archival material, initially suggested. Some of the documents that appear in the volume came from countless files of material that fill his office. Because he has inspired two generations of students at the University of Southern Mississippi and because he continues to shape understanding of the state's past through his editorship of the *Journal of Mississippi*, I dedicate the volume to him.

MISSISSIPPI

Chapter 1

EXPECTATIONS AND ENCOUNTERS

In the sixteenth century, the Lower Mississippi Valley captured the attention of Spain. With colonies scattered throughout the Caribbean and Latin America, the Spanish crown and Spanish adventurers looked to the northern shore of the Gulf of Mexico for new empires to conquer. Early Spanish explorers of the region reported Native American rumors that a fountain of youth and cities of gold might be found in the southeast. They also reported that a great river emptied into the Gulf of Mexico, igniting among Spaniards a lust to locate the river that they hoped would provide a shortcut to Asia. In 1537, King Charles V of Spain named Hernando de Soto governor of Florida. Soto was a conquistador and slave trader, who had achieved extraordinary wealth through his exploits in Central and South America. Upon his appointment, Soto made a reconnaissance of his dominion, hoping to find, as he had further south, an abundance of gold, silver, and other riches. Soto expected that accomplishing his mission would require a long time and necessitate the subjugation of Native Americans. Consequently, he traveled with 650 men (mostly soldiers but also priests and skilled craftsmen), more than 200 horses, hundreds of pigs, and dogs specially trained for warfare. Between 1539 and 1542, Soto carved a circuitous route through the southeastern part of the United States, leaving in his wake a legacy of death, disease, and distrust.

For all concerned, the Soto expedition proved disastrous. Indeed, Soto himself died near the banks of the Mississippi River.

More than one hundred and fifty years passed before a permanent European settlement appeared within the boundaries of the state now called "Mississippi." But, it was not the Spanish who established a lasting colony. In 1699, Pierre Le Moyne Sieur d'Iberville, a French naval officer long associated with the French colony of Canada, landed at the modern-day city of Biloxi and ordered a fort to be built on the east side of the Biloxi River. Fort Maurepas, located at the modern city of Ocean Springs, became the first capital of the Louisiana colony. French royal interest in establishing a presence in the Lower Mississippi Valley owed to anxieties about Spanish intrusion into the valley from Mexico and English intrusion across the Appalachian Mountains. Should either Spain or Britain occupy the valley, Louis XIV feared, his hold on Canada and the Illinois Country would be threatened. Thus, the crown primarily intended the nascent Louisiana colony to serve as an anchor for established French colonies further north, though, of course, the crown also hoped to extract wealth from Louisiana. French intentions for the colony shaped the nature of relations with Native Americans in Louisiana, and the long French experience of dealing with Indians in Canada offered early settlers in Louisiana a model for establishing relations with indigenous people. Even though the French, like the Spanish, believed Native Americans to be mere savages, they, unlike Soto, sought to establish a colony and thus needed to cooperate and negotiate with, not only to subjugate, Indians.

A GENTLEMAN OF ELVAS[1]

The following account of the Soto expedition begins with the Spaniards crossing the Tombigbee River near what would become the location of Cotton Gin Port. Much to the lament of the Chickasaw and other Indians in the area, Soto remained in Mississippi for much of the winter and spring of 1540. The account was written by a member of the Soto expedition, who is known only as the Gentleman of Elvas.

. . . Having crossed the river next day, December 17, the governor reached Chicaca[2], a small town of twenty houses. After they were in Chicaca they suffered great hardships and cold, for it was already winter, and most of the men were lodged in the open field in the snow before having any place where they could build houses. This land was very well peopled, the population being spread out as was that of Mavilla.[3] It was fertile and abounding in maize, most of this being still in the fields. The amount necessary for passing the winter was gathered. Certain Indians were captured, among whom was one who was greatly esteemed by the cacique [chief][4]. By means of an Indian the governor sent word to the cacique that he desired to see him and wished his friendship. The cacique came to offer himself to him, together with his person, land, and vassals. He said that he would cause two caciques to come in peace. A few days afterward they came with him accompanied by their Indians, one being named Alimamu and the other Nicalasa. They presented the governor with one hundred and fifty rabbits and some clothing of their land, namely blankets and skins. The cacique of Chicaca came to visit him frequently and sometimes the governor ordered him summoned and sent him a horse to go and come. He [the cacique] made complaint to him [the governor], that one of his vassals had risen against him, withholding his tribute, and asked that he protect him against him, saying that he was about to go to seek him in his land and punish him as he deserved—all pretense, for it was planned that while the governor went with him and the camp was divided into two parts, some would attack the governor and others those who remained in Chicaca. He [the cacique] went to the town where he lived and came with two hundred Indians with their bows and arrows. The governor took thirty horse and eighty foot and went to Sauechuma,[5] as the province of the principal man was called, who he [the cacique] told him [the governor] had rebelled against him. They found an enclosed town which had been abandoned by the Indians, and those who were with the cacique set fire to the houses in order to conceal their treachery. But since the men taken by the governor were very watchful and prudent, as well as those who remained in Chicaca, on that occasion they did not dare attack us. The governor invited the cacique and certain of the principal Indians [to visit him] and gave them some pork to eat. And although they were not accustomed to it, they lusted after it so much that Indians would come nightly to certain houses a crossbow shot away from the camp where the hogs were sleeping and kill and carry off as many as they could. Three Indians were seized in the act, two of whom the governor ordered to be shot with arrows and the hands of the other cut off. In that condition he sent him to the cacique, who expressed regret that they had troubled the governor and was glad that justice had been executed on them. He [the cacique] was in an open plain a half league from where the Christians were. Four of the horsemen went thither without orders, namely Francisco Osorio, a servant of the Marquis de Astorga, named Reynoso, and two servants of the governor, one his page, named Ribera, and the other his chamberlain, named Fuentes. They seized some skins and blankets from the Indians, at which the latter were greatly offended and abandoned their houses. The governor learned of it and ordered them [the four horsemen] seized. Francisco Osorio and the chamberlain he sentenced to death, as being the principals, and all to the loss of their possessions. The friars and secular priests and other principal persons importuned him to leave Francisco Osorio alive, and to moderate the sentence, which he refused to do for anyone. And while he was already giving the order to take them to the public place to behead them, certain Indians came who being sent by the cacique to make complaint against them. Juan Ortiz,[6] at the request of Baltasar de Gallegos and other persons, changed their words, telling the governor that the cacique said that he had learned that his Lordship had seized those Christians on his account; that they were not guilty nor had they done any wrong to him; that if he [De Soto] would do him a favor, he should let them go free. To the Indians, he [Ortiz] was to say that the governor said that he had seized them and would give them such punishment that it would be an example to others. The governor ordered the prisoners released. As soon as March was come, he determined to leave Chicaca and asked the cacique for two hundred tamemes [burden bearers]. The latter replied to him that he would talk it over with his principal men. On Tuesday, the eighth of March, the governor went to where the cacique was to ask him for the tamemes. He said he would send them next day. As soon as the governor came to Chicaca, he told Luis de Moscoso, the maestre de campo, the Indians looked ill-disposed to him, and that night he should keep careful watch, which the latter heeded but slightly. The Indians came at the quarter of the modorra [i.e. the second watch] in four companies, each company coming from a different direction. As soon as they were perceived, they beat a drum and with loud cries rushed forward, and so rapidly that they arrived at the same time as the spies who had carelessly gone out a distance from the camp; and when they were perceived by those who were within the town, half the houses were burning from the fire which they kindled. That night, three horsemen were by chance at watch, two of whom were of low degree, the most worthless of the camp, and the other was the governor's nephew, who until then had been considered a good man. There he proved himself as cowardly as each one of them, for they all fled, and the Indians not finding any resistance came and set fire to the town and awaited the Christians outside behind the doors, who came out of the houses without having time to arm themselves; and as they rose, maddened by the noise and blinded by the smoke and flame of the fire, they did not know where they were going nor did they succeed in getting their arms or in putting saddle on horse; neither did they see the Indians who were shooting at them. Many of the horses were burned in their stables, and those which could break their halters freed themselves. The confusion and rout were of such a nature that each one fled whenever it seemed safest, without any one resisting the Indians. But God who punishes His own as is His pleasure, and in the greatest needs and dangers holds them in His hand, blinded the Indians so that they might not see what they had done, and they thought the horses which were running about loose were the horsemen gathering together to assault them. The governor alone, and with a soldier called Tapia, got mounted and attacked the Indians, and giving the first one he met a thrust with his lance, went down and his saddle with him; for in the haste he had badly fastened the girth and fell from his horse. All the men who were afoot and were in flight through a wood outside the town, sought protection there. And as it was night and the Indians thought the horses, as above said, were mounted men who were attacking them, they fled away and only one remained there dead, namely, the one the governor had struck with his lance. The town was consumed by fire. A woman was burned there who had gone there with her husband. Both of them going outside the house, she returned for some pearls which they had forgotten; and when she tried to get out, already the fire was at the door and she could not, and her husband could not help her. Three other Christians got away from their houses so badly hurt by the fire that one of them died three days later, and each of the other two was carried for many days in his bed upon some poles which the Indians carried on their shoulders, for they could not have journeyed in any other way. In that turn of fortune eleven Christians and fifty horses died. Of the swine, one hundred were left, and four hundred were burned. If, perchance, any one still had any clothing left from the fire at Mavilla, it was now all burned up in that place [Chicaca]; and many were naked as they had no time to snatch their jerkins. There they endured great suffering from the cold, for which they got relief in large fires. The whole night was passed turning from one side to the other without sleeping, for if they were warmed on one side they froze on the other. They managed to make some mats out of dry grass woven together, and placed one mat below and the other above. Many laughed at this contrivance, but afterward necessity forced them to do likewise. The Christians were become so demoralized together with the lack of saddles and weapons, which had been burned, that if the Indians had returned the second night, they would have routed them with little trouble. They moved thence to the village where the cacique usually lived as it was a site in the open field. A week later they had made many saddles and lances. . . .

IBERVILLE'S EXPLORATIONS, 1699[7]

Pierre Le Moyne, Sieur d'Iberville was born in 1661 in the Canadian village that would become Montreal. As a young man, he received a commission in the French navy. In the 1680s and 1690s, his exploits against the British on Hudson Bay and along the Atlantic coast of North America earned him a reputation among his enemies for ruthlessness and cruelty. For his achievements as a naval officer, the crown commissioned Iberville to establish a colony near the mouth of the Mississippi River. In 1699, Iberville landed at the modern-day city of Biloxi.

February 10th [1699]. About seven o'clock in the morning, wind in the southeast, we set sail and steered northwest for 3 leagues.[8] We came in, under shelter of an island or the point of an island [Ship Island], where we are protected from winds from the south-southwest, south-southeast and east by the island and from the northeast and north and northwest by the mainland, 3¼ leagues from us, and from the west and southwest by an island 2 leagues away. We have found no less than 23 feet of water, and we anchored a cannon's shot off the island in 26 feet of water. The *Francois*, being unable to come in, is anchored at the entrance.

The *11th*. We warped a little farther east and put our animals ashore, and we have men busy rigging up the Biscayan[9] that M. De Surgere has on his ship, and I am making ready to leave with the Biscayans and go and discover the Myssysypy. For a part of the day it was misty.

The *12th*. At noon we saw a column of smoke to the northeast, 5¼ leagues from here, on the shore of an island.

The *13th*. I crossed over the land 4 leagues north of here in my Biscayan, with eleven men, and my brother in a bark canoe with two men. I went ashore and there found two trails of Indians made yesterday, which I followed overland with one man, my brother coming along in the bark canoe, and the Biscayan following half a league behind us, to avoid frightening the Indians. I followed them 2 leagues, going in an easterly direction; here night caught me, and I made camp. From the ships over to this land it is fully 4 leagues, due north. Between the two, I found 15 feet of muddy water. The approach to the shore is quite shallow: half a league off shore, 4 feet of water. This coast runs west by south and east by north. The trees here are very fine, mixed: We are seeing many plum trees in bloom; tracks of turkeys; partridges, which are no bigger than quail; hares like the ones in France; some rather good oysters.

February 14th. I continued to follow the tracks of the Indians, having left at the place where I spent the night two axes, four knives, two packages of glass beads, a little vermilion;[10] for I was sure that two Indians who came at sunrise to watch me from a distance of 300 yards would come there after we left. A league and a half from the spot where I spent the night, walking as on the day before, I noticed a canoe crossing over to an island and several Indians waiting for it there. They joined five other canoes, which crossed over to the land to the north. As the land where I was separated from them by a bay 1 league wide and 4 leagues long, I got into my canoe and pursued the canoes and overtook them as they were landing on the shore. All the Indians fled into the woods, leaving their canoes and baggage. I landed 500 yards beyond them and went across land with one man to their canoes, where I found an old man who was too sick to stand. We talked by means of signs. I gave him food and tobacco; he made me understand that I should build a fire for him. This I did and, besides, made a shelter, near which I placed him along with his baggage and a number of bags of Indian corn and beans that the Indians had in their canoes. I made him understand that I was going half a league from there to spend the night. My longboat joined me there. I sent my brother and two Canadians after the Indians who had fled, to try to make them come back or to capture one. Toward evening he brought a woman to me whom he had caught in the woods 3 leagues from there. I led her to the old man and left her, after giving her several presents and some tobacco to take to her men and have them smoke.

The 15th. Three of those Indians and two women, having been met by one of my Canadians, came along to sing the calumet[11] of peace to me. The old man died about ten o'clock in the morning. One of those men sang, carrying a little plank of whitened wood, which he held up in the air, offering it to me. I met them at their canoes, where they made a sagamite[12] of Indian corn to feast us; I sent for something with which to feast them, in return, and gave them presents of axes, knives, shirts, tobacco, pipes, tinder boxes, and glass beads. More of their men joined them. They went off and spent the night half a league from there.

The 16th. In the morning, during foggy and rainy weather, I went overland and joined them. There I found only ten men with their weapons, entirely naked, wearing *braguets.* All their canoes and baggage were gone, indicating to me that they were suspicious of me. We smoked together all over again, although I never smoke. I persuaded three to go aboard our ships, having left with the Indians my brother and two Canadians as hostages. I got to my ship at two o'clock in the afternoon. There they were greatly astonished at all they saw. I had some cannon shots fired for them, which they greatly wondered at.

The 17th. At noon I went back and joined my brother and brought the three Indians back, who belong to the nation of the Annochy and Moctoby.[13] They are 3½ days from their village. They mentioned to me the name of a village of their neighbors, Chozeta. They are on a river the mouth of which is 9 leagues east; they call it Pascoboula. I gave them several presents to take to their nations. They assured me that there are 4 fathoms of water in their river.

At six o'clock in the evening I got to the place where my brother was. Here I found a chief of the Baggily with twenty-one of his men and some Mougoulascha,[14] who had got there as early as yesterday evening. They live on the bank of the Myssysypy and, being on a hunt on this side, came on at the noise of the cannon to see who we were. They caressed my brother many times; he gave them some tobacco and feasted them that night. They wanted to know whether he had come in the canoe they saw he had and whether he was of the people of the Upper Myssysypy, which in their language they call Malbanchya. He told them yes.

When we got to where my brother was, the chief or captain of the Baggily came to the seashore to show me friendliness and courtesy in their fashion, which is, being near you, to come to a stop, pass their hands over their faces and breasts, and then pass their hands over yours, after which they raise them toward the sky, rubbing them together again and embracing again. I did the same thing, having watched it done to the others. They did the same thing to the Annocchy, their friends. After our meeting and amenities on both sides, we went to my brother's tent, to which all the Baggily made their way to show friendliness to me and all my men, all embracing one another. I had them smoke, and together we all smoked an iron calumet I had, made in the shape of a ship with the white flag adorned with fleur-de-lis and ornamented with glass beads. Then [I gave it to them] along with a present of axes, knives, blankets, shirts, glass beads, and other things valued among them, making them understand that with this calumet I was uniting them to the French and that we were from now on one. I feasted them with sagamite made with plums and had them drink brandy and wine, of which they took very little, marveling greatly at the brandy that we set on fire. About eight o'clock at night the chief and seven others came and sang the calumet to me, giving me a present of three of their blankets made of muskrat, making me the ally of four nations west of the Myssysypy, which are the Mougoulascha, Quascha, Toutymascha, Yagueneschyto;[15] and east of the river, of the Byloccy, Moctoby, the Ouma, Pascoboula, Thecloel, Bayacchyto, Amylcou.[16] At my camp they sang till midnight, and my men sang with them.

February 18th. When we showed the Indians some maps in order to learn where the east fork of the Myssysypy was, we decided that they were indicating that it was the Pascoboula River, which they marked for us. I later learned that they wished to show that, from that river, they went to the Myssysypy by way of rivers that connect with one another. I made them understand that I was going in my longboat to the mouth of it to take soundings and that I would come back and join them. My brother and three men, in the bark canoe, would stay with them. The chief of the Baggily came to me to tell me that he was going hunting for buffalo and turkeys and in four nights would be back at the place where I had slept the first time I went ashore and that there we would feast one another. I set out for the Pascoboula River, which I could not get to because of a head wind. I turned back, expecting to find the Indians again and keep them from going hunting and persuade them to come with me to the west branch, for I could not see how this Pascoboula River could be big enough to have sufficient water at its mouth, which broadened too much. I found that they had gone. I spent this night ashore.

The 19th. At noon I proceeded to my ship with all my men to get ready to set out for the west branch of the Myssysypy upon the arrival of the Indians. That day I got 16 casks of wine from M. De Chasteaumorand for 150 livres; 10 small barrels of flour; 97 pounds of butter, so that I would not lack provisions, not knowing what I would do on the coast.

The 21st. At noon two columns of smoke became visible at the rendezvous I had given the Baggily. I had four cannon shots fired to let them know that I saw them, although the rendezvous was not until tomorrow.

February 22nd. We set out, M. De Surgere and I, to go to the rendezvous in the two Biscayans. We got there about noon. We found nothing there. The columns of smoke came from fires sweeping through the woods. . . .

February 25th. M. De Surgere returned to his ship, and I sent my brother in the bark canoe to within 2½ leagues of the rendezvous to see whether he could get any news of the Indians. He found two of them and two women. One, an Annocchy, came with him to see me and spent the night with us. He made me understand that the Baggily had gone back and had spent only two nights with them and that they had made some columns of smoke, which we had seen, to notify us that they had set out from there during the morning, the wind being right for them to go to the Malbanchya, and they had no provisions at all.

The 26th. I sent the Indian back to his camp, and I came on to my ship, having ordered MM. Desordys and Lavilature, sent by M. De Surgere to me in the two feluccas,[17] to go 6 leagues east and examine the Pascoboula River and take soundings of it and proceed from there to the ship. I got to the ship at two o'clock in the afternoon and made ready to set out tomorrow.

The 27th. I set out from the ships with two Biscayans and two bark canoes with the Sieur de Sauvole, a sublieutenant on the *Marin*, and my brother, and the Recollect Father, and forty-eight men, with provisions for twenty days, to go to the Myssysypy, which the Indians of this area call Malbanchy. . . .

JEAN DE SAUVOLE[18]

When Iberville left for France in May 1699, he named Jean de Sauvole "Commandant of the Post of Biloxi." Even though Sauvole kept a journal during his tenure, he long remained a mysterious figure. Until Jay Higginbotham published his findings in *Fort Maurepas: The Birth of Louisiana* (1998), scholars did not even know his Christian name. The young ensign had enrolled in the French navy in 1683 at Toulon and accompanied Iberville on his first expedition to Louisiana. In August 1701, Sauvole died of a fever.

M. d'Iberville, having given me the command of the fort which he had constructed, I have labored our men to make shelter for protection from the injuries of the elements; that which he had not been able to do before his departure, pressed by the small amount of supplies that he had. Their lodging being finished, I made them enclose the storehouse

that had been erected; afterwards, we made a hospital, and we gave ourselves as many days around the fort as we could, in felling the trees of
the surrounding area which are of a prodigious size. I have devoted
myself to begin to know the fort and the weaknesses of each man, to
establish discipline which is necessary for everyone to observe. It will
not be without pain, especially to the heavy-set men, who have never
had the least smattering. Our chaplain has said daily, as he did on our
ships, the usual prayers of the Mass. M. de Bienville and Levaseaur, and
M. Bordeneau, our chaplain have given us very good example.

The 17th of May, we saw smoke to the west of the fort, from the
other side of the roadstead. I sent a canoe to see what it was—our men
brought the chief of the Bayogoulas with three other savages. I gave
them the best reception that was possible for me, and put the garrison
on the alert; which did little to alleviate their fright. As it was the first
of their visits in this fort, I have given homage to the chief, and let him
eat to the point of surfeity: it is their biggest pleasure. Fortunately, this
day our hunters had killed three deer. Having put a shirt on the body
of each man, I showed them the fort: They were surprised that in such
a small time, we had put such big pieces of wood above one another;
our cannons have caused them no little surprise; they have found them
monstrous, although they were only pieces of eight. I have made two
shots of the cannon, in front of them. They did not know where to
hide they were so frightened of them. They spent a very peaceful
night among us, except for a scare that the sergeant gave them with
his halberd[19] when coming to take his order, and whispering in the
ear of the major; that made them wonder profoundly. Having noticed
this, I reassured them with embraces.

The next day, in the morning, they told me that their wives were
on the opposite shore and they would be delighted to let them come
see the fort. The chief seeing them debark made me a sign to put the
soldiers on the alert and looked in the fort, hollering that his wife was
there, and that they must give her the same homage as they give him.
I hadn't considered that the savages were sensitive in that matter. After

having stayed three or four days among us, they left. I gave them two of our young boys to learn their language; they will send one of them to the Ommas and they will keep the other with them. This chief calls himself Antobiscania. He is the craftiest savage that I have yet seen, and the one who goes to the farthest ends (to achieve his purpose). He told me that the blanket that M. d'Iberville had given him, had met the same fate as his house which had been burned. Although I didn't believe any of that, I gave him a red cloth or hood; but I made it clear to him that I just gave it to him so that he would take better care of the young man that I had placed in their confidence. I gave to each one of the others small presents, some beads, some knives, some axes; and by this I enticed them to conduct M. de Bienville to the Quinipissas, to whom I also sent a present of a hood, of a calumet, of beads, and other things to win such people. The chief of the Bayogoulas meditated a long time whether to go or not, telling me that he could not assure us that the others would not kill our people. I told him that we were not afraid of anyone and in case they took a false step, I would go and kill them all. Seeing that he could not keep him [Bienville] from going there, he decided to relent. He said all of this only in view of having everything for himself and not to give us knowledge of any other nation. . . .

I sent [a party] to reconnoiter the bay of Mobile the ninth of June, and the fort of Pensacola; to see if the Spanish had abandoned it for lack of food, as their deserters had assured us, which they hadn't done at all according to the report of M. de Bienville who has been there. . . .

I can only occupy our people two hours in the morning and two hours in the evening, because of the great heat, to clear the land and to burn around the fort, so hot it has become. The majority of our people have been hit with dysentery. The bad waters without doubt have caused it; again, one cannot find it when one needs it. In regard to the land, it is certainly unproductive. It is nothing but burning sand—our men have planted very often, and unprofitably. The trees are at the bottom pierced by worms, and our bastions, the long-boats have been damaged. It has not been without effort that we have put them back in shape, nobody having been prepared to do it, and once again, that wasn't too good; I admit very ingeniously the responsibility for that which comes to my knowledge. . . .

The 13th [of July], the chief of the Pascoboulas has come singing the calumet of peace. He had at his side seven men of the same nation. I have never seen savages less inhibited. They have embraced us, something that I have never seen the others do; they rub their hand tenderly on their breast at their approach, having lifted their arms to the sky. They have brought me, as a present, some deer-skins, which I have given as presents to our hunters to make Indian shoes, a little smoked meat and half of a deer. They have gone after having received their presents, like the others. . . .

The 27th [of August], I have sent two bark canoes, commanded by M. de Bienville, with six men, including himself, to go make a portage on the river Mississippi, and to go down all the way to its mouth. He has found more water in the channel where we came up than in the other ones; he has gone up to the Bayogoulas and to the Quinipissas. He calls the Mogoulachas Quinipissas, because we want to revive this nation, whose chief is really a Quinipissa.

He has found these two nations very sad about the loss of several men that the Ommas have killed, having surprised them during the time they were working in their fields, according to what the small [French] boy who is with them has said. I do not know the other causes of their differences.

In descending the river to within twenty-three leagues of its mouth, M. de Bienville has met an English frigate of twelve cannons to which he has mad opposition, according to the order that I have given him. It was the 15th of September. The captain of the frigate, named Bank,[20] confessed naively that he had only investigated this river to make an establishment for a company there; but seeing that we had taken it before them, and believing us to be established further up, he has taken the path to go back, assuring us that we would see him again next year. . . .

The 17th of October, there has come a pirogue of Pascoboulas, in which there were thirteen savages, among them there was one, who came from the nation of the Choctaws, which he told us was very numerous, and has forty-five villages. He talks about it with much reverence and fear. He made clear to us that the Choctaws and the English had had dealings together. The English were going, he said, to Chicachas.[21] I believe very well that from Caroline he could have passed by the Chicassas, where two of their men are established, according to the report of M. d'Avion, one of the missionaries who has been here, who has been to the Chicachas with them, leaving together from Tonicas[22] where they have been to buy some slaves from the other savages. The frigate that one has found in the Mississippi could well have given a rendezvous to other Englishmen to meet at the base of the river, if it is true that the English and the Chactas[23] have done battle. A savage had on him a blue blanket that he claims to have found near a dead man, which makes me believe it. The Chactas are enraged because they [the English] buy their slaves from other savages.

The more I know of these kinds of nations, the more I am struck by their poverty. If the hope of finding some mines is not realized, the Court will not be able to be reimbursed for the expenses it had to make, unless it permits the descent of the beaver trade by here, which will not be ruinous for Canada, for it will always have its source and the same abundance one would do much damage by this to the English.

The wool of the ox [buffalo] is still an article not to neglect. The savages, in a short time, would make a heap, instead of losing it, after they have killed the animals, they would take it down for nothing, or at least for some trifles.

M. d'Iberville informed me furthermore of his successful entrance into the river that he has climbed for eighteen leagues. He has chosen a land although very low which is not flooded, from the report of a savage that he had after having given orders and squared the posts for house where he has to put six cannons. He went to the Bayogoulas from where his letter is dated. M. [Henri] de Tonty[24] who has joined him at the place of the establishment that he has made, is of his expedition. He came down from the Illinois where I had written him by the missionaries to tell him approximately the time that our ships might arrive . . . M. [Pierre-Charles] Lesuer stays at the Bayogoulas with his fifteen men, until the return of M. d'Iberville. I wish that good luck accompanies him on this occasion for the good of the King, and that he finds something to compensate himself for the expenses that he has made. It is certain that it is impossible to give oneself more trouble than he has done. Nothing is too difficult for him; if there is any possibility of him accomplishing something, one can surely count on it. I am outdone from not being part of the expedition by the information that I could have drawn out of it. I hope that the Court will put me on a firm footing next year, if one establishes on the river, to make some discoveries which I am not able to do here, because the surroundings are so inconsiderable.

I dare to flatter myself that the savages will do blindly everything that we want, although they are very lazy; they have confidence in what we tell them. I have taken the chief of the Mobille to see the ships, since the departure of M. d'Iberville He was ecstatic to see such big contraptions, and he has been very satisfied with the reception that one has made him. He had with him two Chactas and the chief of the Pascoboulas also. Being back at the fort, they have told the others that they had been on the ships that went up to the clouds, that there were more than fifty villages on each one and crowds that one cannot pass through, and one made them climb down to a place where they did not see sun or moon; they have left to go to the Chactas to teach them these wonders. I hope that they induce them to return. . . .

The other traversier has left the 18th [perhaps January] for Pensacola and for the Apalaches,[25] by order of M. d'Iberville who will reclaim those people there. He writes a letter of sincerity to each governor, and give them notice of the intention that the English have for establishing themselves in these countries. I am of a great impatience for the reception that these gentlemen will give our boat, and how they will receive our honorable men. I have also written to the Governor of Pensacola.

Our bastions will be well advanced at the arrival of M. d'Iberville, for the posts are entirely square for the two bastions; that of the west is half made, its posts are extremely heavy. I don't neglect one moment to put them in the state that is necessary. There have died, in the fort, four men who have carried the disease of France. Since the arrival of the ships, there have died three of those who had arrived here sick.

In regard to the pearls, I have not seen any real ones. A man of integrity has told me of having seen a real one which came from the river of Colapissas.[26] He is certain that there are many, according to the report of the savages.

Chapter 2

FRENCHMEN, AFRICANS, AND INDIANS IN COLONIAL LOUISIANA

After establishing a fort along the coast of the Gulf of Mexico in 1699, French and Canadian soldiers began to spread out into the interior of the Lower Mississippi Valley. Large-scale immigration to the vast Louisiana colony, which included the modern state of Mississippi, however, did not occur immediately. For much of the first two decades of the colony's existence, the French crown considered Louisiana a costly and unsuccessful debacle. In 1717, hoping to turn Louisiana into a prosperous enterprise, the crown gave the colony to the Company of the Indies, a business venture headed by the Scottish financier John Law. Where the crown had hoped to create a peasant's paradise of small farmers, Law's vision for the colony focused on the creation of plantations. A scheme that allowed investors huge concessions of land helped to implement his vision, as pockets of settlement, particularly along the rivers, began to appear. But, outside of cities like Mobile and New Orleans, settlements remained small and oriented toward agricultural production, though they also served as home to military outposts.

One of the early French settlements was located in the vicinity of modern-day Natchez. For a number of years, Europeans, slaves, and Indians near the

French Fort Rosalie on the Mississippi River at Natchez lived in an uneasy peace. Yet, in 1728, fed up with the land-hungry French, the Natchez infiltrated the fort and with the help of slaves wiped out the majority of the European population living there. Over the next five years, the French expended much energy tracking down perpetrators of the so-called Natchez massacre.

The Natchez massacre and the French effort at retaliation shaped French-Native American relations for many years. Prior to the massacre, the French had shown a tendency toward dealing with Choctaws rather than Chickasaws, if largely because the latter were firmly entrenched in the English network of trade that radiated from the east coast colonies. To the French, it was important to cultivate Choctaw allies as trading partners and as military/diplomatic allies capable of squashing English expansion across the Appalachian Mountains; likewise, Choctaws acquiesced to French entreaties of friendship to obtain an ally against their rivals, the Chickasaw. Throughout much of the 1730s and 1740s, French officials in Louisiana and Choctaws cooperated to seek out the remnants of the Natchez group and to block Chickasaw forays against French and Choctaw traders. The relationship between the French and Choctaws was complicated by the fact that each Choctaw village was relatively autonomous, and achieving a uniform system of Indian policy was therefore impossible, even when dealing with only one language group, since the interests of Choctaw groups often conflicted. The documents that follow illustrate the contentious nature of French, Choctaw, and Chickasaw relations, particularly the complications that stemmed from the Natchez massacre and English efforts to expand their political and economic domain westward.

RÉGIS DU ROULLET, 1731[1]

Régis du Roullet was a French military officer who lived among the
Choctaws, serving as an emissary or agent of the French colony.
His report not only reveals much about French-Native American relations
but also the role of African slavery in the colony.

. . . On the fifth [of March 1731] the three negroes entered my house as I was speaking to the chief and told me that they asked no better than to go to Mobile, but that they did not want to be taken by the Indians. I asked them the reason why. "The reason why," they told me, "is the Indians make us carry some packages, which exhausts us, mistreat us much, and have taken from us our clothing down to a skin shirt that we each had." In fact one of these three negroes had a tomahawk wound on the head which went as far as the bone, which made me think.

The reasons that the negroes presented to me and the fear that they might escape from the Indians made me decide to send Huche to take them with the Indians, and I advised him not to allow the Indians to mistreat these three negroes belonging to the Company, to M. Dubreuil of the Chapitoulas, and to M. Bonneau. M. Dubreuil's negro told me that there were still thirty-two negroes at the Choctaws, including six negresses belonging to the Company and eighteen belonging to private persons; that seven negroes and negresses had died, viz., four of the Company's and three belonging to private persons.

This same negro added that he was in the Great Village at the time when Ymiatabe, Chickasaw chief, arrived there, and that this Chickasaw, finding at the time almost all the negroes assembled in the house of the Great Chief, invited them to go to the Chickasaws, telling them that they would be much better off with the English than with the French, and that he would take them there himself, that when the negroes did not wish to go he had returned very discontented. I asked this negro how it happened that they ran away when I sent some Frenchmen to trade for them. "Because," he told me, "the Indians do nothing but tell the negroes continually that all those that you trade for are burned on arrival at New Orleans, and the fear that the negroes have causes them to run away when they learn that they are going to be traded for, but when you go to the Choctaws you have only to bring with you a negro from those for whom you have traded to bring you all those who are among the Indians, who would already have come to find you if it were not for the fear that they have of being burned." . . .

On the eighth the chief of the Cushtushas arrived at the Yowani[2] with two negroes. I asked this chief if he was taking them to Mobile. He told me no. I wanted to pay him for the two negroes in jackets, guns, [a] kettle, and *limbourg*. He did not want [that]; he asked me for the payment in *limbourg*. Since I only had enough to pay him for one, we agreed that I would pay him for the other upon the arrival of the pirogues. After [I gave] him the payment for one negro, he told me to give him some trinket. I gave it to him, since the negroes did not belong to him. The next day he came to tell me that M. Diron had promised him a chest [and] that he was going to get it. I wanted to give him the two negroes to take them to Mobile. It was impossible for me to convince him, because, he said, he wanted to make this trip quickly and the negroes would slow him down. I wrote to M. Diron that this chief had handed over to me two negroes, that I had paid him for one, and that I had made him a present of such and such a thing, knowing that these people try only to play all the angles. This chief told me that the English let him know that they will come into his village with twenty horses loaded with merchandise as soon as the peach flowers have fallen, and that they are to go to the Great Chief at that time.

He added that the English had said that the fear of being pillaged will not stop them from entering the nation and even if they are pillaged one or two times, that will not discourage them; that they will come again a third time; that if they are pillaged then, they will see what they have to do, meaning by that that they will have the Choctaws attacked by the nations that are their allies.

I asked this chief what the Great Chief said about the fact that the English are to come to him. "What do you want him to say," he answered, "since it is he who is seeking them out?" This same chief continued, "I am going to speak to M. Diron about that, and find out from him if he wants me to go and attack the Chickasaws."

I replied to him, "You will do perfectly well to declare yourself to him, but I cannot prevent myself from telling you that I do not understand you. You are dying to attack this nation because they brought you, you say, the sickness that the English made, in order to make you die, and you ask the French whether you should destroy this nation. Do you not know what you are dealing with? What advice do you want us to give you? For my part I will not tell you to kill the Chickasaws because the Great Chief of the French does not order me to tell you that, but also if you attack I will not ask you why you are doing it, because I know that this nation seeks only your ruin and only invites you to receive the English in order to destroy you and to conquer you when you are few. As for the Englishman, if he come into your village you have only to pillage him, capture him, and bring him to me, and you will make the Great Chief of the French understand that your heart is truly inclined to listen to his word." That, Sir, is what I replied to the chief of the Cushtushas. I do not know if you will think it fitting.

The captain of the Yowani, being at my house at the arrival of the chief of the Cushtushas, said that Alibamon Mingo was going to Mobile to find out from M. Diron if he wanted him to attack the Chickasaws, and that according to what M. Diron tells him, he will act; that, however, the warriors of the Yowani were holding themselves ready to march whenever he has word sent around.

The brother of the chief of the Chustushas replied, "Say what you will, we will not attack the Chickasaws. The Red Shoe is obligated to them, and will prevent it." But a warrior of the village of the Chustusha replied, "The warriors know perfectly well that there are chiefs who are sorry for this nation, but the warriors, who are not sorry for it, have agreed to go there without telling the chiefs about it, and for that we are only awaiting the return of those who are hunting. The chiefs of the Chustushas Iajo and of the Yowani will follow us, the warriors," they said, "having as well as they desire to kill some Chickasaws."

On the tenth the chief of the Chickasawhay arrived at the Yowani. He brought me a negro whom a warrior from his village caught in the forest. This negro had escaped from Alibamon Mingo, and it was found that the Indian who had him received a mare in payment, and that he would have been paid a second time if he had not fallen into my hands. The negro belongs to a tailor in New Orleans. The negro was not able to tell me the name of his master. . . .

On the fifteenth, at the moment when I was finishing my letter, two different couriers arrived at the Yowani. These Indians told me that the Natchez had escaped to the Chickasaws; that fifteen of these latter were at their head leading them; that the Chakchiuma,[3] having learned of the flight of this nation, had warned several Choctaws who were hunting in that direction so they might join them to stop them from passing and to attack them, but that not finding themselves sufficiently numerous they had not dared to attack them, and they passed; that after that the Yoyoux [i.e. the Yazoo Indians] wanted to pass but that they attacked those and killed them all and took all their wives for slaves; that the Choctaws who have struck this blow are going to arrive very soon with the scalps that they took, and that they sent a courier to warn the nation to go and attack the Chickasaw because they are giving asylum to the Natchez whom they ought to have handed over; that the warriors, delighted to find a reason to attack the Chickasaws, were ready to depart but that there were some among them who said that first it was necessary to inform the Red Shoe [a medal chief] of it and to wait until the chiefs who went to Mobile had arrived. These chiefs are the chief of the Chustushas and [a Choctaw chief named] Alibamon Mingo. The Red Shoe has not yet left the Yowani when these two couriers arrived there. As soon as he learned this news he told me, "You are right to tell me that the Chickasaws have bad hearts. They are showing it today, because they are taking the enemies of the French and ours into their home. If I was obligated to them, I am not any longer." This news having spread through the village, first everyone assembled at my house, the Red Shoe being lodged there. After all the chiefs and warriors of the village were assembled, the Red Shoe harangued them and spoke to them thus: "It is true," he told them, "I was obligated to the Chickasaws. I even prevented the warriors from going to attack them. Today, when they have taken the Natchez into their home, I declare that I wish to attack them; thus I invite you to do the same." Everyone applauded. Then he commanded them to dance, he rose, he made the death cry, and discharges of musketry followed. He started the dance himself. When the dance was finished, he told them that he was going to leave to arrange everything, and that he would send an express messenger to carry the bundle of sticks for the day of departure, and that he would also let them know the day he would leave to go and spy out what is happening at the Chickasaws, and that when he sees that they are halfway there, he will go and join them.

The Red Shoe told me, "Since we are marching without anyone's asking us for Natchez scalps and those of the Chickasaws, we will be paid for such." I answered him, "Since the other nations are paid for the Natchez scalps they take, I believe that you will be paid likewise for the scalps of the Chickasaws. . . ."

As soon as the scalps that the Choctaws take have arrived I will know everything better, and I will have the honor to dispatch a courier to you. . . .

ETIENNE DE PÉRIER, 1731[4]

Between 1727 and 1733, Etienne de Périer served as governor of Louisiana. He played an important role in the transfer of authority from the Company of the Indies back to the royal government. His letter, written to the French Minister of the Marine, chronicles the perpetual conflict between the French and Natchez and the disruptions that conflict caused in French-Native American relations.

. . . As for the Indians, I think that I know them better than did those who have preceded me. I have profited by the mistakes that they made, as those who come after me will profit by mine. If another than I had had to contend against a multitude of Indians in a conspiracy with as small a force as I have had for it, perhaps he would have been less fortunate and the king would have lost the colony. I know that the general conspiracy of all the Indians to slaughter the French of Louisiana has been regarded as a deliberately prepared story; nevertheless, my lord, nothing was more true, and if it had been as easy to win over the western Choctaws as it was those of the eastern part, the thing would have been carried out; so your Lordship will never make this colony safe for the King except by putting sufficient troops in it to cope with the Indians, who ordinarily respect only those whom they fear, and [troops who are] able to quell them when they do anything foolish. The officers who state to the Court that they will manage the Indians by the devotion and friendship that they will have for them are deceiving it. The Indians of all Louisiana can be managed at present only by force or self-interest. This latter means increases in proportion as we make gifts to them. They are by no means savages in whatever procures them some advantage, by which they know how to profit as well as more civilized people. That is why if the colony were left feeble in troops all the merchandise of France would hardly be sufficient to satisfy them. . . .

On my return from the Balize [at the mouth of the Mississippi River] in the month of April of this year, where I had gone to have made the official report on the channel, which my brother has had the honor to deliver to your Lordship, I found here the chief of the Tunicas, who told me that when he had gone hunting, four Natchez had come to surrender to him in order to beg him to have reconciliation made for them; that all those who were dispersed both among the Chickasaws and elsewhere would be very glad to be received with forgiveness; that they would settle where I wished and on whatever site I wished, but they would be very glad to settle near his village. I replied to the chief of the Tunicas that I was quite willing that they settle within two leagues from him, where they would remain without arms, but that I did not wish them to settle in his village because of the daily disputes that would occur between his warriors and the Natchez. He promised me that he would execute carefully what I ordered him to do. Consequently he went to his village, where he received thirty Natchez, whom he disarmed. At the same time fifteen Natchez and twenty women surrendered to Baron de Crenay at our fort of the Natchez. While things were in this state the Flour Chief, who was the only one who remained to the Natchez, came to the village of the Tunicas with about one hundred Natchez [and] their wives and children while fifty Chickasaws or Coroas[5] were hidden in some canes around the village. The chief of the Tunicas told them that he had orders not to receive them with arms, whereupon they told him that they would hand their arms over to him, that they were keeping them only to reassure their wives. The Tunica believed this too readily, and following his first impulse had food given to all the Natchez families, after which each one slept or danced as he wished until an hour before daybreak on the fourteenth of June, when the Natchez sprang at their arms and at those of the Tunicas and began to kill their hosts, of whom they killed a dozen immediately, among whom was the chief of the Tunicas, who had already killed five of his enemies, although they had overwhelmed him by [their] great number. His war chief was not confounded by this loss any more than by the flight of the greater part of his warriors, who had been made to flee by the surprise. He rallied about a dozen of them with whom he regained his chief's cabin, and by means of harangues he made return those who had been made to flee by the first fright, with whom he recaptured his village after a combat of five days and five nights. This was one of the most vigorous struggles that has ever taken place among Indians. The Tunicas had twenty men killed and as many wounded, together with [the loss of] eight women [who were taken] prisoner [and] whom they afterwards recaptured. The Natchez left thirty-three men dead and three who were taken prisoner, who were immediately burned. If our French inhabitants, who were only seven leagues distant, had gone to the assistance of the Tunicas instead of fleeing here, only a few Natchez would have escaped, but they lacked a man of judgment to lead them. . . .

When I saw the blow that the Chickasaws together with the Natchez had just struck the Tunicas, in which we had lost a man and a woman, I sent orders to Sieur Regis [du Roullet], an officer who had been living among the Choctaws since the beginning of the war [against the Natchez], to have a party of three hundred men set out to try to intercept either the Chickasaws or the Natchez, but the latter had retired to the lands of the Ouachitas [i.e. modern-day northern Arkansas] where I defeated them last year. At the same time I ordered this officer to induce the Choctaws to declare war on the Chickasaws, whom I had resolved to treat with caution until [the arrival of] new assistance, which I was expecting from France, with which I was intending to attack them this winter, but their underhanded activities among the Illinois, the Arkansas, and part of the Miamis and among us ourselves show that they are not led by Indians, since they sent one of the negroes who was with them to come here to tell our negroes that they would get their liberty and that they would lack nothing with the English, who would take care of them. Since this negro was a Banbara, of a nation [whose language] the others do not understand, [he] had attached to his party all the negroes of his nation. I was warned of it by a negress, a domestic servant of the town, who had herself entered this conspiracy, which I tried to clear up thoroughly. I found that they had agreed to take the time when everybody would be at mass at the parish church; that they would set fire to different houses of the town in order to scatter those who would not be in the church. When the thing was proved we had five of the leaders broken on the wheel and a woman who had led part of the affair hanged.

We have also had four soldiers hanged at Mobile and two here for having stolen from the Company's [i.e. the Company of the Indies] warehouses. This band of thieves had been formed for seven years without the keepers of the warehouses having complained that they were being robbed. All these disorders, which I have fortunately remedied in time, have obligated me to have war declared on the Chickasaws in order to cut the ground from underneath all the negotiations that they were conducting with all these nations, which were all anxious to receive the English into their midst. I have had more difficulty than I expected in making the Choctaws declare [war] on the Chickasaws. The latter had won over more than half of the former. It was only by means of a war chief who was a friend of ours that we succeeded in having an attack made upon the Chickasaws, while the rest of the Choctaw nation had been deliberating about the policy that it was to adopt for three months, since the end of July when the Chickasaws had killed some of their people to the number of thirty to forty persons. The Choctaws appear to be well united among themselves and are more attached to us, which comes from the need that they have of us for their munitions and weapons, but unfortunately we lack light trade guns of the sort the Company used to send. The quantity of powder and of lead both in bullets and in shot that is consumed in this province will appear surprising to you, my lord. We cannot do without it, both for making a living and for the safety of the country, and it is of the utmost importance that we should not be in want of it.

    . . . The province of Louisiana will never be tranquil until the Chickasaws have been destroyed or until they have been obliged to go and settle outside the lands of the province. They have entrenched themselves in their villages, which are defended by small forts, which it will not be possible to take without cannons or double grenades. . . .

DIRON D'ARTAGUETTE, 1734[6]

In 1722, Diron d'Artaguette was the Inspector General of the Troops of the Province of Louisiana, but throughout his years in the colony he held a variety of positions. When he wrote the letter that follows, he was the King's Commissary, or accountant, at Mobile.

The just apprehension that the Choctaws have given us by their activities, that they might make peace with the Chickasaws and that they might enter into an alliance with the English, caused M. de Bienville to decide to write to me in these terms on the second of last July.

"As the southwest winds are prevailing and as it is difficult for you to be able to give me news promptly of what is happening at the Choctaws, the longboat having taken eighteen days to get here, I beg you to act and to do everything that you think advisable to divert the Choctaws from the trade with the English. If you think even that by taking the trouble to go to the Great Village you could have better success than by giving your orders to the officer who is there, you must not postpone going there. I shall approve all the agreements that you make with them. Perhaps at the time that I am writing to you the news is more favorable."

The same letter contains another article, which states: "I greatly fear that these negotiations with the English may break up their plan to go to war in the month of August, as they had proposed to do. . . ."

It appears, my lord, that the situation of our affairs was very bad and that we had everything to fear from a rupture with this nation, but no matter how urgent M. de Bienville's orders were, I could not go to them [the Choctaws] until a month and a half later, because I was recovering from a severe illness and it would have been impossible for me to travel 150 leagues through the forests and [over] impracticable roads without having recovered at least a part of my strength, to travel during the heat of the dog days, to make part of the journey on foot, and to live like the Indians. . . . Finally I set out on the fourth of the past month, after having received information from the officer who resides in the nation that the English were winning them over by the presents and the offers that they were making them and that he was despairing of the plan that it [the Choctaw nation] had formed of sending a party against the Chickasaws. I passed through the principal villages and I came here in twenty-seven days. . . . My presence was very necessary at the Choctaws, who were only waiting for one of their chiefs named Red Shoe, whom the entire nation had sent as a delegate to Carolina to agree upon the articles of their treaty with the English. I learned there also that the small parties that are apparently preparing to attack the Chickasaws had no desire to do them any harm, and that they were only seeking to put us off by this external appearance of good will until the delegate was back. Several among them have admitted it to me, and the majority of the chiefs have made it quite plain by their resistance in the assemblies to which I called them, by haranguing vigorously about the interest that they had in not continuing the war. Since M. de Bienville threatened them with not giving any presents to those who refused to go it, they drew from this the inference that when they had destroyed the Chickasaws they would no longer be given anything. It was in vain that I told them that the presents would never fail them so long as they remained attached to the French nation, and that what M. de Bienville had done about them was only in order to excite the lazy to become warriors; [in vain I] added to that everything that could alienate them from the English, the difficulties that the latter would have in keeping their agreements because of the great distance, whereas on the other hand they were so to speak within our reach; everything was useless and finally since I no longer knew how to influence them, I determined to try a method that, as singular as it is, was perfectly successful to me.

The Choctaws like all the others are very much given to superstition, and I am considered by some of the cleverest of them as a man who knows the future because I have foretold to them events that were going to happen to them in the natural order of things. I decided then, my lord, to take advantage of their credulity and to tell them that I had foreseen that they were going to fall into the utmost misfortune if they resorted to the English; that I had seen the shades of the ancestors who were suffering infinitely from their lack of gratitude to us, who had armed them and clothed them and from whom they were every day receiving new benefits. I accompanied this speech with several metaphors in their manner, which made more impression upon them than all the offers that I could have made them. They passed from great chattering to profound reflection, and having left the assembly without saying anything they came on the next day to the house of the missionary where I was staying to tell me that they had all agreed to

march to the war and no longer allow the Englishman who was leading them to peace to set foot in their country. As the great chief of the
Cushtushas and the principal men of the nation who had been won
over were in this assembly, I threatened those who were not there with
summoning their warriors of valor and with assigning to them the
portion of the presents that [the chiefs] received every year if they
refused to do as the others. These threats had the effect that I was
expecting from them, and we then saw nothing but ardor for the war.
They talked only of attacking the enemies even in their forts, adding
that they would regard as true dogs those who retreated. I turned
them over in this mood to M. le Sieur, according to the intentions of
M. de Bienville, and I withdrew after having fulfilled my mission in
the manner in which I have just, my lord, related to you, although they
tired to persuade me to go in their company for at least two days to
show me, they said, that not one remained at home. In fact they all
departed on the twentieth of last month, and they must have nearly
two thousand me. I told them in parting that I was mortified not to be
able to give them the satisfaction that they asked of me by accompa-
nying them, because I did not march without my warriors, and I would
be censured if I did so, but that I exhorted them to establish their reputation by a brilliant exploit, which by procuring them the friendship
and esteem of the French would cause them to be respected by other
nations. The great chief, who was at the head of this little army, told
me anew that in addition to the fact that he had to avenge the death
of his brother and of one of his children, he was inclined to follow the
fraternal advice that I gave him. . . .

ALIBAMON MINGO, 1739[7]

A Choctaw leader who was friendly toward the French, Alibamon Mingo
helped shape French-Native American relations. The letter that follows
was written by a French official, but it consists largely of transcriptions of
speeches by Mingo. In the speeches, Mingo describes the difficulties that

pro-French Choctaws experienced with the Chickasaw and the agents of the English colonies on the Atlantic seaboard.

. . . After having made an explanation of the purposes of my journey, I exhorted my two chiefs to state to me frankly all that they knew about the sentiments of the Choctaws and to second me in the desire that I had to bring them all back to our side, whereupon Alibamon Mingo, taking the floor, replied to me:

"The French ought to attribute less to the Indians than to the English all that has happened contrary to their interests since they came to settle these lands, but to speak to you only of the things of which I have had personal knowledge, I begin with the Natchez massacred, the cause of which the French have perhaps never well understood, and I shall inform you that the English alone were the authors of that conspiracy, to join which they had proposals made to us by the Chickasaws a hundred times, and it was only by convincing the Natchez that we had accepted the plan that they convinced them to be the first to raise the standard of rebellion. It is true, however, that the proposal had been rejected by all the Choctaw chiefs. The promptness with which we marched against the Natchez at the first signal is a proof of the truth that I assert.

"Since that time the English, thinking indeed that our attachment to the French would always be an invincible obstacle to their evil plan, have spared nothing to win us over. They began by asking to be received [in] the nation as traders, [promising] that they would sell us merchandise more cheaply than the French. Red Shoe, whom they had won over by presents, declared himself their protector and even made she share his intentions, which were meant, he said to me, only to oblige the French to sell us merchandise at the same prices as the English did. Is it astonishing," continued this Indian, "that men who are poor and who are fond of opulence should let themselves be taken in by these enticements? I entered into Red Shoe's plans on condition that when the French had granted us trade at the rate of the English we would dismiss the latter in order not to get into a quarrel with the others, whom our action could not fail to please. The English were therefore brought into the nation. I even established one of their warehouses in my village. My policy had in part the success that I expected from it; the French traders reduced the price of their goods, but it made me lose a great deal more than it made me gain, inasmuch as it involved me in a quarrel with the French chief, who to punish me deprived me for two years of the presents that I had been accustomed to receive.

"In the meanwhile," continued Alibamon Mingo, "the English, who had other intentions than those of trade, arranged a conference between Red Shoe and the Chickasaw chiefs, in which they agreed upon a suspension of hostilities, which, although it was really disapproved by the majority of the nation, has, however, been very carefully observed. That comes," added he, "in the first place from the fact that the Great Chief of the nation, who is truly devoted to the French, did not have the strength to oppose Red Shoe; in the second place from the fact that the disfavor that I was in with the French had made me lose all influence in the nation; and finally from the fact that all the warriors returned last winter very much dissatisfied from Mobile, where the presents were delivered to the chiefs who divided them among themselves and their relatives".

"This action of Red Shoe," continued the Choctaw chief, "made me open my eyes to the mistakes that I had made in seconding his plans. I hesitated no longer about the course that I was to follow. I had already driven the English from my village. I sent back to the Alabamas, who consider me their chief, the flag that these traders had brought me on behalf of their governor so that they might send it back on my behalf to the one who had made a present of it. At the same time I begged the nations of those districts to refuse passage to the English, or at least not to furnish them any more guides to come to us, because we did not wish to have any dealings with them any longer. This declaration did not prevent two troops of them from coming under the escort of Red Shoe, who went to find them at Kaapa; but his presence did not prevent one of our young warriors from going and killing on their journey three of their horses, the finest of which belong to Red Shoe. Since that tie I have opposed him on all occasions, so that we have several times been on the brink of coming to blows. The French traders, who have often attended our assemblies, will give you testimony about it." . . .

Alibamon Mingo took the floor again and said to me: "If Red Shoe thought like other men the first means that you propose would doubtless be successful and would be more to the liking of all the Choctaws, inasmuch as it would unite all minds and all sentiments, but because of the character that we all know this man to have, the measures that the French would take to win him back would only make him more haughty, and the favors that he would receive would embolden him to do them more harm by providing him with the means of acquiring more partisans. Besides, his decision is made. He has assured me himself that he was irrevocably on the side of the English; that nothing would be able to detach him from them, and I inform you that he departed a week ago for New Georgia, from which he expects to bring back sufficient presents to compensate his partisans for those that they are losing from the French side, but I do not think that will happen, and since I have promised you to tell everything, I declare to you that when I had learned that this man had formed the intention of going to the English, I went and found him to order to try to divert him from it and to induce him to come with me to Mobile. He replied to me at first rather gently that he was afraid that he would be badly received there after what he had done in opposition to the French. I replied to him that my example ought to reassure him in this respect, and I represented to him that the interests of the nation demanded that he should take this stop. 'Let come what may,' he replied to me angrily, 'my decision is made. I shall be as loyal to the English as you wish to be to the French, and we shall see whether my warriors or yours will return better satisfied with the presents that they have received.' This reply made me catch fire. I called him in the presence of his friends a reckless, young fellow who, while destroying himself, wished to destroy those who were crazy enough to follow him, and I left him making threats that will possibly be put into execution. I had taken the precaution to bring with me the chief of the French traders, who was a witness to everything that I said to him and who will confirm to you what I say".

"It is therefore useless," continued Alibamon Mingo, "to think of detaching Red Shoe from the English faction. It will be much easier and much more expedient to make him lose the influence that he has acquired by lies and by promises that he will never be able to fulfill, for it is not possible that he will bring back from the English all that he has promised his partisans. . . ."

CHICKASAW CHIEFS, 1743[8]

> Desirous of peace with French Louisiana, a group of Chickasaw chiefs wrote Governor Pierre Rigaud, Marquis de Vaudreuil to state their intentions.

Great Chief of all the French and of the red men, hear our word. We have learned of your arrival and that all the red men of the North are your children; that for a long time you have been their chief; that you have always kept peace among them; that you have never broken your word to them nor did your father, the great chief of all the nations of the North; and that you have not let them lack coats, blankets, powder and bullets, vermilion, or beads.

If you wish to regard us as your children, listen to our word, which is true. We do not wish to attack the French any longer. We shall hold out our hands to them when we find them. There are no longer any Natchez in our villages. The Choctaws are madmen to attack us. We shall no longer paddle our canoes on the Mississippi. When we came there we were not seeking to make attacks upon the French.

We captured them in order to make you listen to our word. We were seeking red men on the Mississippi.

We love your Frenchmen. We regard them as our brothers. All the Chickasaw chiefs ask you for peace. Marianne, whom we are keeping as our prisoner with your Frenchmen, begs you to grant us peace and to send us powder, bullets, guns, and coats, and we shall deliver Marianne and the Frenchmen who remain in our villages. Send us everything that we ask of you and do not refuse us, otherwise we shall paddle our canoes on the Mississippi and we shall attack all the French and the red men.

PIERRE RIGAUD, MARQUIS DE VAUDREUIL, 1744[9]

For ten years, Pierre Rigaud, Marquis de Vaudreuil, served as governor of Louisiana. He left office in 1753 to become Governor-General of Canada. In the letter that follows, Vaudreuil analyzes the overtures for peace that the Chickasaw had offered. Despite the hopefulness of his communication, better relations with the Chickasaw never came to fruition.

The frequent steps that the Chickasaws have taken for peace had made me really think, my lord, that they were disposed to obtain it. I had given all the necessary attention to this negotiation and at the same time taken all the measures necessary to secure its groundwork, but the fact that I should have found it impossible to supply them with the things they need has contributed no little to diverting them from the design that they had of driving the English off their land, as they had promised to do and as you will see, my lord, by all the accounts that I have had the honor of rendering you about them since the twelfth of last February, from which it will not be difficult for you to judge that if we had not fallen into such indigence, the Chickasaws would today have made peace with us and driven the English out of their country. This was really the reason why I was not willing to grant it to them, in addition to the means that I would thereby have given the English of coming and establishing themselves in the Choctaw nation, which would have been successful through the use of the Chickasaws, as was certainly their intention if one may judge by the steps that they have had the latter take so that they might become reconciled with our allies. This had led me to make every effort to have war declared on them again. The steps that these Chickasaws took last spring to come and see me, when the Choctaws killed two of their principal chiefs and a warrior . . .; when some deputies of that nation came again to our fort of the Alabamas to treat there for peace; the blow that has just been struck at them by a Choctaw party that I had induced to go raiding in their direction, which killed five of their men last month; [all that] in addition to the fact that they have not made any expedition upon the river this year proves clearly enough the determination of the Chickasaws to give up the commerce with the English and the desire that they had to live on good terms with us. They would undoubtedly have done this if they had thought us able to supply them with the things they need, but as they could not believe it by the report that our Alabamas had given them about it, they did not wish to run the risks. I have not been sorry about it because of the harsh necessity in which I would have found myself of refusing them, which would have made a much worse impression on the minds of these Indians, who would very quickly have called the English back into their country, so that since we have not deceived them, it will be less difficult for us to succeed in making peace with them when they have been thoroughly harassed by the different nations of this continent and those of the north and when you have put me, my lord, in a position to be able to supply them with their needs by means of the merchandise for which I have had the honor to ask you on all occasions that have presented themselves.

Chapter 3

ANTEBELLUM WHITE
SOCIETY

Between the close of the War of 1812 and the mid-1830s, the population of Mississippi grew exponentially. Three phenomena sparked the population boom. First, the war itself helped settle lingering conflicts with Native Americans and led to the eventual removal of Choctaws and Chickasaws from Mississippi, opening fresh lands to settlement by white farmers and their slaves. Second, the state of Mississippi's admission to the union encouraged potential settlers to believe greater stability on the southwestern frontier loomed. Most importantly, between the early 1790s and 1830, Mississippi emerged as one of the chief cotton producing states in the nation. The invention of the cotton gin, as well as Mississippi's fertile soils and good climate, made possible the spread of cotton cultivation and the concomitant growth in the state's population.

White settlers who rushed to occupy and purchase land in Mississippi brought with them their dreams for economic success. Poor farmers found in Mississippi cheap land that they could occupy or purchase and on which they tended livestock and raised row crops. Many remained forever on the move, seeking that perfect patch of land. Middling folk also found Mississippi attractive as a place where they could attempt to enter plantation society by cultivating cotton. And, of course, wealthy planters from other southeastern states relocated to Mississippi.

Although the popular image of Mississippi in the antebellum period places a grandiose plantation home at every bend in the road, the reality of life in pre-Civil War Mississippi was quite different. Transportation was difficult because roads were crude and treacherous. Diseases that modern Americans rarely think about were deadly killers. Rivers, as yet unbounded by levees, overflowed regularly. And homes, even the homes of large planters living outside of significant cities, were often little more than log cabins with dirt floors. Literacy rates among whites in the antebellum period were relatively low, in large part because Mississippi did not create a system of public schools until Reconstruction. Diversions from day-to-day life included church, hunting, fishing, and the occasional party or political gathering. At many of the events, great quantities of food and alcohol often feted guests. But for most white Mississippians their daily lives were routinely shaped by the labor of the prevailing season. Fences were erected, and ditches were dug in the winter; and the soil was prepared for cultivation, too. The spring was occupied with planting. Summer was the season for hoeing and nurturing crops; late summer signaled the start of picking time. Picking continued into the autumn, but autumn was also the season for rounding up livestock to slaughter or sale. The documents that follow portray the interests and concerns of many classes of white Mississippians as they lived their daily lives.

CARTER FAMILY LETTERS

In the early nineteenth century, the Carter family, consisting of Casandra and Matthew and their children, moved to Mississippi from Bullock County, Georgia. The letters that appear below capture the loneliness and hazards of life in the antebellum Piney Woods; and they describe the forces that motivated the Carters to migrate to and remain in Mississippi. The letters also describe what the Carter clan and undoubtedly others, too, most valued.

Casandra Carter, 1811[1]

These few lines comes in love to you to let you know that we are all well at present, thanks be to God for His mercy, hoping that may find you in the same state of health as we are at present. The old man has a pain in his arm and I am afraid will lose the use of it.

We all held out on our journey better than we expected. We have not had one day's sickness since I left you all, thanks be to God for it. Matthew has got a fine son and calls his name Joseph, and William has got a dator [daughter] and calls her name Sabra.

I have nothing remarkable to relate to you. We have bought a little improvement in the piney woods. The range is very good for cattle and hogs. We sold a horse and bought 30 head of hogs. We settled the sixth of September [1811]. We have got a few cows. We have never suffered. As for being satisfied I can't relate. The men seems to be satisfied; as for the two girls they are often in tears for you all and wishes to be with you. Naomy and her family is well at present. My heart is so full I can't say no more, but remain Your loving Aunt and Mother tel Death. We do all desire to be remembered to you all.

Pray don't fail wrighting all opportunities. The last words that ever you git from my mouth I am afeared.

Matthew Carter, Jr., 1813[2]

I now gladly embrace an opportunity of writing a few lines to inform you that through the Mercies of God we are all in perfect health at present, hoping these lines will find you and your family the same. We have enjoyed our health in a wonderful manner ever since we have been in this country and I feel myself very well satisfied with respect to the country, though the loss of my father and the talk of war[3] together with other things has caused me great trouble and uneasiness of mind, though I have good reason to believe that my loss is his eternal gain. He was taken in October with a pain in his shoulder which continued several weeks and in the time he hurt his leg and a fever fell in it and it was likely to mortify. He was several weeks not able to get out of the house without his crutches, and in a short time after his leg got well he was taken in a lingering condition which condition continued until he was not able to get out of his bed. He was then taken with fits which continued until he died. He lay several weeks not able to get out of his bed and continued to get weaker until the 2nd of April, in the afternoon, when it pleased God to take him out of this troublesome world.

I think he bore his affliction with the most patience that I ever saw any person in all my life. He told my mother a short time before his death he was willing to go anytime when it pleased the Lord to take him.

My dear brother and sister, I am sorrow to hear that you are not satisfied where you are. Peter Cone told me that he understood that you wanted to go back to Ogeechee [Georgia]. I would not wish to persuade you to do anything against your inclination but it is my opinion that it would be much better for you to come to this country than to go back to an old worn out place. This is a fine fresh country, well watered and healthy, and the land produces very well. It is the opinion of the citizens of this country that it will be the best place of trade that is in America, and if you are disposed to come to this country I want you to write to me as soon as you can to let me know what time you can be ready to start for if nothing happens William or myself will be there in October and we will assist you all we can in moving. I do not think you will ever repent coming. It is only 40 miles from where I live to Mobile where I can buy shugar and coffee on better terms than ever I did in Savannah, and the schooners pass up and down the river and we can get any kind of necessaries from them, and they give a good price for our produce. As for the land I can give you no true account of [it] at this time; some people is of the opinion that we shall have a donation rite but it is not yet known how we shall get it. . . .

Matthew Carter, Jr. and Ann Carter, 1822[4]

We received your letter of the 21st July within 13 days from the time it was mailed and was very glad to hear from you. Our family at present is in good health. My brother and sister and families is all in good health at present. Our mother is also well and desires to be remembered to you. She has quit housekeeping and is living about amongst us.

Our crops this year is not very good. We had a storm on the 9 of July that hurt our corn and cotton very much but I hope I shall make a plenty for [my] part. . . .

My dear brother, I thank you for the advice you gave me with respect to having preaching in our settlement. We have had regular preaching this year once in three weeks within 4 miles and once in 6 weeks at my house. Some few has joined our Society and I hope we shall have better times than we have had. I want you to write me every opportunity and I will endeavor to do the same. . . .

Matthew Carter, Jr., 1825[5]

I take up my pen once more to let you know that through the mercies of God myself and family with all the family connection is in good health at present. My old mother is yet living and in tolerable good health. She has no particular place of abode; she lives sometimes with one and then another of us. She is at William Goff's at this time.

We have had a very healthy season in the country though Mobile has been very much afflicted with the yellow fever. There has been a great many people died there this summer. We have made tolerable good crops this year. . . .

I feel somewhat dissatisfied with the place where I now live in consequence of the overflowing of the River, though I have a plenty of good land and good trade and enjoy good health, yet the inconveniences occasioned by the freshets makes me feel rather dissatisfied, though I have not determined whether I shall try to move or not. I wish you to write to me whether you have any thought of moving or not. If you have I hope there will be a probability of our getting nearer together. . . .

And now, my dear brother and sister, I am about to close my letter and if we never should see each other again in this world I have a hope that we shall meet in a better [world] where parting will be no more. Farewell!

Matthew Carter, Jr., 1828[6]

I once more take up my pen to write a few lines to you to let you know that we through the mercies of God enjoy pretty good health at present. We have had a very healthy season this year. Our relations in this country are all in good health. Mother is yet alive and in good health. She is at this time with Sister Casandra.

Our crops are generally pretty good except cotton; that is almost entirely ruined by the rot. We have been very much plagued this year with the blowing-flies. I never saw the like before. They have killed a number of cattle and sheep and injured our hogs very much. They have even blowed our horses and dogs but I hope the frost we had last night will put a stop to them.

I will give you some account of our Camp-meeting which commenced on Thursday the 2nd of October, last, and concluded 9th Monday. Though there was nothing very extraordinary occurred during the meeting it was a very solemn time and I hope much good was done. How many was converted I have not as yet ascertained but I have reason to believe there was a considerable number, and I think I can say a truth that it was as happy a time among the people of God as I ever saw. . . .

Matthew Carter, Jr., 1829[7]

I once more take up my pen to let you know that we are all well and alive and enjoy pretty good health at present, for which we desire to be thankful. . . .

Our crops is very backward and not very likely. We have had a hard winter and a backward spring. It was a fatal time among our cattle. Five cows out of your little stock is missing this spring, and, I expect, dead. The times is dull in this part of the county but not as much so I expect as where you live. We have the advantage of a good market. I have declined the idea of moving at present as I hope it will not be long before we shall have better times. There is now a town laid out at the mouth of Pascagoula River and several houses put up in the course of a few months past, and there is the largest kind of vessels can come in. I think if you wish to move you would do well to take your horse next fall and come and see us. It would not cost you much. . . .

BENJAMIN LAFAYETTE SMITH[8]

Benjamin Smith was born in Lowndes County to parents who had moved from Georgia. The selection of his hand-written memoir that follows describes his father's effort to secure financial success, as well as the hallmarks of his success.

About the year 1840, my father bought four negroes, three men, John, Henry, and Abram, and a woman, the wife of Abram. . . . With these men, he built three cabins made of small logs or round poles, without hewing or peeling them, with wooden chimneys. Ribs of small logs were put on top of these, forming a frame to nail the oak boards to, instead of rafters with sheathing. These cabins were built on the ground without floor, and cracks were filled and daubed with mud, which made them warm and comfortable. In a similar manner he built a crib for corn and log stables. My father lived in one of these until he could build him a better one. He fenced these and horse lot and garden with ten foot rails split of oak. He also fenced his farm in [the] same way. . . .

I was born October 11th 1842 in one of the above mentioned cabins. . . . Soon after this my father quit teaching school, and ever after this devoted his whole time to farming and stock raising. He soon built for himself a double loghouse, of large hewn logs, with ten foot hall between floored with rough plank. At each end of this hall was a small board shelter, which answered for a porch, resting on two peeled poles set in the ground. There were no floor to these shelters. The chimneys were of wood, and the cracks in these as well as cracks in the house, were filled with wood and daubed with mud in which hog hair was placed. The floors were of dressed matched timbers, with batton [i.e. batten] doors made of similar timber. The rafters of this house were made of small round poles peeled and sheathing was of split laths, three inches wide and three fourths of an inch thick, and covered with oak boards thirty inches long. The furniture consisted of a cheap plain bedstead, in each room, fastened together with cotton rope cords, and a trundle bed under my mother[']s bed, six unpainted plain split bottom chairs, and a similar rocker, which was known as my mothers, a cheap wardrobe, bookcase and table, the two latter made by a neighbor carpenter, also two small hanging mirrors.

JOSEPH B. LIGHTSEY, 1852[9]

When Joseph B. Lightsey made the following entries in his diary, he was a twenty-one year old, bachelor who lived in his father's household. He worked for his father alongside two adult slaves. His diary, which covers the years 1849 to 1852, includes many terse entries describing the day-to-day activities of a yeoman farmer, as well as several short essays and dialogues. The dialogue that follow reflects Lightsey's values and also the fact that Mississippi, despite several efforts in the 1840s, failed to build a system of public education in the antebellum period.

Sunday [August] 15: I staid at home today and wrote this dialogoue On Education
Enter Tom: Well I am sitting monstrous tired a-waiting for dad but yonder he comes I guess no, it aint neither its that larned chap Henry May I wander where he is going today
Enter Henry May: Good morning Son I am glad to see you are going to school to Mr Barnes
Tom: No I guess not
Henry: Why Tom

Tom: Cause dad says I have got education enough allready and he will not let me go if I wanted to

Henry: How much education have you got Tom

Tom: Well I went to Mr snatches school 6 months in that time I got to practice in smileys arithmetic and could read all the New York reader without missing more than halfe the words

Henry: Can you wright any

Tom: yess a little

Henry: Can you spell good

Tom: Well I can hossfly I used to stand head in my class all the time

Henry: did you ever study Grammar

Tom: No I didnt go to school long enough for that

Henry: Did you ever study Geography

Tom: No Mr Snatches was going to put me to studying Peter Parleys geography with Peter Pet but I had to stop going to school and haint went no more

Henry: and dont you want to go again

Tom: Well I dont care much about hit but I believe if dad was willing I would go a while and try my hand

Henry: Well I am glad to heare you say so for if your father is the man of sense I take him to be I can soon make him to let you go to school But yonder he comes now, Enter Farmer.

Farmer: Good morning henry how do you do

Henry: Pretty well I thank you how are you

Farmer: Well I am about as common but what are you and Tom confabulating about here so soon this morning

Henry: Why I have been pursuading of Tom to go with me to school

Farmer: I dont see any use of toms goin to school any more for hes got more larning than I have now and besides I cant spare him out of the crop

Henry: Well sire I have just been escamining Tom and I find he has lain a pretty good foundation for an education but nothing more and you know sir that if you were to stop building one of your fences when you had but just laid the foundation it would be of but little use in keeping out the pigs

Farmer: Yess but it looks to me like in six months a boy ought to git plenty of education to make a farmer I never went to school but 3 months in my life and I dont see but what I git along as well as the common run of peopple

Henry: Yes sire but you see you have learned a great deal by experience and experience is a dear school you know and if you will but send Tom to Mr Barnes one year he will learn more that will be useful to him than he could in 2 years of experience staying at home

Farmer: Well Well but theres no use in given Tom a lawyer nor doctor larning for I want to make a farmer of him

Henry: Very well sir but if Tom had a good education he would make a better farmer

Farmer: I don't know for I dont believe in this book farming much no how cause didnt the squire lend me a paper tother day called the Southern cultivator and I couldnt see no sence in it for they talked about gininiseing this and iligatering that with such hard names as colbin mitginhugin[10] and gracious [k]nows what not

Henry: Well well now Mr Discon but you do not take a right view of the subject of education why sir suppose our forefathers who were mostly farmers had been as much opposed to educating their sons as you are to educating Tom what kind of country would this have been by this time.

Farmer: Well I dont know

Henry: Well sir I do it would have degenerated into a land of heathenism and we been no better than the red man of the forest had it not been for love our forefathers had for the arts and sciences you say sir you want Tom to be a farmer well sire give him a good education I expect to be a farmer myself but that does not keep me from wanting an education and besides sir you do not know what place Tom may ocupy in society when he becomes a man he has a chance of makeing a great man with a good education why sir I could tell you of several

great men who were farmer boys but one will suffise you have heard
of Henry Clay have you not

Farmer: Oh yess I voted for him for president *once*

Henry: Well sire he was once a mill boy with no more education than
Tom has but by aplication and studey he became one of the greatest of
our great men and no[w] sir let me pursaude you once more to let
Tom go to school for Mr Barnes is a competent teacher and Tom
would larn very fast under his guidance and believe me sir if Tom does
get a good education he nor you will ever regret the time nor expense
of obtaining it

Farmer: Well Tom may go but I spects upon Six months he will be like
Mr Snatch taling bout the worlds turning around and sich like nonsesce

Henry: Why sir do you not believe that the world turnes around once
in every twenty four hours

Farmer: No cause dont sperience teach us that if our heads were
turned down we would drop off and you know that if the world turned
around our head would be down sometimes

Henry: That is tolerable reasoning sir but up and down are mere relative termes in Phylosophy and there is a property called attraction of
gravity which tends to draw things towards the centre of the earth and
therefore there is no chance of dropping off

Tom: Yess dad that what mr snatch said about it

Farmer: I don't know any thing about losophy and 'tractions but this
much I know this earth is as flat as a pancake and dont no more turn
round than nothing

Henry: how do you account for the rising and setting of the sun moon
and stars then sir

Farmer: Oh thats easy enough they go around the earth to be sure
dont the bible tell us that much didnt Joshua command the sun and
moon to stand still and wouldnt he have been a great fool to have
commanded them stand still whers they are already still

Henry: You say Joshua commanded the sun and moon to stand still
do you

Farmer: Yess I do

Henry: Well did you ever here of his setting them to going again

Farmer: Well I guess not but I recall they started again after a while

Henry: Very likely. Now sire I can tell you the reason why Joshua commanded the sun and moon to stand still it had not been discovered in his day that the earth is round and turned on its axis once in every 24 hours and every person believed as you do that the sun went around the earth it is therefore reasonable I supose that Joshua knew no better than others of his day the laws by which the planets are governed and he therefore spoke as he thought

Farmer: Well well that will do for this time go Tom and get your books and toddle on to school for I guess this is the school master coming this way now

Tom: Yes sir.

Exit Tom.

Enter Barns.

Farmer: good morning Mr Barns

Barns: good morning mr Discon (shakes hands. Barns and Henry shakes hands[)] how are you Henry how are you mr Barnes

Farmer: I suppose you commence your school this morning Mr Barnes

Barnes: Yess sire

Farmer: how many schollars have you got signed

Barnes: I have got 29 sir

Farmer: Would you take another

Barnes: Yess sir I would be glad to get another to make out 30 schollars

Farmer: Well sir you may put down one for me

Barnes: [(]Wrights in his book[)] thank you sir

Farmer: My son has studied arithmetic reading wrighting and ciphering but it has been so long since he has been to school til he has forgot most all he knowed you will soon find out what he knowes though and just put him to studying what you think best for I have come to the [']clusion this morning to give him a good education if I hant got none myselfe

Barnes: Very well sire I will attend to him and now I will be going will you go down with us and see how we make a start this morning

Farmer: I believe I will sire.

AMANDA D. WORTHINGTON

The Worthington clan of Washington County was a wealthy one. As the letters below indicate, the Worthingtons hired a tutor for their children and sent their oldest son to the University of Virginia. The value that the planter class placed on education and good cotton crops stand out in the letters. Likewise, the letters describe the social life of an ambitious, planter family.

The First Letter, 1857[11]

Altho' no letter has yet reached me from you, I take it for granted you have answered mine, written to you a long time ago & I begin this, my second, in the hope that now you are settled we shall have a weekly epistle from you at least. You must write soon & oftenest to your Father, but I shall expect to come in every now & then. Mr. Hazelton got here a week ago, but only organized the Pt. Worthington Academy day before yesterday, I have no doubt but he misses the Senior Class very much & if Aron & you shouldn't be able to squeeze in at the University, would be very glad to reinstate you at your old desks—he brought a Mr. Peterson to tutor Bob Lashley, but I understand Mr. Lashley says he does not care about Bob learning much as he will have a fine fortune & it will consequently not be necessary—I however do not put quite so high an estimate on money & think the more he has in his pocket the more he ought to have in his head, in order to keep his balance. Mr White arrived here the day after Mr Hazleton did & after starting the Sewing machine proceeded to overhauling gins as usual. . . .

The Second Letter, 1857[12]

I received your very welcome & affectionate letter a day or two after I started my last to you; I need hardly say how glad I was to learn you were quite well again nor how deeply I sympathized in your stage-ride suffering. Your Father says when you get back home you must practice & learn to ride anywhere, inside or out, backwards or forwards.

I am sorry you do not think the University [of Virginia] a first rate place for improvement as I expected you to be greatly enlightened & polished off, but I hope by the time you write again you will have come to a better conclusion. You must try hard & get the little good that is going, as it is all important you should *learn many things* somehow or somewhere. If a writing master comes along you must give him a trial & be particular to spell well. I do not think it important for a farmer to be a Greek & Latin scholar, but to transact his plantation business creditably & satisfactorily he must compose, write & spell well & to enjoy himself in the society of gentlemen he must be versed in the literary pursuits & topics of the day.

But for fear I should tire you with my long lecture on education I will pass on to something else for the present, but I expect to give you a little bout in every letter.

Mr. Hazelton is teaching at your Uncle William's & if he comes here at all, will come the first of Feb.; two months you know is our proportion of the time. Amanda and Sam appear very industrious & as ambitious as ever to excel. Mary has not gone to New Orleans yet, nor will she go until money matters are easier there. The Merchants have decided to sell no more cotton until more money comes in & better prices are offered. Our last sale was at 9½ [cents per pound] but it was only a small lot & we are not shipping any now, but storing it up until there is a fairer demand for it. We cannot tell yet how much we will make but the crop will not be large. We dug our sweet potatoes yesterday & have a much better turnout than last year.

Last week your Brother & Cousin Tom killed a bear & a deer & this week Cousin Willie has gone up to join them & try his luck; I look for them all home tomorrow & hope we shall have a good time eating venison & slicking up with bear oil. Our quarterly meeting commences day after tomorrow & our new church is so far finished as to admit of our occupying it; we expect several strange preachers & hope to have a protracted meeting. . . .

You speak in one of your letters of the high price of wood in winter, would it not be a good notion to lay up a supply at five dollars instead of waiting until it gets to ten—as you have money on hand. . . .

The Third Letter, 1858[13]

We have not had a letter from you this week but expect that in a day or two we will get two or three at once, as is often the case. We have all been in a state of "tremendous excitement" over Masie's wedding & at last it is all over & we have calmed down. But I must give you some account of the jollification; in the first place it commenced rainning just as hard as it could pour & continued at it till next morning, but we went down in daylight & got along very well; the people gathered early but the marriage did not take place until after eight. Masie & Cy were as badly scared a couple as I ever saw—& Vic was so drunk when he got there that he could barely stand up so you may judge Maimie had a delightful time as he was her attendant. Ben took Miss Julia & Willie took Jane; the very minute D Camp pronounced them man & wife Jane pounced upon Cy & gave him the loudest kiss, it popped like the old woman's yeast bottle; then the kissing went round generally. Don't you wish you had been there. Then the supper was "gorgeous" as your Cousin Tom would say—I know that will make your mouth water, oysters, ice cream & all that sort of thing. Mrs Caughey helped to fix up & she is the nicest person at any thing of that sort that I ever saw. I have bespoken her for your *infair* & William's, but I must tell you about the disperson. About 12 o'clock we began to think about coming home & found it dark as pitch & raining as hard as it ever did rain since the days of the flood I reckon, but we lighted our lamps & started, mary, Amanda, Sam & I in the carriage & Tommy Wright & Mrs. T. C. Wright in the buggy just behind & your Uncle Wickliffe just behind them—all had lights but they seemed just to make the darkness visible. Mr. Wright & Lady got lost between here & the Point & had the greatest time wading round in the ditches and climbing over the levees but they got righted, up toward day & got home to Andy & the baby. Just as we were going to bed your Uncle Wickliffe & party got in, he having lost his hat & as wet as a drowned rat & the muddiest folks you ever saw; they staid all night with us of course. Your uncle William mired down & had to send back to your Aunt Anne's for help to prize him out. The rest of the company staid all night & slept at the rate of 15 for two beds. The infair is to come off on Tuesday next & I enclose you a ticket to it, but I guess you will hardly come as you did not attend the wedding. . . .

Willie & your Uncle Wickliffe & Willie H. are all waiting on the river bank to go to New Orleans; they expect to take the Diana, the Miss Millers went down on the Powell yesterday & I think some our gents were sorry they had engaged the Diana to call for them; they tried to persuade Mr. M[iller] to defer & go with them on a finer boat, but it would have cost him two dollars apiece more, so of course they did not prevail with him—I should have been glad if our folks had saved their money & gone on the cheap boat, for I assure you I never have known such tight times about a little money. You must be economical & not waste a single red cent as we are all trying to curtail; all the necessary expenses of your expensive school must be met of course, but what I mean is do not be extravagant or wasteful & study hard & try to get the worth of your money out of the profit.

. . . We had preaching in our New Church today tho' it is not finished, Mr Tucker is dead slow & has not even finished our cotton carriers yet & you know he was to have them ready for the past crop. Our cotton has fallen far short of what we expected, not much exceeding 1,100 bales on both places & the latter part selling for little or nothing. . . .

MARTIN W. PHILLIPS, 1840[14]

Martin W. Phillips left South Carolina for Hinds County, Mississippi in 1831. He eventually established his "Log Hall" plantation near Edwards. From there, he conducted agricultural experiments and raised a variety of crops, concentrating on cotton cultivation. Through the articles that he wrote for agricultural publications and his co-editorship of *Southwestern Farmer*, he became one of the most renowned advocates of agricultural reform in the South.

January 1840

1. We have now gathered the whole crop, although not yet done pressing, but will to-morrow. Our cotton-book calls for 104,908 lbs. of seed cotton, and we have pressed 66 bales, weighing 30,009 lbs., averaging 75 bales and 99 lbs.

Housed about 1,000 bushels, having been using sometime previous, using about 10 acres of the very best of the corn. If corn had been better cultivated we would have exceeded expectation. 25½ loads (frame body) cut and housed of the oat crop; not having threshed any we know not the number of bushels.

Threshed out 21 bushels of peas and hauled in a great number of pumpkins.

25. Since the 1st day of January we have been engaged in clearing the new ground, cleaning up, deadening and grubbing in the piece of ground added to field No. 1 in front of house. Jacob has laid off piece No. 1 for corn, and is now plowing with two mules and large plow, followed by Viney in the same furrow deepening the furrows, but not exposing subsoil to atmosphere. Sowed 22 acres in oats. Finished ginning this night. . . .

February 1840

3,4. All hands cleaning and burning brush. Amanda, daughter of Peyton and Amy, born A.M. 4th.

5,6. Jacob and Viney plowing in No. 1, other hands in clearing.

10,11. Cutting up logs in our oat field and working in old burn.

12. Rolling logs with 4 hands in oat field. Jacob and Viney finished plowing No. 1. Women and Charles in old burn. Jerome sick.

13. Women and Charles in old burn, Jacob and Viney plowing in oat field, Nanny and Jerome sick.

14. Peyton and Ned mauling; Jacob and Viney plowing; balance clearing; Jerome and Nanny sick.

15. Four hands cutting up and rolling in oat field the logs that were burnt down and blown down since the 12th; Green hauling logs out of new ground; Jerome and gilbert with women in clearing; Jacob and Viney plowing. . . .

18. Rolling logs in new ground with 8 hands; Louisa and Viney grubbing; balance burning brush; a beautiful spring day.

22. Since the 18th been working in new ground; 2 hands mauling; putting up grass fence north side; to-day rolling logs in new ground with 8 hands; commenced pulling and knocking down cotton stalks with the small chaps; Nanny and Viney firing log heaps. . . .

25. Cleaning out new ground fence row with 4 hands; women and children burning brush; hauling cotton seed in potato patch; Charles, Jacob and Viney breaking it up; finished at 3:30 o'clock, then went to oat field; M. W. P. left for Sharon[, Mississippi]. . . .

March 1840

2. Rolled logs with 6 hands in new ground; finished plowing in oats; Gilbert breaking out baulks in corn field; women rolling and beating down cotton stalks; Jacob sick; Amy commenced work this day; rain about midday. The spring has every appearance of having opened; forest trees budding out; cotton up where good seed thrown out; planted peas in garden this day.

3. Jacob and Cyrus cross-plowing for corn; Gilbert and Charles breaking out baulks; Ned and Viney hauling cotton seed for manuring corn; balance of fellows chopping; women and children beating down cotton stalks; preparing to plant corn. . . .

18. Rolled logs to-day in cotton field with 5 hands; Cyrus Jacob and Viney plowing; Louisa clearing up hollows; Nanny firing log heaps; Amy and children threshing down cotton stalks till evening, then picked up chunks; Ned sick; the logs in the cotton field have been very hard to roll on account of the negligent overseers that have been here for the last three or four years. I have had nearly as much trouble to clear up the hollows of bushes, briers and logs as would have rolled the cotton field entirely. Very heavy rain last night, thundered and lightened a great deal.

19. Finished rolling logs in cotton field, had 6 hands at it; Louisa, Viney, Gilbert and Amy cleaning up hollows; Nanny firing log heaps; a very heavy rain last night; Jacob commenced laying off about mid-day; the small chaps threshing down cotton stalks; remarkably warm; many planters in Warren [County] have their cotton planted and corn up ready to scrape; 24 lambs. . . .

April 1840

4. An uncommon heavy rain this morning; fellows cutting rail timber; women raking up manure; holiday in afternoon; . . . corn out; enough was made to have done the farm, but extra hands and extra stock with some extravagance have consumed all; corn selling this year at 50 cents per bushel. The frost on the morning of the 31st killed gourd leaves, squash, nipped corn, a stalk several inches high several blades cut off, but no cotton the least killed—much up as volunteers where stock has fed, and in the garden. . . .

9. Four hands plowing and planting cotton, part of the mules being in the swamp; women cutting out fence row of pasture; Jerome and Green splitting rails.

10. Same work as yesterday with fellows; women and children clearing in burn field. . . .

May 1840

8. Sad havoc with cotton, gullies now where never a wash; all loop heaps in burn field afloat, water over spring and all the field, except form hill to spring; fence gone at the back of field. What a pretty day after so hellish an afternoon!

All hands in the woods, mauling and putting up pasture fence. In the afternoon, took 3 boys in burn to float out logs, etc.; succeeded finely; try again to-morrow.

9. The day was so cold we did not try the water again; falling only about 30 inches since yesterday at 5 o'clock, now 8 o'clock P.M.

Plowed up cotton in the flat of gin house cut, washed up and died out. On finding so much of sweet potato ground washed up, took all hands in it, gave it a thorough working and replanted all missing, now a full stand and in fine order. Planted some drawings amongst corn where missing. Part of new ground corn covered an inch or more with earth from the adjoining field by the very heavy rain. . . .

15. Two plows in new ground corn, part of a good stand, some 2 acres must be planted over. Hoe hands in front of gin house.

Have visited Alex[ander] Montgomery's [his brother-in-law] place today. The rain has ruined his crop, one-half of his cotton crop washed up, levee washed away in many places, fencing gone for about a mile, low ground washed greatly, no idea of the injury. No one can describe, water higher on the levee by 11 inches and in low ground by three feet. He will lose at least 100 acres of cotton—will plant over. This freshet has been general in this section. . . .

July 1840

17. . . . Louisa sick for two days past, disease "prolapsus uteri," with some fever. Gave her rhubarb and cr[eam of] tartar and pills (out of calomel), rhubarb and aloes, 2 doses. Sibley sick, taken with vomiting, dose of pills.

18. Sibley, biggest kind of ague. Dose of pills, then quinine. A very fine rain. Planting potatoes. . . .

20. . . . We mortals are hard to please. We are now fearing too much rain, every appearance tonight of more rain. Rain will now injuure cotton, and any more at present will benefit nothing; the entire crop is now promising. Cotton is now about 3 feet high, but very full of bolls, forms and blooms. I counted today a chance stalk and find 25 bolls, nearly grown. New ground corn in full silk, spring field corn about head high (6 feet); the corn for stock not a good stand up, it has been too dry; peas very fine. . . .

25. Sowed turnips on the 23rd, about 1–5th of an acre, having plowed, cross plowed, harrowed, sown and harrowed. Jerome and his gang working young corn (for stock). Fellows getting rails and hauling to fence row. Have cut out fence row for lots and brushed off sheep lot and cow lot, about 6 acres.

Cotton growing very fast, shedding forms. Counted bolls and forms on "ocra cotton;" average about 70. Corn very fine. Cut tops on old corn past week, one-half badly wilted. Very heavy rain on the night of 22d. Frequent rains since 18th; enough, enough.

August 1840

13. All hands in clearing except Cyrus making baskets. Nanny has been in bed since Saturday; Amy down since Monday, chill and fever; Viny down yesterday, out today; Jane sick since Tuesday, fever; an emetic yesterday, oil this morning, now a hard chill. Last turnips sowed, up. . . .

21. Ned and Woodson topping cotton yesterday and today; Sibley hauling timbers for shed at gin house, etc., yesterday and today; Cyrus assisting in getting the timbers at gin house yesterday and today; all else in the cotton, except Viny and Green—not much the matter with either, but sick, they say. Fodder taken up without rain, 4 loads now hauled in and one more shocked up. . . .

28. Picking cotton in burn field. Woodson very sick. Cyrus and Frank laid up, but not bad off. Sibley sick yesterday, and Moses much better. A great deal of sickness now everywhere. Mr. Montgomery has

some fifteen or more down, and all of the neighbors equally as bad. There has not been a case here this summer that I would call a difficult one to handle. Woodson is now bad off on account of stuffing himself with meat and greens after a dose of calomel and ipecac.

30. Sunday. Finished yesterday picking over the whole field first time, turned out 13,229 lbs, gin house cut turning out 1,510; big cut, 7,370; and burn field, 4,349. All hands (except Peyton and Jacob) have been down with fever; now sick, Frank, Cyrus, Woodson, Sibley, Jack, Jane and Paris. I have never heard of so much sickness in my whole life, everybody down. . . . Bacon out.

September 1840

8. From last date up to present time the hands have been picking cotton, except what were sick. As much sickness as necessary. Ned and Bartlett are now down and have been one week laid up. . . .

11. Finished taking up fodder in spring field, turned out but little more than half that I expected, making in all two double stacks, well cured and without a rain. I don't know whether it is always the case, but new ground fodder has been more trouble to pull than old ground and not half the turn out, owing to the small size of the blades. Ned and Bartlett better, Maria with slight fever. . . .

29. Finished picking over the gin house cut yesterday about 2 P.M., yield, third time, 10,358 lbs.

October 1840

10. . . . Jane a little sick yesterday and today—Cr[eam of] tartar and rhubarb; Milly sick—Cr[eam of] tarter and rhubarb, yesterday, calomel and ipecac, 4 doses of 5 grs calomel and 1 ipecac today. Complains of head, some fever, but skin moist. . . .

21. Hauled in 12 wagon loads of corn out of field in front of the house, turning out over 400 bushels. I think 450, as most of the corn was tramped in by myself from the start. No doubt that the old part

of the whole yield averaged full 35 bushels per acre. The hands were employed yesterday and today breaking in and hauling corn and pulling peas. Pressed 8 bales on the 15th, averaging 482, another in the press, and ought to have got out 10 bales, but the rope was so infirm that much time was lost in breaking ropes. . . .

31. Pressed the residue of cotton now ginned, 4 bales—No. 15, 441; No. 16, 467; No. 33, 435; No. 34, 451. Cyrus and maria, with four mules, have ginned at the least calculation 16 bales in ten days, remarkably—bad work.

November 1840

3. Yesterday being regular sale day of the Marshal of the Southern District of Mississippi, all property I owned in 1839 in this county, except what was sold on August 17, was sold, and A. K. Montgomery became the purchaser, 16 negroes, cattle, sheep and hogs selling for $4,090.

Thus we are sold out, but fortunately a friend was able to advance the money and give my wife time and opportunity to redeem; so we can take a new start, and with prospects flattering, that is, a fair prospect of paying ultimately the honest debts contracted by us, and in the meantime afford a support to our family and educate those [who] providence has placed in our charge. *May the period soon arrive when we may owe no person.* . . .

26. We have this day finished gathering corn, having one-half of our corn crib full, say 1,000 bushels. This with what we have used gives an average of full 30 bushels to the acre. Hauled in a vast number of pumpkins, far more than we ever made before, and more in the field. Threshed out now altogether 21 bushels of peas. . . .

December 1840

14. Killed the sorrel steer today and weighed as follows: 170, 208, 188, 182–728 pounds, which cost $20 and trouble of butchering—in fine order, 30 pounds of tallow. . . .

15. Put up the beef today, having had it well soaked in water so as to get the blood out; then took 4 pounds of salt, 4 pounds of sugar, ½ ounce of saltpetre, and would have taken ½ ounce of pearl ash, but used only a small portion of the cwt. of beef. . . .

19. Received from A. K. Montgomery 3 hogs weighing 204, 230 170–604 pounds, for 3 pigs in exchange. Killed four hogs this morn— 142, 180, 118, 164–604 pounds. . . .

29. Killed 5 hogs this day–184, 144, 192, 133, 150–803 pounds.

31. Finished ginning today.

This day closes the year 1840, with all its sorrows and joys with all its pains and pleasures. May the Ruler of all things so order all that the coming year may be more propitious to all men, and if it can be, that I may have less of the bitter dregs incident to man. This year has been to me full of sorrows and anxieties. Thou Ruler of the world, judge with mercy and punish with moderation, guard and protect us, guide our footsteps, that we many not stumble in thy paths, and keep us ever in the same.

To the close of the year 1840, ever gone.

Chapter 4

ANTEBELLUM SLAVERY

During the early eighteenth century, French colonists began importing slaves from Africa and Caribbean islands into the colony of Louisiana. By 1724, a sufficient number of slaves lived in the colony to justify the creation of a law code—the Code Noir—which defined the rights and responsibilities of owners and slaves alike. Although slaves arrived early in the colonial period, sustained growth in the slave population did not occur until the 1790s, when white planters shifted away from tobacco and indigo production and began to plant cotton on a large scale. As Mississippi farmers planted more and more cotton, the demand for slaves increased. Census reports illustrate the increased presence of slave labor. Before the great cotton boom, a Spanish census of the Natchez District taken in 1784 counted 1,619 whites and 500 blacks; a census completed in 1796 found 5,318 whites and 2,100 blacks in the District. By 1820, slaves constituted 43.5 percent of the new state's population, and by 1860, more than 436,000 slaves, or just over 55 percent of the state's total population, lived in Mississippi.

Throughout the antebellum period, slaves built Mississippi. They maintained roads, constructed levees, drained swamplands, washed, cooked, cleaned, tended livestock, and worked at various jobs that required skilled labor. The vast majority of slaves, however, cultivated cotton and other row crops on plantations and farms. Whether they lived on a vast plantation or a small farm, the lives of slaves consisted largely of work, short rations, and dread—the dread of arbitrary violence, cruel taskmasters, and forced separation from their families. Yet, despite the fears with which slaves daily lived, they constructed worlds of their own, worlds often invisible to whites. Slaves built not only the wealth of Mississippi through their labor, but they also built a dynamic culture that celebrated family and religion. In the late antebellum period, with black enslavement deeply entrenched in Mississippi, the institution reached maturity. The accounts that follow portray slavery at its zenith.

SLAVERY IN THE LAW[1]

Laws governing slavery changed over time, but the changes were never revolutionary in antebellum Mississippi. The selection of laws that follows represents the 1822 slave code as amended by the legislature prior to 1848.

Article 2. An Act to Reduce into one the several Acts concerning Slaves, Free Negroes and Mulattoes—June 18, 1822

8. *Slaves not to go from Home without Pass.* No slave shall go from the tenements of his master, or other person with whom he lives, without a pass, or some letter or token whereby it may appear that he is proceeding by authority from his master, employer or overseer; if he does, it shall be lawful for any person to apprehend and carry him before a Justice of the Peace, to be by his order punished with stripes, or not, at his discretion, not exceeding twenty stripes; and if any slave shall presume to come and be upon the plantation of any person whatsoever, without leave in writing from his or her master, . . . [he shall receive up to thirty-nine lashes].

10. *Slaves not to keep Weapons or Ammunition.* No slave shall keep or carry any gun, powder, shot, club, or other weapon whatsoever, offensive or defensive, except the tools given him to work with, or such as he is ordered by his master, employer or overseer, to carry from one place to another; but all and every gun, powder, shot, club or other weapon found in the possession or custody of any slave or slaves, may

be seized by any person, and upon due proof thereof, made before any Justice of the Peace of the county or corporation where such seizure shall be made, shall, by his order, be forfeited to the seizer for his own use; and moreover, every such offender shall have and receive, by order of such justice, any number of lashes not exceeding thirty-nine, on his or her bare back, for every such offence: *Provided, nevertheless,* that any Justice of the Peace may grant, in his proper county, permission in writing to any slave, on the application of his master, employer or overseer, to carry and use a gun and ammunition, within the limits of the land or plantation of his master, employer or overseer, for a term not exceeding one year, and revocable at any time within such term, at the discretion of the Justice of the Peace granting the same. . . .

12. *Free Negroes not to keep Weapons or Ammunition without License.* No free negro or mulatto shall be suffered to keep or carry any fire-lock of any kind, any military weapon, or any powder or lead, without first obtaining a licence from the court of the county or corporation in which he resides, which license may at any time be withdrawn by an order of such court. Any free negro or mulatto who shall so offend, shall, on conviction before a justice of the peace, forfeit all such arms and ammunition to the use of the informer.

16. *Riots, Routs, Unlawful Assemblies, Trespasses and Seditious Speeches by Slaves, how Punished.* Riots, routs, unlawful assemblies, trespasses and seditious speeches, by a slave or slaves, shall be punished with stripes, at the discretion of a Justice of the Peace, and should any quarrel or fight take place with any free negro or mulatto, and any slave or slaves, such free negro or mulatto, being proved before a Justice of the Peace to be the aggressor in such quarrel or fight, shall be punished with stripes, at the discretion of the justice not exceeding thirty-nine lashes; and he who will, may apprehend and carry him, her, or them, before such justice. . . .

19. *Punishment of White Persons found in Company with Slaves at an unlawful Meeting.* If any white person shall at any time be found in company with slaves, free negroes or mulattoes, at any unlawful

meeting or assembly, and oath thereof being made before a Justice of the Peace of said county, such justice shall forthwith issue his warrant, commanding such person to be brought before him, whose duty it shall be to bind over such person, with good security, to appear at the next Superior or Circuit Court of said county, to answer to said charge; and on conviction thereof, such person shall be fined in the sum of twenty dollars for every such offence, to the use of the informer and shall, moreover, receive not exceeding twenty lashes on his bare back, at the discretion of the court. . . .

31. *Punishment of Free Negroes for Furnishing Slaves with Ardent Liquors.* Any free negro or mulatto who shall give or sell to any slave or slaves any ardent or other intoxicating liquor, upon conviction thereof, before a justice of the peace, shall receive not exceeding thirty-nine lashes, by order of such justice, well laid on his or her bare back.

32. *Punishment of Negro or Mulatto for Abusive Language, or Assaulting a White Person.* If any negro, or mulatto, bond or free, shall, at any time use abusive and provoking language to, or lift his or her hand in opposition to any person, not being a negro or mulatto, he or she so offending, shall for every such offence, proved by the oath of the party, before a justice of the peace, of the county or corporation, where such offence shall be committed receive such punishment as the justice shall think proper, not exceeding thirty-nine lashes, on his or her bare back, well laid on; except in those cases where it shall appear to such justice, that such negro or mulatto was wantonly assaulted, and lifted his or her hand in his or her defence. . . .

44. *Cruel Punishments not to be inflicted on Slaves.* No cruel or unusual punishment shall be inflicted on any slave within this state. And any master or other person, entitled to the service of any slave, who shall inflict such cruel or unusual punishment, or shall authorize or permit the same to be inflicted, shall on conviction thereof, before any court having cognizance, be fined, according to the magnitude of the offence, at the discretion of the court, in any sum not exceeding

five hundred dollars, to be paid into the treasury of the state, for the use and benefit of the literary fund. . . .

📝 50. *Punishment of Slaves Conspiring to Rebel or Murder any Free White Person.* If any negro or other slave shall, at any time, consult, advise, or conspire to rebel, or make insurrection, or shall plot or conspire the murder of a free white person or persons whatsoever, every such consulting, plotting, and conspiring, shall be adjudged and deemed felony, and the slave or slaves, convicted thereof, in manner hereinafter directed, shall suffer death.

🖋 51. *Of Free Person Advising or Conspiring with a Slave in Rebellion or Murder.* If any free person shall advise or conspire with a slave or slaves, to rebel or make insurrection, or shall in any wise aid, assist, or abet, any slave or slaves, making rebellion or insurrection, or shall advise or assist, such slave or slaves, in the murder of any person whatsoever, or shall consult, advise, or conspire with any other free person, or with any negro or other slave, to induce, entice, or excite any slave or slaves to rebel or make insurrection, every such free person so counselling, advising, plotting, or conspiring, or so aiding, assisting, or abetting, on conviction of any of the aid offences, shall be held and deemed a felon, and shall suffer death.

🖋 52. *Punishment of Slave for Assault and Battery on a White Person, with intent to Kill.* If any slave or slaves, shall, at any time commit an assault and battery, upon any white person with intent to kill, every such slave or slaves, so committing such assault and battery, with intent to kill, as aforesaid, and being thereof convicted, in manner hereinafter directed, shall suffer death. . . .

🖋 54. *Slaves, how Punishable for Felonies not Capital.* When any negro or mulatto slave, shall be convicted of any felony not punishable with death, such negro or mulatto slave shall be burnt in the hand, by the sheriff, in open court, and suffer such other corporal punishment as the court shall think fit to inflict, except where he or she shall be convicted of a second offence of the same nature, in which case such negro or mulatto slave shall suffer death.

55. *Certain Capital Offences.* If any slave shall maim a free white person, or shall attempt to commit a rape on any free white woman or female child under the age of twelve years, or shall attempt to commit any capital crime, or shall be voluntarily accessary before or after the fact, in any capital offence, or shall be guilty of the manslaughter of any free person, or shall be guilty of burning any dwelling-house, store, cotton-house, gin or out-house, barn or stable, or shall be accessary thereto, or shall be guilty of any of the crimes aforesaid, or any other crime made capital by law, or shall be accessary thereto, every such slave shall, on conviction, suffer death. . . .

SLAVE LIFE

The memories of Smith Simmons, Charlie Bell, and Ebenezer Brown offer descriptions of slave clothing, food, the rhythm of agricultural labor for men, women, and children, the treatment of slave children, and slave culture, including folk medicine and songs. The selections that follow are from oral histories recorded by white employees of the Works Progress Administration during the 1930s. The dynamics of the interview process raise difficult questions about how historians should treat them. For example, Lizzie Fant Brown, who was interviewed by Netty Fant Thompson—likely a relative of the ex-slave's owner—presents a particularly peculiar situation, and the text of her interview plainly points to some of the difficulties that historians must consider.

Smith Simmons[2]

I came to Coahoma County from the hills. I was born in Montgomery County about six miles from Winona. I never heared anybody say what year I was born, and I don't know how old I was when the Civil War was fought but I wasn't big enough to work, I knows that, but I had sense enough to know what was going on. . . . I can remember good and well going out with one of Master's sons and catching birds under a trap and cooking them in the field. I never will forget that, cause it was the most fun I ever had.

My father Charles and my mother Calline was both from North Carolina. I had four brothers Frank, Sollie, Murry, and Bryan; and four sisters Minerva, Susie, Mollie, and Margaret. . . . The place we lived on was small. There was only three large families on it. Each family ate in their own house. There wasn't no quarters or eating kitchen like the big places had. Our beds was home made stead, with rope cords to hold the mattress. . . . The place had a great big garden for the white folks and the slaves. We was always fed mighty good, peas, greens, meat, lasses, and plenty of milk. I liked everything to eat and still does. Above everything I is a crank about my milk. I likes it yet as well as I did then. We didn't have no game like possums and rabbits. Didn't have no way to kill them.

In them days there wasn't no money paid for work. Everybody worked for their owner for their keep. The clothes we had wasn't nothing to brag on. The children wore shirt tails the year round. When the weather was cold, they put one on over the other. The children didn't wear shoes neither winter or summer. Their foots would crack open from the cold if they went outside in bad weather. The grown folks had good shoes cause they had to go outside to work.

My Master's name was Mr. Dick Baylock. His wife's name was Miss Janie. They had seven children. . . . My white folks lived in a common box house. They was very respectable people, but they didn't care for no fine doings. They didn't have no overseer or driver. Master looked after everything hisself. I don't believe there was more than one hundred acres in the place. Master blowed the horn at daylight for the field hands to get up. The children lay in bed as long as they pleased. At sundown the work stopped. No work went on at night. When the hands came in from the fields, they could do what so ever they pleased. Master sure wasn't hard on nobody. There was very little punishment that went on; if any of the slaves ever got whipped I is never heared of it. Such thing as jails was not known. They didn't need such as that for slaves. They was taught better than to do all the things, people is put in jails for now. . . .

None of the slaves on our place could read and write. None them knowed so much as the A.B.C. There wasn't no body to teach them. Old Miss and Old Master couldn't so much as write their own name. . . .

We didn't know nothing about religion. There wasn't no church to go to, and we never as much as heared about the Bible or Baptizings. . . .

It was very seldom a slave ever ran off. My oldest brother tried that once. He was caught by the patrollers and brought back so quick he never tried that no more. My father lived on a different place from us. My master didn't own him. He had a pass to come to our place so there wasn't no trouble about that. Any of us could visit around if we had a pass. When we do the visiting, we tell all the news we knowed and receive news in the same way. . . .

Saturday at twelve o'clock we was let off from work. The women did their washing, but the men didn't do nothing. Saturday nights we most always had a dance. The banjo and the pat of the hands was the music we had. Sundays was rest and play day. No church to go to, no work to do. In the summer the grown folks walked about and visited. The children had a rail they skilled the cat on and plant across a log for to see-saw. My mother sang a song she had learned in North Carolina. "Come ye that love the Lord and let your joy be known." Everything was lazy like and peaceful the whole day Sunday. The old folks told ghost stories to the children. They would think about them ghosts every time dark would come. That's how come folks grow up to believe in them. I am going to come clean and say straight out I got no faith in such as that. If them things could be seen I would run across one of them some time or other, but I ain't so I telling you I got no faith in it. I don't believe in them Hoo Doo doctors neither. I don't pay them no attention when I hears all this and that 'bout what they can do. I just says to myself, "Seeing is believing" . . .

Charlie Bell[3]

I b'longed to Mr. Mo' frum Poplarville in Pearl River County. They was 'bout fo' hund'ed slaves an' up'ards of six hund'ed acres in

cultivation; hit aint no tellin' how many acres they was in all. I disre-
members his fus' name 'cause I wasn't but nine year old when de
Surrender come in sixty-five an' Mr. Mo's oldest girl mar'ied, an' me
an' my mama an' my daddy an' six others was part of her settin'-out.
So we jes stayed on.

My mother was bornd between Poplarville an' Picayune an' my
father was bornd at Red Church forty mile below New Orleans. . . . My
father was a carpenter an' a blacksmith, could make a whole wagon,
go out an' cut him a gum tree an' make a whole wooden wagon, an'
hubs an' ever'thing. That's how come they didn' take him to de War;
leave him at home ter make mule shoes an' things. He was a powerful
worker.

I 'tended de cows an' calves—give 'em water—an' fed de chickens
what roos' in de big hen-house. But 'fo I got big enough ter do that, I
stay in de 'long house' with de other little fellers. It was just hewed out
er logs. They was notched ter fit—like this—an' dobbed with mud an'
pine straw—wouldn't never wash out. Three of de old women 'tended
ter de chullun an' cooked they sompin'-t'eat. They'd po' syrup in
ever'one of 'em's plate an' ever'one of 'em had tin cup ter theyse'f fer
they milk. They had a big oven like a frog-stool house [i.e. a mush-
room], made out er mud. In de summer they moved hit out in de yard
'cause de chullun didn' stay in de 'long house' 'cep' in de winter. Hit
was plum full then, though, an' Miss Mo' she come out ever' day an'
teached us out'n a Blue Back Speller.

Mr. Mo' built a log church for his labor on de plantation. A white
preacher come twice a month ter speak ter us. His tex' would always
be 'Obey yo' marster an' mistress that yo' days may be lingerin' upon
God's green earth what he give you.['] We didn' have no nigger
preachin' ter us when I was little.

Some of de colored folks was pretty sociable. Some of 'em was
pretty good scholards, could read well enough ter go anywhere an'
enjoy these'fs. De niggers on de plantation danced a heap—seemed ter
me like hit was mos' ever' night. You takes a coon skin an' make a

drum out of hit, stretch hit over a keg—a sawed-off one—dat make a fine drum. An' banjos an' fiddlers! . . .

I've heard say they didn' never buy medicine. Whenever one of 'em got sick, they give 'em peach-tree leaves fer chils an' fever an' biliousness; hit was boiled an' steeped. An' they give 'em red-oakd bark fer dysentery; put hit in a glass an' po' cold water over hit an' drink off er hit all day. Fer jes plain sprains, the'd make a poultice out er okra leaves; hit ud show draw you! You know what they'd put on a bad sprain? Put a dirt-dobber's nest an' vinegar. When de chullun had dem bad colds like they has now, they give 'em hic'ry bark tea, drink hit kinder warm, drink hit night an' mornin'. Hit kep' dat cough from botherin' 'em. . . .

Ebenezer Brown[4]

I is now eighty five years old; I was born 'bout twelve miles south uf Liberty, on de road dat goes frum Liberty to Jackson, Louisiana, on Mr. Bill McDowell's place, an' dat wus er big farm. Marse Bill wus mi'ty tough on his slaves. I was jes' a boy, but I will niver fergit how he whup'ed his slaves. I ken name ebry one uf his slaves: dar was Viney— she done de cookin' 'Zias wus er fiel' han' an' he driv de carriage; my uncle Irwin, he fed de hosses, an' he wus a bad nigger an' got whup'd fur stealin' all de time; Jim wus de rice beater, an' he beat de rice ebery Friday; Sara wus er fiel' han'—Relia wurk in de fiel' an' milked, an' had ter go to de cow pen bar' fotted an' her feet got frost bit, an' dat made her cripple; Hager wus er fiel' han' an' Peggy wus er fiel' han' an' afte' Relia got crippled Peggy he'p milk; Monday wus er fiel' han' but he was bad 'bout runnin' way from home an' de patroller wud git him; Patience, dat wus my mammy, she milked an' wurk in de fiel' an' den dar wus sum big chulluns dat wurk in de fiel' an we all hed ter wurk round de house. . . .

Marse Bill hed a big fine two story house, an' it wus white, an' de front uf it wus to de west; on de north side uf de house wus a dug well, sity five feet deep, an' it had er pulley over it, an' two buckets, an' when one bucket wud come up de udder wud go down. My! But dat wus cold water, but de buckets wus heavy. De gard'n wus on de south side uf de house, an' de pigeon house wus on de northwest side uf de big house, jes' over de Carriage house. . . .

My pappy wus a carpenter, an' wurk in de fiel' an' dun de buildin' dat wus dun on de place, an' he drive de ox team to Osyka to git sugar an' flour, an' he allus hed ter grease de wagon wid tar. Dat wud make it run easy.

Marse Bill had no overseer dat I remember; he an' young Marse Russ toted de whup, an' wud ride ober de fiel' an make de slaves wurk an' dey wud shore whup iffen dat wurk wusnt dun. . . . Marse Bill wud tie dem slave an' whup hard, and all de slave wud say "O, pray, marster; O, pray, Marster!"

When de slaves wus wurking good dey wud sing like dis—

> *Watch de sun; see how she run;*
> *Niver let her ketch yo' wid yer wurk undun.*
>
> *Howdy, my brethern, Howdy yo' do.*
> *Since I bin in de lan'*
> *I do mi'ty well, an' I thank de Lord, too,*
> *Since I bin in de lan'*
> *O yes, O yes, since I bin in de lan'*
> *O yes, O yes, since I bin in de lan'*
> *I do mi'ty well an' I thank de Lord too,*
> *Since I bin in de lan'—*

Dar wus 'nudder song dat went sorta like dis—

> *See my brudder down de hill; fall down on he knees;*
> *Send up your prayers; I'll send up mine; de good Lord ter please.*
> *Raise de heabens, high as de skies; fall down on yer knees;*
> *Send up your prayers; I'll send up mine; de good Lord ter please.*

When cum quitin' time dem slave wud sing all de way ter de house.

Marse Bill had plenty uf ebery thing 'round him. He hed er drove uf cows an' more milk dan dey knowd whut to do wid. He hed hosses, mules, hogs, sheep, yard full uf chickens, geese, guineas, peafowls, pigeons, and he had two jennies an' er jack, an' he made big money offen dem; he made plenty cotton, corn, rice, taters an' peas an' ebery thing good ter eat. He planted more taters dan eny body in de country; dem taters wus red on de outside and white inside an' dey wud choke yer iffen yo' didn't drink water wid 'em. He made as many as 50 tater banks.

When he kilt his hogs, he wud smoke dat meat an' wrap it in shucks ter keep it frum spilin' an' dat wus better dan yo' can buy right now.

He made his slaves pull fodder an' stack it high, an' den he put sum uf it in de loft uf de big barn. He had a rack in de lot an' put dat fodder in dat rack so his stock culd eat it.

He made lots an' lots of rice ebery year, an' ebery Friday he made old Jim put sum rice on a big cloth like er sheet, an' git switches an beat an beat dat rice; den old Jim wud hold dat rice high up and let it fall to de ground a lil'l atter time, an' de wind wud blow de chaff off an' den he had good rice left. Dat wus de way he hulled his peas, an' he fed us on peas an' rice.

Ebery Sat'day dat cum, Marse Bill wud rashun u de slaves. He wud call dem up an' giv ebery fambly a lil'l flour, rice, peas, meat an' meal, an sum times a lil'l soda; we had flour 'nouf to make biskits ebery Sunday mornin an de rest uf de time dey et corn bread. Iffen de rashuns giv out 'fore next Sat'day—well, dat wus too bad, fur yo' had ter do wid out. . . .

When de wimen who had babies wint to de fiel' dey took dem babies wid 'em, an' made a pallet out uf a old quit in de fence corner, an' put dem babies dar while dey hoed and plowed. Den sum uf de wimen had bigger chulluns, dat dey wud put dar to watch de babies, an' wehn de babies wud cry, an' de mammies got to de end uf de row, dey wud stop an' nurse deir babies. Den sum uf de big chaps had to tote water to de field fur de han's. . . .

When it rained de wimen had to go in de loom house an' wurk. Dey made all de jeans an' lowells, an' cloth right dar an' dyed sum uf it wid copperas an' maple bark. Dem women cud make pritty cloth. Dat cloth niver wore out. . . .

De wimen had no combs, an' seed my mammy comb her hed with a cob, then wrap her ahir, and tie it up in a cloth. My mammy cud tote a bucket uf water on her head and niver spill er drap. I see her bring dat milk in great big buckets frum de pen on her head an' niver lose one drap. . . .

Lizzie Fant Brown[5]

I was born in 1861 on the Fant plantation, three and one- half miles due west from Holly Springs. . . .

Marse Jeemes Fant and Miss Liza wus my master and mistress. Our plantation (I always calls it "ours" 'cause being a Fant nigger makes me a Fant too) wus a great big one but I can't say how many acres. And they sho taken good care of us. Them wus better days. Everybody had a good time and they wasn't no hard times. . . .

Yes'm, the patarollers wus always hanging around at night to catch the niggers that wus visiting away from they own plantations.

And of course when they told a nigger he couldn't go away from home, that is just what he wanted to do. Niggers is just like chillun; when you tell 'em they can't do a thing, then they want to [know] whats in it, that you don't want 'em to see.

Patarollers couldn't whip a nigger what had a pass, but they got tired askin' Old Marster for passes ever' night, so they just lit out anyway.

Uncle Tony Moore use to tell us about when he was young. One night he wus visiting his gal on another plantation. They wus setting in front of a big log fire a-talking and a-talking. Sudden-like, the gal's pappy come in and say, "Tony, the patarollers is at the do' a-knocking, what must I do?" Tony say, "Open the do.'"

Ole man didn't want to open the do' so he say agin, "Tony, they's knocking hard, we got to do something quick. And Tony say, "Go on and open the do."

All that time, they wus a big wore-out spade what they had been using on the railroad, a-laying on the hearth. Tony shoveled that spade full of red hot coals and when the gal's pappy swing open the do', Tony pitched them red hot coals right out the do'.

Them patarollers scattered in a hurry and Tony followed them coals out the do' as fast as he could run. Then it wus a race between him and the patarollers. As he clum over a fence, one of 'em grab his foot but he wriggled loose.

All that time, Tony wus hollering, "Mamma, Mamma, open the do," because it was the law that no pataroller could git you in your own house.

Tony's mammy open the do' and Tony make a run for it, just as a pataroller grab his foot agin. But Tony falling in the do' so hard and fast, nobody could hold on to that foot—and he was safe.

One time niggers from the different plantations sneak off and had preaching in a big ditch. Uncle Pat made him a pulpit out of a log and the niggers stand up at the other end and listen to him.

Uncle Pat wus a-zorting and a-zorting them sinners, when all a-sudden, they see him reach behind him, slap on his cap, fall backwards off that log and run like the Devil wus after him.

They turned around the patarollers wus all around 'em. They wus surrounded. Some of 'em got away but the patarollers got a lot of 'em. And did they whip 'em!

Yes'm the patarollers sho wus a 'noyance to the niggers in them days.

SLAVERY IN THE WHITE MIND

The Fear of Rebellion[6]

On September 20, 1835, Jesse Mabry wrote the following letter to Thomas Shackleford, describing an uprising supposedly planned by peddlers, northern doctors, and slaves living near Livingston, Madison County. Shackleford included Mabry's letter in a book he wrote about the Madison County affair.

Dear Sir:—I now attempt to comply with your request, in giving you what information came to my knowledge during the late investigations had before the citizens in the vicinity of Beatie's Bluff, in regard to the late contemplated insurrection in Madison County. I had been absent from the county until the Sunday before the 4th of July; when I arrived at home, I learned that there was some apprehension that the slaves of the vicinity intended an insurrection—that Madam Latham had over-heard a conversation between one or two of her house girls and one of Mr. Landfair's men, in which she distinctly understood the man to say that the negroes were going to rise and kill all the whites; and when being asked by one of the girls what they would do with such a child as she then held in her arms, (having one of her master's grand children in her arms,) he replied, that they intended to put them to death, as it would be doing them a service, as they would go to heaven and be rid of much trouble in this world, &c. On the first day of July we had a small meeting at the Bluff, when I was requested to examine the two girls—they both said, in unqualified terms, that the boy above alluded to had informed them that the negroes intended rising and slaying all the whites. Mr. James Lee, who resides near the Bluff, a very close observer of men, both white and black, had his suspicions aroused from what he had seen and heard, and was consequently on the alert both day and night—he had overheard conversations which confirmed him in his suspicions; and this was of great service to the Committee in the investigations, among the slaves he had heard two of Capt. Sansberry's boys, Joe and Weaver, (a preacher)[.] There was a motion made that a committee of three be appointed to arrest Joe and examine him; where-upon Capt[.] Beattie, James M. Smith and myself were appointed, and immediately proceeded to the plantation of Capt. Sansberry, who promptly delivered up Joe for examination. This man, Joe is a black-smith, and works for the public. I had sent one of my men to the shop twice some short time before this. This man of mine, Sam, I consider a great scoundrel, and I felt confident that if Joe knew any thing of the intended insurrection that Sam was also in the scrape. This I communicated to Capt. Beattie and Mr. James M. Smith, before we commenced the examination of Joe. The first question we put to Joe was this: do you know who we are? Joe replied that he knew Capt. Beattie and Mr. Smith, but that he did not know me. I immediately insisted that he did know me, and continued to look him full in the face for some minutes, until he began to tremble. When I saw this, I asked him if he knew Sam, and when he saw him last? Joe replied that he knew Sam, and had seen him twice not long since, at his shop. I then told him that our business with him was to know the conversation that passed between himself and Sam, at their last interview. He declared that nothing had passed between himself and Sam but what was usual when fellow servants met. We then called for a rope, and tied his hands, and told him that we were in possession of some of their conversation, and that he should tell the whole of it; after some time he agreed, that if we would not punish him that he would tell all that he could recollect. He said that he knew what we wanted, and would tell the whole truth, but that he himself had nothing to do with the business. He said that *Sam* had told him that the negroes were going to rise and kill all the whites on the 4th, and that they had a number of white men at their head: some of them he knew by name, others he only knew when he saw them. He mentioned the following white men as actively engaged in the business; Ruel Blake, Drs. Cotton and Saunders, and many more, but could not call their names, but that he had seen several others. He also gave the names of several slaves, as ringleaders in the business, and was understood to be Captains under those white men. He said that one belonging to his master, by the name of Weaver & one belonging to Mr. Riley, by the name of Russell, (*a preacher also,*) and my old carpenter, Sam, were on the list of captains. Joe stated that the insurrection was to commence the 4th of July; that each plantation of slaves were to commence with axes, hoes, &c, and to massacre all the whites at home, and were then to make their way to Beatties Bluff, where they were to break into the store houses, and get all the arms and ammunition that was in that place, and then to proceed to Livingston, where they would obtain reinforcements from the different plantations; and from thence they were to go to Vernon and sack that place, recruiting as they went, and from there they were to proceed to Clinton; and by the time that they took the last mentioned place the calculated that they would be strong enough to bare down any and every opposition that could be brought against them, from there to Natchez; and that after killing all the citizens of that place, and plundering the banks, &c., they were to retire to a place called the *Devil's Punch Bowl*—here they were to make a stand, and that no force that could be brought could injure them, While Joe was going on with his confession, Capt. Sansbury and his overseer, Mr. Ellis, brought up old Weaver: he would not confess any thing; said that Joe had told lies on him, and that he did not know any thing about the matter at all. He was put under the lash; and Mr. Lee being present, who had overheard his conversation with Mr. Riley's boy, Russell, in which he heard them pledge themselves to each other that they would never confess any thing, either on themselves or any others; and although he frequently repeated these words to Weaver, yet he would not confess. Joe was set at liberty, and Weaver remained in confinement. We then went to Mr. Riley's and took up Russell: all was as mystery with him, he knew nothing, nor could he conceive what we were punishing him for; we now concluded that we would hand him over for safe keeping, to Mr. Ellis, who took charge of him, and just as he arrived at home with him, Mr. Lee rode up, and told Russell that he had overheard Weaver and himself in conversation at a certain place and time, and that he should tell him what had passed between them. Mr. Lee, at this time, struck him twice; Russell asked him to wait, and that he would tell him all about the business; he then went on to make a full statement of all that he knew. His statement was, in all particulars, precisely like the one made by Joe. Next day we again met at the Bluff; a number of slaves were brought in; among the rest, one belonging to Mr. Saunders, by the name of Jim, a very sensible fine looking fellow. I was appointed to examine him; he would not, for some time, make any confession, but at length agreed that if I would not punish him any more that he would make a full confession, and proceeded so to do. His statement was very much like that of Joe's; implicating, however, more white men by name than Joe had done, and some more slaves. There was a man present on the ground by the name of Dunavan, who he pointed out as deeply implicated; he also pointed out a man by the name of Moss, and his sons, as being very friendly to the slaves; that to him they could sell all that they could lay their hands on; that he always furnished them with whiskey; and, also, that these bad white men, while in the neighborhood, always made Moss's house their home; but that he did not know whether he, Moss, intended to take any part with them in the intended insurrection. Jim further stated, that it was their intention to slay all the whites, except some of the most beautiful women, those they intended to keep as wives; said that these white men had told them that they might do so, and that he had already picked out one for himself; and that he and wife had already had a quarrel in consequence of his having told his wife his intention. Jim gave the names of Blake, Cotton, Saunders, and Dunavan as deeply engaged in the business.

Bachus, a boy belonging to Mr. Legget, stated, in substance, all that Jim stated; added one more white man's name to Jim's list. The name given by Bachus I understood to be *Sliver, a pedlar*; and that *Sliver* was making up money to buy arms, &c.; and that he, *Bachus*, had given him six dollars for that purpose, and that he not seen him from that time. This man we could never get hold of. After getting through with these examinations, Jim, Bachus, Weaver, Russell, and Sam, were all put to death by hanging. And being sent for to-day to take my seat on the committee, organized and appointed at Livingston, I do not know any thing more that transpired at Beatie's Bluff, except this, one of Mr. Landfair's boys who was implicated, made his escape, and when he was brought back to the Bluff the people met and hung him. I was present at this hanging.

The above is all that I now recollect that took place at the Bluff while I was present.

James M. Wesson[7]

James M. Wesson was president of the Mississippi Manufacturing Company at Bankston. His 1858 letter to John Francis Hamtrack Claiborne was intended to serve as a pro-manufacturing article in Claiborne's journal, *Sea-Shore Farmer*. Most importantly, Wesson discusses the importance of providing manufacturing jobs for poor whites so that they could be assured that despite their status in society they were different from black slaves.

. . . The capital stock of our Company is now 100,000 dollars, with a surplus of 10,000, and 178 Souls are fed by labour for us in and about the Mills. All of whom have the benefit of weekly preaching, as well as sabboth school instruction, so that while the children are brought up to industrious sobriety, and taught the doctrine of economy of time as well as money, they are instructed in letters and elevated in morals. The improvement in Character and standing of the men and their families who have been for any length of time in our imployment is such as hardly to be believed—only by those who may have witnessed it!

And when all the resources and inergies of the South shall have been fully developed and improved and diverted, what a large and prosperous class of population will have been created out of the very dregs of society (and it may be in some instances worse than dregs)!

For if we are permitted to stop here and take a political view of the Subject and see what an influence a general system of manufacturing in the South would have upon this verry numerous class of our population, we think it would far accell all pecuniary considerations. It is a debatable question whether they are benefitted by the peculiar institution, or not. And as we have some doubts about their interest, we may doubt their political position upon a direct issue disconnected from party ties and love of the Union. A general system of Manufactoring would raise them above the manual labour performed by the Negro, and identify them with the institution, and make them the connecting link between the producer and the consumer which they would most certainly be in the manufacture of wool hats, shoes, and the coarser fabrics. When they become the manufacturers of these articles consumed by the Negro on the one hand and manufacturers of the articles produced by the Negro on the other, they are as clearly identified with him as the owner is, for by him they both get their bread. . . .

We use white labour, except in some of the preparatory departments which are very dusty, not because black is not equal to the task, but because white is cheapest and really more efficient. And it affords the means of an honest living acquired by their own labour to many poor destitute families, widows and orphans, who would otherwise be compelled to live upon what they could get from their friends and from charity. . . .

Chapter 5

THE SECESSION CRISIS

In the presidential election of 1860, a plurality of American citizens cast ballots for Abraham Lincoln. Lincoln won the office without receiving a single vote from a Mississippian—or for that matter any resident of the Deep South. That Lincoln failed to garner support in Mississippi should hardly surprise: white Mississippians approved of neither Lincoln nor his party, which they regarded as the party of abolitionism. Lincoln's election placed Mississippians in a precarious situation. Since 1856, when the Republican party first ran a candidate for the presidency, Mississippians had promised that if the northern states elected a president without the support of southerners, they would not submit to the results of the election. True to their promise, two months after Lincoln's election, representatives attending a statewide convention voted to sever the state's ties to the union. The road to secession ended in January 1861.

The origin of the secession movement in Mississippi can be traced to a much earlier time. During the early 1830s, a State Rights Association formed to oppose President Andrew Jackson's stand during the nullification crisis, but fervent support for secession mounted only during the Mexican War, particularly in response to the Wilmot Proviso. The proviso, a congressional resolution offered in 1846 by Pennsylvanian David Wilmot, called for the Federal government to exclude slavery from any territory acquired from Mexico during the war. Even though the proviso never passed in congress, it provoked great fear among white southerners, who suspected that northern

85

congressmen and ordinary citizens wanted to end slavery. In 1850, when Congress considered the admission of California into the union as a free state, southerners, including Senator Jefferson Davis, howled that admission of a free California would be tantamount to enacting the Wilmot Proviso in another form. Mississippians divided over how to respond to the admission bill, which was a part of the bundle of laws known as the Compromise of 1850. Some politicians, like Governor John A. Quitman, wanted Mississippi to secede, while others, including Senator Henry Stuart Foote, called for support of the compromise. In 1851, a Mississippi convention refused to issue a secession ordinance, and for a short time, unionists held secessionists at bay.

Yet, they could not restrain the secession impulse indefinitely. Throughout the 1850s, the rush of events augered the impending failure of unionists. The 1854 Kansas-Nebraska Act, which opened two new territories to settlement, stirred again the debate about the expansion of slavery. Northern state legislatures angered Mississippians when they effectively abrogated the Federal fugitive slave law by passing personal liberty laws that protected suspected runaway slaves from re-enslavement. In 1859, John Brown's raid on Harper's Ferry, Virginia sent shockwaves through Mississippi, as whites assumed that Brown represented the violent sentiment of every northern man and woman. To many whites in Mississippi, secession seemed like the only way to secure the blessings of black enslavement and white liberty. After all, one half of the nation, a new political party, and perhaps the Federal government as well seemed committed to the destruction of the South's "peculiar institution." Thus, Mississippians interpreted the election of Lincoln as evidence of northern determination to end slavery. Citizens of Mississippi believed that they faced a clear choice: they could submit to the rule of the Republican Lincoln and live with the consequences of emancipation, or they could resist abolitionist influence and leave the union in the hope of preserving slavery. Mississippi chose to secede, and the election of Lincoln, though not the cause of secession, was the trigger that propelled the decision. As indicated by the documents that follow, Mississippians were not unanimous in their decision to secede. However, all agreed that submission to evil—in some cases, the evil of abolition; in other cases, the evil of secession—must be avoided.

HARRY DICKINSON, 1860[1]

Just before the November 1860 presidential election, Harry Dickinson, a member of the moribund Whig party, responded bitterly to a letter written by the state's best known Whig, William Sharkey. Since the Whig party's inception as the leading anti-Andrew Jackson party in the 1830s, Sharkey, the chief justice of the Mississippi High Court of Errors and Appeals, had been an forceful leader of the party. But in 1860, Sharkey called for cooperation between Mississippi Whigs and Democrats. According to Dickinson, Sharkey's appeal, if heeded, would sound the death knell of the already withering Whig party in Mississippi and propel the state toward secession.

. . . The position you assume is that the South should be united. I have very often heard this proposition proposed, and with every desire to view it fairly and impartially, I must say that it has seemed to me to be destitute of force, and ever dangerous in its consequences, though I am satisfied you honestly believe in its importance. Now for what are we to unite? For resisting the encroachments of the north on the slavery question of course. Are we not united on that question? I think as much so as a people could possibly be. Can we be better united in the democratic party than in the opposition? To assert this to assert that the democratic party is sounder on the question than we ourselves have been. This I deny; on the contrary the democratic party has done more to agitate and unsettle that question, and has done more to injure the south than all other parties have done. They have given up the interests of the south for the interests of the party, and my friend, I warn you that they will do it again. I told them in 1856 what they had done, and what Douglass had done and what he was. They admit now that I was right. Shall I go to a party that has then erred itself, and now seems to be penitent. You belonged to the Union party in 1850; look at the democratic party of Mississippi then, and look at it now. The party you then opposed is democrat, and its aims now are just what they were then. Who has unsettled the compromise of 1850; the democratic party. But I will only allude to the past, you of course are familiar with its history. Now I will ask what shall we gain by uniting with the democratic party? This question may be answered, it seems to me by asking, what has the democratic party of the south done for us on the slavery question? . . . They have done nothing—nothing but agitate, excite and alarm the people, and this is all they will do. But I would ask again, what has the democratic party of the nation done for us? Nothing, although it has had possession and control of the government for thirty odd years. Why then join a party that has been always promising and has done nothing? Will it improve by an increase in members? No, the stronger it gets the more corrupt it will become. Now if we are going into battle where bayonets counted I could see the force of your proposition, but not so, this is a mere political contest, in which united as we may be, we do not increase our strength. We are sure not to vote for a black republican, either in the one party or the other; then why join the democratic party? I am inclined to think the party will present a black republican as a candidate, and he who joins the party must vote for him. I think the success and the safety of this government depends upon the conservative patriotism of the people, and that party is injurious and even dangerous. The democratic party is now the government. And it would be even worse if the party in power should be exclusively a sectional party. Now if we unite in the south merely for the sake of a union, what can we expect of the north? Do we not drive it to unite also? Necessarily, as it seems to me. And when we arrive to that condition the government must end in revolution of course. We must depend upon the conservative element of the north, and it is right we should do so, for that constitutes our safety. We cannot put down the abolitionists; it must be done at the north, and if we say to the north we intend to unite as a southern people, they may say we will unite as a northern people. By this sort of union we throw off—set at defiance [—] that conservative element at the north whose great object is opposition to the democratic party. We drive them to the republican party. We all know that [John C.] Fremont would have been elected but for

[Millard] Filmore. There is a noble host of men then, sounder than northern democrats, who are not willing to give us up—shall we abandon them by going to their inveterate enemy. I hope not. But we must moreover expect that if we unite, even the northern democrats will soon drop off from us. But what is quite as bad, we thus admit that there is such a diversity of sentiment, such an antagonism of principle between the north and the south, that the union cannot long exist under such circumstances; and this, in my opinion, is just what the leaders of the party south desire. Depend upon it there are thousands of them that would rather see [Henry] Seward elected than any other man because they hope it would result in disunion. I cannot see that we can have any well grounded hope from the democratic party— its tendencies are to dis[union]. I think our hope should be in an effort to elevate some conservative man to the Presidency who will look to the welfare of his country, and not to the success of the party, as the democratic Government has done, and is now doing. I look upon the democratic party as including all parts of ultraism. I have not one sentiment in common with it—principles it has none. I think the opposition to the democratic party will unite. . . .

My Dear Sir, I have given the foregoing only in general terms; I could not elaborate more. I shall be most sincerely reluctant to part with you, and write you this in a spirit dictated alone by sincere friendship, and it is of course *confidential*. I hope you will not take it amiss, and that it may at least induce you to pause and reflect.

LUCIUS QUINTUS CINCINNATUS LAMAR, 1860[2]

L. Q. C. Lamar holds a distinction that few Americans can claim: he served in all three branches of the United States government. First elected to the U.S. House of Representatives in 1872, Mississippi named him U.S. Senator in 1877. In 1885, he joined the executive branch of government when he became the Secretary of Interior. Four years later, he was named a justice on the Supreme Court. In 1860, while still a professor at the University of Mississippi, Lamar wrote a lengthy letter to an acquaintance in Carrollton explaining why Mississippi should secede after Lincoln's election.

. . . The result of the recent Presidential contest has inflicted a dangerous, perhaps a fatal wound on the confidence of the southern States in the integrity of the Federal Government. . . .

Let us look at this event in its mildest aspect, dissociated from the sectional hostilities in which it originated, and apart from the purposes which it was designed to accomplish. It is the first step towards the subversion of American representative liberty.

There is, as you know, a northern and a southern theory of the Constitution; the latter regarding the United States as a confederacy of States, sovereign, independent, and equal; the former regarding it as one political community—a consolidated republic, in which a majority of the people govern under the forms of the Constitution. Either theory may be adopted for the purpose of my argument. Let us, for the sake of argument, adopt the latter. It is an essential condition of representative liberty, that the powers of Government, (of which the choice of rulers is not the least important,) be distributed through the entire mass of the nation. This is the point from which all representative liberty starts, and to which it must return. That the central authority must derive its nutriment, and draw its force from all the parts of the entire body of society, so that, by their reciprocal independence, they can counteract the tendency of any one part to usurp the sovereignty of the whole. It is required that all the parts should seek and contribute to legitimate rule in common; and, if any part, whatever be their number, insulated from the rest, assumes the common Government over the others by virtue of a prerogative which it arrogates to itself as its exclusive possession, the result is not liberty; it is tyranny unmixed. Test the recent Presidential election by this principle. The northern States—or if you prefer the expression of—the northern people, have usurped an entire branch of the Government, to the exclusion of the southern people. I do not wish to be understood as saying that the southern people have been deprived of the privilege of depositing their ballots and having them counted with all the formalities of law. My proposition is, that the *principle*, not the *form* of representative Government, has been violated. The policy of a conquering power has ever been to disguise its grasp upon the liberties of a people under the sameness of external forms; not to startle the people by any striking alterations, but to cheat them by respect for their usages and customs into acquiescence in the control which it covertly assumes over their public affairs. The Greek Republics retained all their forms of municipal government: the freedom of legislative and judicial proceedings unchanged, while all Greece lay, at the feet of Philip, a subjugated nation. This is the relation which the southern people, if they quietly submit to this election, will sustain to the Executive department of the Government on the 4th day of March, 1861 [i.e. the day of Lincoln's inauguration]. They will live under a Chief Magistrate whose power touches them at every point, penetrating into their States, their towns, cities, villages, and settlements, their business arrangements, and family relations—a Chief Magistrate elected, in no part *by them*, but *over* them, by another people widely distant from them in locality, and still more widely distinct in passions, prejudices, interests, civil and domestic institutions, than they are in geographical position. The obligation to submit and live under a Chief Magistrate thus elected, one Presidential term, implies the obligation to do so under an indefinite number of terms—forever. The right of the North to place the Executive Department in such a relation to the southern people, involves the right to place all the departments of the Government in that relation. But would that be representative liberty? Liberty does not exist where rights are on one side and power on the other. To be liberty, rights must be armed with vital powers. A people cannot be free, who do not participate in the control of the Government which operates upon them. If it is irresponsible to them, if they cannot contribute to the check upon its operations, they are not a free people, but subjects dependent for their rights and interests, upon the moderation and justice of irresponsible rulers; or upon those revolutionary remedies which constitute no part of the machinery of civil society. Such will be the condition of the southern people if they remain in the Union until after the 4th of March next. You will observe that it is a matter of no importance to the people of the South, whether Mr. Lincoln was elected according to the forms of the Constitution or in disregard of those forms. Had he been appointed by the Governors of the northern States, or nominated by the Crowned Heads of Europe, his selection as Chief Magistrate would have been, in either case, no more in disregard of the wishes, interests, and feelings of the entire South, than his election has actually been. When one of the vital principles of a political system has been destroyed, society, in all its elements, is thrown into disorder. In this election the Democratic element of our Government shares the fate of the representative idea. Mr. Lincoln is elected by a minority of nearly a million votes—the South being thus subjected to all the terrors of a passionate Democracy, and the tyranny of a selfish oligarchy. It may be said that this is a mere temporary displacement of the political forces, and that another Presidential election will readjust them, and restore the harmonious operation of our political system.

But our people cannot shut their eyes to the fact, that this revolution in the *Government* only manifests and embodies a mightier *moral revolution*, which has for fifty years upheaved the bosom of northern society—a revolution which has never gone backward, and whose very law is progression. They cannot but see, in this election, the sword of empire drawn by a fanatical majority section, in a contest which cannot be declined, and yet, on the issue of which, the existence of the minority section is staked; that it is a movement impelled by a fanaticism, whose footsteps have never been seen in voluntary retreat; that it is a victory secured by the citizens of States whose Legislatures have solemnly recorded their determination that no oath shall bind them to observe the constitutional compact in respect to slavery. They are convinced that this anti-slavery fanaticism is rife at the North, and that society, in all its elements, is surcharged with the deadly poison;

that it infects their literature, pervades their jurisprudence, is the animating spirit of their theology, is taught in their academies and schools, and they behold the party which represents this spirit, entrenched, (by overwhelming majorities in all their States save one,) in the departments of the Federal Government, armed with the sword in one hand, and the purse in the other. . . .

. . . I feel it my duty to say, that I think acquiescence on the part of the South, in the results of the late Presidential contest, is fraught with more danger to the safety of her society, the stability of her institutions, the freedom of her citizens, and the lives of her people, than can possibly attend any of the plans of resistance to Black Republican rule.

Upon the stability of slavery in the southern States, as an institution of society, government, and property, entitled to the recognition and protection of the Federal Government at home and abroad, and the right to carry our property upon the common territories of the Union, and to enjoy it there, without bar or hindrance from any quarter, I am prepared to advise firmness. Believing, as I did, that a vast majority of the southern people prefer a Union of the southern States to the existing connection with the North—provided such a result could be secured without radical changes in their fundamental system, or shock to existing conditions—I submitted, for the consideration of the Legislature of our State, the plan to which your letter refers. It is intended to avoid the perils that attend transitions from dismemberment to reorganization, and also the evils of provisional governments.

The leading feature of that plan is the adoption of the present Government either by a General Convention of the Southern States, or by commissioners appointed by their authority, who shall provide that the Constitution of the United States shall remain in full force and effect among the States withdrawing; that the laws and decisions of courts which are now of force in the Republic of North America under the authority thereof, shall be adopted as a body of laws for the Federal Government about to be established; that the people of the States so withdrawing will bind themselves to observe and sacredly carry out the stipulations of all treaties subsisting between the United States of North America and foreign Governments anterior to the date of said ordinance, until such treaties are changed or altered, or are disregarded by such nation with this Government about to be established. . . .

THE SECESSION CONVENTION, 1861[3]

On January 9, 1861, delegates to the Mississippi secession convention voted to sever the state's bond with the union. The convention published the secession ordinance, as well as a document written in the style of the 1776 Declaration of Independence, outlining the reasons for the convention's decision to remove Mississippi from the union.

A Declaration of Independence

In the momentous step which our State has taken of dissolving its connection with the government of which we so long formed a part, it is but just that we should declare the prominent reasons which have induced our course.

Our position is thoroughly identified with the institution of slavery—the greatest material interest of the world. Its labor supplies the product which constitutes by far the largest and most important portions of the commerce of the earth. These products are peculiar to the climate verging on the tropical regions, and by an imperious law of nature, none but the black race can bear exposure to the tropical sun. These products have become necessities of the world, and a blow at slavery is a blow at commerce and civilization. That blow has been long aimed at the institution, and was at the point of reaching its consummation. There was no choice left us but submission to the mandates of abolition, or a dissolution of the Union, whose principles had been subverted to work out our ruin.

That we do not overstate the dangers to our institution, a reference to a few unquestionable facts will sufficiently prove.

The hostility to this institution commenced before the adoption of the Constitution, and was manifested in the well-known Ordinance of 1787, in regard to the Northwestern Territory.

The feeling increased, until, in 1819–20, it deprived the South of more than half the vast territory acquired from France.

The same hostility dismembered Texas and seized upon all the territory acquired from Mexico.

It has grown until it denies the right of property in slaves, and refuses protection to that right on the high seas, in the Territories, and wherever the government of the United States had jurisdiction.

It refuses the admission of new slave States into the Union, and seeks to extinguish it by confining it within its present limits, denying the power of expansion.

It tramples the original equality of the South under foot.

It has nullified the Fugitive Slave Law in almost every free State in the Union, and has utterly broken the compact which our fathers pledged their faith to maintain.

It advocates negro equality, socially and politically, and promotes insurrection and incendiarism in our midst.

It has enlisted its press, its pulpit and its schools against us, until the whole popular mind of the North is excited and inflamed with prejudice.

It has made combinations and formed associations to carry out its schemes of emancipation in the States and wherever else slavery exists.

It seeks not to elevate or to support the slave, but to destroy his present condition without providing a better.

It has invaded a State, and invested with the honors of martyrdom the wretch whose purpose was to apply flames to our dwellings, and the weapons of destruction to our lives.

It has broken every compact into which it has entered for our security.

It has given indubitable evidence of its design to ruin our agriculture, to prostrate our industrial pursuits and to destroy our social system.

It knows no relenting or hesitation in its purposes; it stops not in its march of aggression, and leaves us no room to hope for cessation or for pause.

It has recently obtained control of the Government, by the prosecution of its unhallowed schemes, and destroyed the last expectation of living together in friendship and brotherhood.

Utter subjugation awaits us in the Union, if we should consent longer to remain in it. It is not a matter of choice, but of necessity. We must either submit to degradation, and to loss of property worth four billions of money, or we must secede from the Union framed by our fathers, to secure this as well as every other species of property. For far less cause than this, our fathers separated from the Crown of England.

Our decision is made. We follow in their footsteps. We embrace the alternative of separation; and for the reasons here stated, we resolve to maintain our rights with the full consciousness of the justice of our course, and the undoubting belief of our ability to maintain it.

The Ordinance of Secession

The People of the State of Mississippi, in Convention assembled, do ordain and declare, and it is hereby ordained and declared as follows, to-wit:

SECTION 1st. That all the laws and ordinances by which the said State of Mississippi became a member of the Federal Union of the United States of America be, and the same are hereby repealed, and that all obligations on the part of the said State or the people thereof to observe the same, be withdrawn, and that the said State doth hereby resume all the rights, functions and powers which, by any of the said laws or ordinances, were conveyed to the government of the said United States, and is absolved from all the obligations, restraints and duties incurred to the said Federal Union, and shall from henceforth be a free, sovereign and independent State.

SECTION 2nd. That so much of the first section of the seventh article of the Constitution of this State as requires members of the Legislature, and all officers, executive and judicial, to take an oath or affirmation to support the Constitution of the United States, be, and the same is hereby abrogated and annulled.

SECTION 3rd. That all rights acquired and vested under the Constitution of the United States, or under any act of Congress passed, or treaty made, in pursuance thereof, or under any law of this State, and not incompatible with this Ordinance, shall remain in force and have the same effect as if this Ordinance had not been passed.

SECTION 4th. That the people of the State of Mississippi hereby consent to form a Federal Union with such of the States as may have seceded or may secede from the Union of the United States of America, upon the basis of the present Constitution of the said United States, except such parts thereof as embrace other portions than such seceding States.

Thus ordained and declared in Convention the 9th day of January, in the Year of Our Lord One Thousand Eight Hundred and Sixty-one.

JEFFERSON DAVIS, 1861[4]

When Jefferson Davis resigned from the U.S. Army, he moved to Warren County, Mississippi to be near his brother, a wealthy planter. He did not remain long in Mississippi. In the 1840s, his neighbors elected him to the U.S. House of Representatives, but he resigned to serve in the Mexican War where he achieved acclaim for his exploits. Afterwards, he served as Secretary of War and won a seat in the U.S. Senate, an office he vacated upon Mississippi's secession. He was the only president of the Confederacy and lived out the majority of his postwar life at Biloxi.

I rise, Mr. President, for the purpose of announcing to the Senate that I have satisfactory evidence that the State of Mississippi, by a solemn ordinance of her people in convention assembled, has declared her separation from the United States. Under these circumstances, of course,

my functions are terminated here. It has seemed to me proper, however, that I should appear in the Senate to announce that fact to my
associates, and I will say but very little more. . . .

It is known to Senators who have served with me here, that I have
for many years advocated, as an essential attribute of State sovereignty,
the right of a State to secede from the Union. Therefore, if I had not
believed there was justifiable cause; if I had thought that Mississippi
was acting without sufficient provocation, or without an existing
necessity, I should still, under my theory of the Government, because
of my allegiance to the State of which I am a citizen, have been bound
by her action. I, however, may be permitted to say that I do think she
has justifiable cause, and I approve of her act. . . .

I hope none who hear me will confound this expression of mine
with the advocacy of the right of a State to remain in the Union, and
to disregard its constitutional obligations by the nullification of the
law. Such is not my theory. Nullification and secession, so often confounded, are indeed antagonistic principles. Nullification is a remedy
which is sought to apply within the Union, and against the agent
of the States. It is only to be justified when the agent has violated
his constitutional obligation, and a State, assuming to judge for itself,
denies the right of the agent thus to act, and appeals to the other
States of the Union for a decision; but when the States themselves,
and when the people of the States, have so acted as to convince us that
they will not regard our constitutional rights, then, and then for the
first time, arises the doctrine of secession in its practical application.

A great man who now reposes with his fathers, and who has been
often arraigned for a want of fealty to the Union, advocated the doctrine of nullification, because it preserved the Union. It was because
of his deep-seated attachment to the Union, his determination to find
some remedy for existing ills short of a severance of the ties which
bound South Carolina to the other States, that Mr. [John C.] Calhoun
advocated the doctrine of nullification, which he proclaimed to be
peaceful, to be within the limits of State power, not to disturb the

Union, but only to be a means of bringing the agent before the tribunal of the States for their judgment.

Secession belongs to a different class of remedies. It is to be justified upon the basis that the States are sovereign. There was a time when none denied it. I hope the time may come again, when a better comprehension of the theory of our Government, and the inalienable rights of the people of the States, will prevent any one from denying that each State is a sovereign, and thus may reclaim the grants which it has made to any agent whomsoever.

I therefore say I concur in the action of the people of Mississippi, . . . ; and this brings me to the important point which I wish on this last occasion to present to the Senate. It is by this confounding of nullification and secession that the name of a great man, whose ashes now mingle with his mother earth, has been invoked to justify coercion against a seceded State. The phrase "to execute the laws," was an expression which General [Andrew] Jackson applied to the case of a State refusing to obey the laws while yet a member of the Union. That is not the case which is now presented. The laws are to be executed over the United States, and upon the people of the United States. They have no relation to any foreign country. It is a perversion of terms, at least it is a great misapprehension of the case, which cites that expression for application to a State which has withdrawn from the Union. You may make war on a foreign State. If it be the purpose of gentlemen, they may make war against a State which has withdrawn from the Union; but there are no laws of the United States to be executed within the limits of a seceded State. A State finding herself in the condition in which Mississippi has judged she is, in which her safety requires that she should provide for the maintenance of her rights out of the Union, surrenders all the benefits, (and they are known to be many,) deprives herself of the advantages, (they are known to be great,) severs all the ties of affection, (and they are close and enduring,) which have bound her to the Union; and thus divesting herself of every benefit, taking upon herself every burden, she claims to be exempt from any power to execute the laws of the United States within her limits. . . .

It has been a conviction of pressing necessity, it has been a belief that we are to be deprived in the Union of the rights which our fathers bequeathed to us, which has brought Mississippi into her present decision. She has heard proclaimed the theory that all men are created free and equal, and this made the basis of an attack upon her social institutions; and the sacred Declaration of Independence is to be construed by the circumstances and purposes for which it was made. The communities were declaring their independence; the people of those communities were asserting that no man was born—to use the language of Mr. Jefferson—booted and spurred to ride over the rest of mankind; that men were created equal—meaning the men of the political community; that there was no divine right to rule; that no man inherited the right to govern; that there were no classes by which power and place descended to families, but that all stations were equally within the grasp of each member of the body politic. These were the great principles they announced; these were the purposes for which they made their declaration; these were the ends to which their enunciation was directed. They have no reference to the slave; else, how happened it that among the items of arraignment made against George III was that he endeavored to do just what the North has been endeavoring of late to do—to stir up insurrection among our slaves? Had the Declaration announced that the negroes were free and equal, how was the Prince to be arraigned for stirring up insurrection among them? And how was this be to enumerated among the high crimes which caused the colonies to sever their connection with the mother country? When our Constitution was formed, the same ideas was rendered more palpable, for there we find provision made for that very class of persons as property; they were not put upon the footing of equality with white men—not even upon that of paupers and convicts; but, so far as representation was concerned, were discriminated against as a lower caste, only to be represented in the numerical proportion of three fifths.

Then, Senators, we recur to the compact which binds us together; we recur to the principles upon which our Government was founded; and when you deny them, and when you deny to us the right to withdraw from a Government which thus perverted threatens to be destructive of our rights, we but tread in the path of our fathers when we proclaim our independence, and take the hazard. This is done not in hostility to others, not to injure any section of the country, not even for our own pecuniary benefit; but from the high and solemn motive of defending and protecting the rights we inherited, and which it is our sacred duty to transmit unshorn to our children.

I find in myself, perhaps a type of the general feeling of my constituents towards yours. I am sure I feel no hostility to you, Senators from the North. I am sure there is not one of you, whatever sharp discussion there may have been between us, to whom I cannot now say, in the presence of my God, I wish you well; and such, I am sure, is the feeling of the people whom I represent towards those whom you represent. I therefore feel that I but express their desire when I say I hope, and they hope, for peaceful relations with you, though we must part. They may be mutually beneficial to us in the future, as they have been in the past, if you so will it. The reverse may bring disaster on every portion of the country; and if you will it thus, we will invoke the God of our fathers, who delivered them from the power of the lion, to protect us from the ravages of the bear; and thus, putting our trust in God, and in our own firm hearts and strong arms, we will vindicate the right as best we may.

In the course of my service here, associated at different times with a great variety of Senators, I see now around me some with whom I have served long; there have been points of collision; but whatever of offense there has been to me, I leave here; I carry with me no hostile remembrance. Whatever offense I have given which has not been redressed, or for which satisfaction has not been demanded, I have, Senators, in this hour of our parting, to offer you my apology for any pain which, in heat of discussion, I have inflicted. I go hence unencumbered of the remembrance of any injury received, and having discharged the duty of making the only reparation in my power for any injury offered.

Mr. President, and Senators, having made the announcement which the occasion seemed to me to require, it only remains for me to bid you a final adieu.

WILLIAM NEED, 1861[5]

> In two separate letters, William Need, a former resident of Mississippi who had moved to Tuscon, Arizona Territory to seek his fortune as a mine owner, wrote to his former political ally John J. McRae, encouraging him to reconsider the wisdom of secession. One of his letters, which appears below, indicates the shock and dismay with which a former resident viewed the arrogance of secession. Need's effort to sway McRae had no influence; in fact, McRae united with the Confederate cause and recruited soldiers in the southern part of the state.

. . . I perceive from a perusal of the "Missouri Republican," that the State of Mississippi in Convention assembled passed the Ordinance of Secession with great unanimity. I regret her hasty action; and it seems to me an inevitable conclusion that her people will live to remember their false steps with a deep and bitter reproach. In 1835, when I sent the Prospectus of the "Free Trader" forth to a reflecting world, certain members of the "Metropolitan Junta" at Natchez belonging to the so-called State Rights or Nullification Party said I was deranged.[6] *They sneered at the Union*, and affectedly seem[ed] to condemn every sentiment . . . intended to uphold its integrity. But as a Union Democrat, of the Jefferson, Jackson, Rives and Livingston school, I passed by their idle sneers and vituperation as I did the passing zephyrs of the fleeting wind. The doctrine of the "Free Trader" Prospectus—get it and read it—had the effect to raise the price of Mississippi Securities in the Eastern and European stock market above par—to Elevate the character and standing of the State. . . . Let us now look upon the *picture* which the Ordinance of Secession when it is read in New York, London and Paris will Exhibit to an admiring or astonished world! I doubt whether Mississippi Securities now would bring 10 cents on the dollar in Wall Street, and certainly not 5 cents in London or Paris. . . . This shows the difference between standing by the Union through good report and Evil report, instead of rushing with a heedless impetuosity to the brink of disunion and destruction. "Peaceable Secession" is impossible; it can never become an accomplished fact. I am utterly amazed at the madness which rules the hour! I know the idea is Entertained among many warm and generous and Enthusiastic minds (yours perhaps among the number) that after "Secession" succeeds, the disunion States will be able to form a new Constitution with *ample guaranties for the protection of Slavery*, and Erect a magnificent Southern Confederacy upon the ruins of the Government Established by the wisdom of Washington, Jefferson, Franklin, Madison and their Compatriots. Fatal delusion! Sir, the people of the Cotton States are insane; great prosperity has made them mad! They look to Mexico and Central America and Cuba to Extend their Empire. It can never succeed! Maryland and Delaware and the other Border States will never join your Slavery-Extending Confederacy! . . . *Louis Napoleon*, the Emperor of the French rules Mexico, and already he has a Treaty with the Government of *Bonita Juarez*, the President of the Republic, by which he finds himself to defend the Territory in fact against all further Efforts on the part of other governments to conquer the country. It is a check against Extension in that quarter on the part of a Southern Confederacy. The whole civilized world, besides three-fourths of the American people forbid the [action of Mississippi], and think you of the South against all this show of face and determined resolution, could [never] make good this boast of planting Slavery *there*. The idea is ridiculous! The first blast of the bugles would place innumerable Garibaldis[7] in your midst, and you would find as much as you could do to protect your altars and firesides, without moving an army 100 miles in the direction of such an object! You would be overwhelmed on land and at Sea!

Dismal Swamp tragedies[8] would break out in Every direction, and who could stop them? Pause, I beseech you in the false step Mississippi has taken. The cotton States cannot *destroy* the Union. They may retard its prosperity, but they cannot Effect its destruction. Impossible! Sir, it is because I think a good deal of you that I address you in such frank and Earnest words. I do not, I cannot believe that your heart is in this Secession Movement. You have suffered your prejudices to lead you astray. If you continue in the "footsteps" of disunion, and resolve needlessly to carry out the dismemberment of the Confederacy, my deliberate conviction is that you will lose the sympathies of the Entire Northern Democrats as well as Republicans, one half of the South and the Entire world, the slaveholding Republic of Brazil included; and in five years there will not be a Slave in all Mississippi. This is my firm belief. It is because I love that State, and regret that I Ever left it ([William H.] Harrison's Election [as president in 1840] rendered the fulfilment of a vow unalterable with me— a fixed determination to leave the State in the Event of his Success) and it is because that I want to see you Elected *President of the United States, to take your seat on the 4th of March, 1865,* that I appeal to your patriotism, to your judgement, to your good sense, and to every consideration that Enlightened man holds dear, to retrace your steps! You can do it—nobly and honorably. Never mind the taunt of *consistency* or being called a "*Retreating Secessionist*". . . . Better be called that than an incorrigible renegade. So I think you had better come back into the Union fold, albeit you should be called a "Retreating Secessionist" or "Submission" man. Better be called that than a Destroyer of your country, a Burrite. Old Arthur Fox once told me on the banks of Pearl River, that he would sooner be called a "d__d rascal" than a Nullifier or Disunionist. . . . By the memory of such old Democrats . . ., the pillars of Eastern Mississippi Democracy, I beseech you to pause! Did they not oppose the "Black basis" of Mississippi representation in the Legislature and think you they would join South Carolina and submit to Slavery rule—a military Despotism? Never, sir; never! I am not opposed to slavery, *per se*; but I would be opposed to Adams and Wilkinson, Hinds and Yazoo Counties ruling East Mississippi; and, on the same principle, I would oppose the idea of South Carolina governing and ruling New York and Pennsylvania and Maryland. . . . [I suggest that] you and your brother Secessionists will take the advice of Sir Pete and Lady Teazle,[9] and conclude the performance of your Drama by winding up and concluding to be better friends of the Union than you Ever were before. That's all.

Chapter 6

WARTIME MISSISSIPPI

In the spring of 1861, white Mississippians, with few exceptions, looked forward to the start of the Civil War. Men and boys rushed to enlist in local militia companies; women and girls formed sewing circles to supply the new soldiers with clothing and company flags. So many volunteers enrolled in the state militia that Governor John Pettus, knowing the state could ill afford to keep and maintain a sizable army, turned away large numbers of volunteers. The flush of victory at Fort Sumter in April 1861 and the rout of the Union army at Manassas strengthened the faith of Mississippians, who believed the Confederate States would conquer the forces of abolition before the crop gathering season ended. But the realities of the Civil War—both those realities known most plainly to soldiers (death, destruction, disease) and those known best by civilians (taxes, conscription, inflation, restrictions on trade)—soon visited Mississippi, dampening enthusiasm for the war.

Bloody military campaigns involving Mississippi citizens, some as combatants, others as civilians, diminished the ebullience of 1861. The Shiloh, Tennessee campaign, which spilled over into Corinth and northeastern Mississippi, brought the hardships of war into the region of the state least supportive of secession. In July 1863, dual Confederate defeats at Gettysburg, Pennsylvania and Vicksburg claimed the lives of many Mississippians, as did the Atlanta campaign in 1864. The long siege of Vicksburg in particular left Mississippi soldiers and civilians with the acrid taste of warfare in their mouths and a crushed collective spirit. With every defeat, southern soldiers came less and less to believe that victory was soon to be theirs.

Likewise, on the home front, warfare and wartime policy brought to civilians greater suffering annually. In addition to the despair caused by war-related loss of life and property, three laws especially caused whites to doubt the virtue of the war. Conscription laws and the prejudiced manner in which they were enforced against ordinary white males left many Mississippians desiring an end to the war. The tax-in-kind, which permitted the government to extract from civilians a portion of their foodstuffs and livestock, as well as impressment, which empowered the military to take from civilians necessary war material, spread among citizens a spirit of resistance to Confederate and state policies and the war itself. Coupled with military failure and oppressive laws, soaring commodity prices and a drought in eastern Mississippi quenched the thirst for war that many white Mississippians suffered in 1861. The selections that follow represent a variety of responses to the war and wartime conditions.

MATTHEW A. DUNN

Matthew Dunn owned a sizeable farm and a few slaves near Liberty in southwest Mississippi. In 1861, he forsook his family and farmstead to enlist in the state militia. Much of his time in the military was spent in Mississippi. The following letters, written in 1863 and 1864, were addressed to his wife Virginia. They contain interesting stories of day-to-day life in the military.

Newton Station, 1863[1]

. . . I will tell you of a little Scrape I got into a few days ago while at Morton [Mississippi]. I was guarding Some prisoners in town and was ordered by the Provost Marshal to take two men and go ahead about 2½ miles in the County to arrest Some men who had acted very impolitely with a Citazen & one of them was finally knocked down by the Citazen and I expect will die—they were all drunk—there were three of them. I was furnished with an ambulance and I and the detail drove out and when I got to the place I found one man lying under a tree asleep. I Posted a guard over him until I got the wounded man in the ambulance. I then awake him & he pitched into us for a fight and we had a nice time of it he was a very stout man and just drunk enough to be a fool[.] I avoided useing our guns on him as he was drinking, but I never will be imposed on by another as I was by him—in the Scuffle I got him by the hair of his head and about that time one of the men who was assisting me let him go and run, he tore loose from me and broke after him. I then ordered the guard to take him which was Soon done—the other one never Showed fight—after I got them to the guard house the one that fought us soon tried to make his escape by the guard at the door. I Saw he would make his escape when I put my gun against his breast and pushed him back into the house he gritted his teeth at me asked me if I dared to treat him so—I told him he could not come through that door—finally he jumped out at a place where there was no guard and made his escape. I have been Sore from the Scuffle ever since. . . .

Meridian, 1863[2]

We are haveing an interesting meeting going on now at night—eight were Babtized last Sunday. On yesterday our Brigade was ordered out [to participate in a] Scene that I hope my eyes never will behold again—but it is to be the case again next Friday—that is Seeing men Shot for Desertion. I saw three Shot yesterday—they were Seated on their Coffins with their arms confined and blind folded—the executioners were placed about fifteen paces in front. Two were shot dead—the third one never fell—one of the non-Com-Officers had him to kill. He walked up to him very deliberately and Shot him through, this was a horrible Sight and painful duty to perform, but the affair was well conducted—one of them had a family—one of them made his escape from the guard yesterday morning before their execution—the

Corporal Shot at him twice but failed to stop him. Skirmishers were immediately thrown out for him when he was found and brought in again—it was him that had to be killed by the sergeant—this war is calculated to harden the softest heart. . . .

Bear Camp, Canton, 1863[3]

As this is a beautiful Saturday evening and I am on duty and but little to do I will spend a portion of it in writing to you. Nero expects to start down home in the morning and it will be a good opportunity to send it. . . . I have made an effort for a Furlough but failed and an order came from Gen[. Robert] Lowry today—not to let any off under no considerations—only according to the old rule which is one Furlough for every twenty five men in the Reg. According to that . . . it will be Some time next summer before I will be entitled to one. It really seems that the best soldiers are the Sufferers in this war. But if it is right I will try and Submit to it with a hope that we will have peace before that time and all be on an equality once more. Some think it will not be long before we will be disbanded, but I dont know what their hopes are based upon. Jeff Davis Said in a Speech he made in Meridian a few days ago that in a Short time we would hear some thing that would be cheering to us. Lo I hope day is beginning to dawn. . . . Our duty would be very light if it was not for the Deserters we have to guard. Our Cavalry bring them in and we keep them under guard until they can be tried by a court martial. Some of them are bad cases. Some are wearing a ball and chain, which they will have to wear during the war and live on bread and water a portion of the time— more of them I expect will be shot. There is not chance now for a substitute we are debarred of all Such privilleges. . . .

I don't know what to tell you about hiring Bob for another year. If you cant pay him in Confederate money I dont See how you can hire him any longer. . . . I dont See how he [Bob's owner, a Mr. Covington] can refuse the money at this time as its all we have. If Andrew Should take a whim to try the yankees, which I hope he never will, Bob would be a great help to you and would be less apt to runaway than a grown one—do whatever your Pa and Levi thinks best. . . .

I suppose people are selling Cotton rapidly Stumpy. It is rumored here in Camp that Sam Chance was Caught by our Calvary with negro dogs in a sink hole—and conscripted. I took the responsibility on myself to contradict the report as I thought it a mistake. Let me know whether there is any thing of it or not—urge the Darkies to keep straight tell them to carry on business as though I was present. . . .

Atlanta, 1864[4]

I am happy to say to you that my life is yet spared and my health is good. But a portion that I will write will be very painful. I sent word to you in Clem [Lea's] letter a few days ago that Tad was wounded on the 22nd, but it was a mistake. But Since then on the 27th he was in another battle and was Shot through the leg below the knee which caused his leg to be amputated above the knee. His Brigade was in the fight before ours, and as we went in I met him lying on the Road Side. I Stopped with him a few minutes and he told me that he did not think the bone was broken. But I supose after the Doctors examined it they thought it best to take it off. I know it will nearly kill Ma to hear of it but it is a portion of the horrors of this cruel war. . . .

Atlanta, 1864[5]

. . . The Yankees for the past few days have made some demonstrations upon our Picket line, but their efforts so far have proven ineffectual. They Shelled us rapidly yesterday all day and one came very near getting me which has been the case several times before. But God for Some purpose, unknown to me, had spared me. He has taken three of my Mess in killed and wounded, since we have been on this Campaign. And not only have I lost mess mates, but I have lost my bed mate, my best friend in Camp, and neighbor at home. Poor Clem

[Lea] is no more. But when I took the last look at him I felt happy to think that he had gone to a better world, and had left so honorable a name to be transmitted to *loved* and *dear* ones behind. I Started Julia a dispatch on the next morning after his death which I reckon has been received by this time. And it makes my heart throb within my breast when I imagine her feelings. With her little Fatherless ones weeping over her lap as She has called them around her to tell them of the fate of *that Father*, which they had so anxiously been looking for and being altogether insensible of the *cause* for which *he* So cheerfully yielded up his life. . . . We have prayer meetings every night when we dont have preaching and it would make one[']s heart rejoice to see the interest taken by our young members. I am glad to hear of the great revival in Liberty[, Mississippi]. I hope the good work will go on until we will receive a great blessing nationally as well as Spiritually. . . .

JEREMIAH S. GAGE, 1863[6]

Jeremiah Gage resided in Richland, Holmes County but attended the University of Mississippi. Soon after secession, Gage joined the University Greys, a company composed of students at the university. Gage's company saw constant action after being attached to the Army of Northern Virginia. Of the nearly 600 soldiers capable of duty in July 1863, approximately 34 percent were killed or wounded at Gettysburg. Gage was one of the Gettysburg casualties. Suffering from his wounds and undoubtedly under the influence of morphine, Gage used his last substantial strength to write his mother a brief letter of farewell.

This is the last you may ever hear from me. I have time to tell you that I died like a man. Bear my loss as best you can. Remember that I am true to my country and my greatest regret at dying is that she is not free and that you and my sisters are robbed of my worth whatever that may be. I hope this will reach you and you must not regret that my body can not be obtained. It is a mere matter of form anyhow.

This is for my sisters too as I can not write more. Send my dying release to Miss Mary . . . you know who. . . .

This letter is stained with my blood.

AN ANONYMOUS VICKSBURG WOMAN, 1863[7]

The author of the diary extract that follows remains anonymous. Perhaps because the diarist appears to be an outsider in Vicksburg, the original editor of the diary, the New Orleans novelist George Washington Cable, refused to identify her. As recounted in the diary, the struggle to find safe haven, food, and clothing stand out. Other themes are also broached: her husband dodges conscription by his maintenance of a local government position; the attitude of slaves toward the war is mentioned; and the role of white women during the war is illustrated.

. . . *May 1st, 1863*: It is settled at last that we shall spend the time of siege in Vicksburg. Ever since we were deprived of our cave [on April 2 when the property owner returned], I had been dreading that H____ would suggest sending me to the country, where his relatives lived. As he could not leave his position and go also without being conscripted, and as I felt certain an army would get between us, it was no part of my plan to be obedient. A shell from one of the practicing mortars brought the point to an issue yesterday and settled it. Sitting at work as usual, listening to the distant sound of bursting shells, apparently aimed at the court-house, there suddenly came a nearer explosion; the house shook, and a tearing sound was followed by terrified screams from the kitchen. I rushed thither, but met in the hall the cook's little girl America, bleeding from a wound in the forehead, and fairly dancing with fright and pain, while she uttered fearful yells. I stopped to examine the wound, and her mother bounded in her black face ashy from terror. "Oh! Miss V____, my child is killed and the kitchen tore up." Seeing America was too lively to be a killed subject, I consoled Martha and hastened to the kitchen. Evidently a shell had exploded just outside, sending three or four pieces through. When order was restored I endeavored to impress on Martha's mind the necessity for calmness and the uselessness of such excitement. . . .

"Oh! H____," I exclaimed, as he entered soon after, "America is wounded."

"That is no news; she has been wounded by traitors long ago."

"Oh, this is real, living, little, black America; I am not talking in symbols. Here are the pieces of shell, the first bolt of the coming siege."

"Now you see," he replied, "that this house will be but paper to mortar-shells. You must go in the country."

The argument was long, but when a woman is obstinate and eloquent, she generally conquers. I came off victorious, and we finished preparations for the siege to-day. Hiring a man to assist, we descended to the wine-cellar, where the accumulated bottles told to the "banquet-hall deserted," the spirit and glow of the festive hours whose lights and garlands were dead, and the last guest long since departed. To empty this cellar was the work of many hours. Then in the safest corner a platform was laid for our bed, and in another portion one arranged for Martha. The dungeon, as I call it, is lighted only by a trap-door, and is so damp it will be necessary to remove the bedding and mosquito-bars every day. The next question was of supplies. I had nothing left but a sack of rice-flour, and no manner of cooking I had heard or invented contrived to make it eatable. A column of recipes for making delicious preparations of it had been going the rounds of Confederate papers. I tried them all; they resulted only in brick-bats, or sticky paste. H____ sallied out on a hunt for provisions, and when he returned the disproportionate quantity of the different articles obtained provoked a smile. There was a *hogshead* of sugar, a barrel of sirup, ten pounds of bacon and peas, four pounds of wheat-flour, and a small sack of corn-meal, a little vinegar, and actually some spice! The wheat-flour he purchased for ten dollars as a special favor from the sole remaining barrel for sale. We decided that must be kept for sickness. The sack of meal, he said, was a case of corruption, through a special providence to us. There is no more for sale at any price, but, said he, "a soldier who was hauling some of the Government sacks to the hospital offered me this for five dollars, if I could keep a secret. When the meal is exhausted perhaps we can keep alive on sugar. Here are some wax candles; hoard them like gold." He handed me a parcel containing about two pounds of candles, and left me to arrange my treasures. It would be hard for me to picture the memories those candles called up. The long years melted away, and I

> "Trod again my childhood's track
> And felt its very gladness"

In those childish days, whenever came dreams of household splendor or festal rooms or gay illuminations, the lights in my vision were always wax candles burning with a soft radiance that enchanted every scene. . . .

May 28th: Since that day [May 1, when Confederate troops retreated from the countryside into Vicksburg] the regular siege has continued. We are utterly cut off from the world, surrounded by a circle of fire. Would it be wise like the scorpion to sting ourselves to death? The fiery shower of shells goes on day and night. H____'s occupation, of course, is gone, his office closed. Every man has to carry a pass in his pocket. People do nothing but eat what they can get, sleep when they can, and dodge the shells. There are three intervals when the shelling stops, either for the guns to cool or for the gunners' meals, I suppose,—about eight in the morning, the same in the evening, and at noon. In that time we have both to prepare and eat ours. Clothing cannot be washed or anything else done. On the 19th and 22d, when the assaults were made on the lines, I watched the soldiers cooking on the green opposite. The half-spent balls coming all the way from those lines were flying so thick that they were obliged to doge at every turn. At all the caves I could see from my high perch, people were sitting, eating their poor suppers at the cave doors, ready to plunge in again. As the first shell again flew they dived, and not a human being was visible. The sharp crackle of the musketry-firing was a strong contrast to the scream of the bombs. I think all the dogs and cats must be killed or starved, we don't see any more pitiful animals prowling around. . . . To-day he heard while out that expert swimmers are crossing the Mississippi on logs at night to bring and carry news to [General Joseph Eggleston] Johnston. I am so tired of corn-bread, which I never liked, that I eat it with tears in my eyes. We are lucky to get a quart of milk daily from a family near who have a cow they hourly expect to be killed. I send five dollars to market each morning, and it buys a small piece of mule-meat. Rice and milk is my main food; I can't eat the mule-meat. We boil the rice and eat it cold with milk for supper. Martha runs the gauntlet to buy the meat and milk once a day in a perfect terror. The shells seem to have many different names; I hear the soldiers say, "That's a mortar-shell. There goes a Parrott. That's a rifle-shell." They are all equally terrible. A pair of chimney-swallows have built in the parlor chimney. The concussion of the house often sends down parts of their nest, which they patiently pick up and re-ascend with.

June 7th. In the cellar: There is one thing I feel especially grateful for, that amid these horrors we have been spared that of suffering for water. The weather has been dry a long time, and we hear of others dipping up the water from ditches and mud-holes. This place has two large underground cisterns of good cool water, and every night in my subterranean dressing-room a tub of cold water is the nerve-calmer that sends me to sleep in spite of the roar. One cistern I had to give up to the soldiers, who swarm about like hungry animals seeking something to devour. Poor fellows! my heart bleeds for them. They have nothing but spoiled, greasy bacon, and bread made of musty pea-flour, and but little of that. The sick ones can't bolt it. They come into the kitchen when Martha puts the pan of corn-bread in the stove, and beg for the bowl she mixed it in. They shake up the scrapings with water, put in their bacon, and boil the mixture into a kind of soup, which is easier to swallow than pea-bread. When I happen in, they look so ashamed of their poor clothes. I know we saved the lives of two by giving a few meals. To-day one crawled on the gallery to lie in the breeze. He looked as if shells had lost their terrors for his dumb and famished misery. . . .

June 20th: . . . I fear the want of good food is breaking down H_____. I know from my own feelings of weakness, but mine is not an American constitution and has a recuperative power that his has not.

June 21st: I had gone upstairs to-day during the interregnum to enjoy a rest on my bed and read the reliable items in the "Citizen," when a shell burst right outside the window in front of me. Pieces flew in, striking all round me, tearing down masses of plaster that came tumbling over me. When H_____ rushed in I was crawling out of the plaster, digging it out of my eyes and hair. When he picked up a piece large as a saucer beside my pillow, I realized my narrow escape. The window-frame began to smoke, and we saw the house was on fire. H_____ ran for a hatchet and I for water, and we put it out. Another [shell] came crashing near, and I snatched up my comb and brush and ran down here. It has taken all the afternoon to get the plaster out of my hair, for my hands were rather shaky.

June 25th: A horrible day. The most horrible yet to me, because I've lost my nerve. We were all in the cellar, when a shell came tearing through the roof, burst upstairs, tore up that room, and the pieces coming through both floors down into the cellar. One of them tore open the leg of H_____'s pantaloons. This was tangible proof the cellar was no place of protection from them . . . I do not think people who are physically brave deserve much credit for it; it is a matter of nerves. In this way I am constitutionally brave, and seldom think of danger till it is over; and death has not the terrors for me it has for some others. . . . But now I first seemed to realize that something worse than death might come: I might be crippled, and not killed. Life, without all one's powers and limbs, was a thought that broke down my courage. . . .

July 4th: It is evening. All is still. Silence and night are once more united. I can sit at the table in the parlor and write. Two candles are lighted. I would like a dozen. We have had wheat supper and wheat bread once more. . . .

But I must write the history of the last twenty-four hours. . . .

Breakfast dispatched, we went on the upper gallery. What I expected to see was files of soldiers marching in, but it was very different. The street was deserted, save by a few people carrying home bedding from their caves. Among these was a group taking home a little creature, born in a cave a few days previous, and its wan-looking mother. About eleven o'clock a man in blue came sauntering along, looking about curiously. Then two followed him, then another.

"H____, do you think these can be the Federal soldiers?"

"Why, yes; here come more up the street."

Soon a group appeared on the court-house hill, and the flag began slowly to rise to the rope of the staff. As the breeze caught it, and it sprang out like a live thing exultant, H____ drew a long breath of contentment.

"Now I feel once more at home in mine own country." . . .

CORDELIA LEWIS SCALES

Cordelia Scales was born in July 1844. In the spring of 1861, she left the State Female Institute in Memphis to return to Oakland Plantation near Hudsonville (eight miles northeast of Holly Springs). Her correspondent was Loulie Irby, a former schoolmate, who lived at Como in Panola County. As the letters indicate, Scales reveled in the war. She was a firebrand, a real "secesh gal," who found immense pleasure in denouncing Union soldiers and boasting of her wartime adventures.

October 1862[8]

. . . I wish you could see me now with my hair parted on the side[9] with my black velvet zouave on & pistol by my side & riding my fine colt, Beula. I know you would take me for a Gurilla. I never ride now or walk with out my pistol—quite warlike, you see. We have had the house full of our soldiers ever since the *Yankees* left. I suppose you know our army is encamped all most in sight of us. . . .

I wish you could see the camps. The tents look so pretty. I must tell you about the Yankees as you are so anxious to know how they behaved. You may congratulate your self, my dear friend, on being slighted by them. They came & staid in our yard all the time. Their camp was where our soldiers are now. And they use to order the milk to be churned any time & they took corn, fodder, ruined the garden & took every *thing* in the poultry line. [Brigadier-General Stephen A.] Hulbert[']s division, the *very* worst[,] staid here with us nearly all the time. I never heard such profanity in all my life & so *impudent*, they would walk around the house & look up at the windows & say, "I wonder how many *dam Secesh* gals they got up there." I did not have my pistol & Ma would not let me go where they were, but one evening she was so *worn out* she sent me down to attend to the skimming of some wine & other household matters, when she thought they had all left. Just as I got out in the yard, two cavalry men & six infantry came up & surrounded me. Pa was not at home. Ma & Sis Lucy were looking on & were frightened very much, for they knew I would speak my mind to them if they provoked me. The first Lt. asked me if we had any chickens. I told him, *no*[.] Any milk? I said, *no*—that some of his tribe had been there that morning & got everything in that line. He smiled & said "they did not pay you for them did they?" I told him a *few pretended* to pay by giving us *federal* money, that *I* preferred leaves to that—he said "why federal money dont seem to be in demand." I said not *down this* way *sure*. The second Lt. a *red* headed pirt [*sic*] thing commenced to laugh about our men running from Holly Springs & said "our men *never* run, Miss." I told him, O *no* we all know what a orderly retreat they made from Bul[l]run, Manassas, & Leighsburg, that it did their army a great deal of credit & I hope *they* felt *proud* of it. One of the pickets remarked then "Oh! *hush Tom* you dont know how to talk to *Secesh* gals." I turned to him & thanked him that we were all *ladies* in the *South*. The 2nd lt. got very mad at what I said about their men running—said "I can inform you Miss *I* was in the battle of Leighsburg & our men did not run far.["] I told him I knew they did not, they ran as far as they *could* & then *jumped* in the *river*. The first Lt. broke out in a laugh & said "Ah! Tom shes *got* you now," & turned to me & said, "I admire your candor *very* much. I had *much* rather see you so brave then for you to pretend to entertain *Union* sentiments." I told him that there wasnt a Union man, woman, or child in the state of Mississippi & the first man that said he was to shoot him right *there* for he did it only to protect his property. He said he would & wanted to know if all the ladies were that brave. I informed him they were & if they whipped this part of our army that we had girls & boys enough to whip *them*. One of the soldiers said "I think you had better *inspire* some of your men with your bravery." I told him that our men needed *no inspiration* what ever. The Lt. then said to me "Now, Miss, you southern ladies would not fight, you are two good natured." I said we *were very* good natured but when our soil was *invaded* & by *such creatures* as they were it was enough to *arouse* any one—he wanted to know what I styled them. I told him Yankees or negro thieves. This made them very mad & they told me they were *western* men. I told him that I judged people by the company they kept, that they fought with them & staid with them that "birds of a *feather* would flock together." . . . I *wish* you could have seen me when I walked away just like the very *ground* was *polluted* by them; the first Lt. asked me for some water when he saw I was going. I told him there was a *spring* on the place if he wanted any, he then told me that such bravery should be rewarded—that nothing on the place should be touched, he made all the men march before him & did not let them trouble anything. Just as I was walking away and congratulating myself that they had not cursed me one of them said "She is the damndest little Secesh I ever saw" & another "she is a *dam pretty gal*, I be-dog if she aint." I could write you a newspaper about them but I reckon you are tired now & it makes me mad to think about them. . . .

January 1863[10]

I really thought some time ago that I *never* should have the pleasure of writing to you againe, & you have no idea how *sad* it made me feel; to think that I was in the *Federal* line, & would never have the pleasure of holding *sweet communion* with the dearest friend I have on earth. Oh! Lou I hope you may never experience such feelings as I did the day the Yankee army passed our house. . . .

The first skirmish I witnessed was in front of our house at the pickett stand; our men were surprised by [Major General James B.] McPhirson's [*sic*] cavalry, they were near enough to use their pistols; I'll tell you what our pickets run like *clever fellows*, they made *rail road* time. After the fight was over three hundred of the Yankees came up to our house—one of the officers asked me "Well Miss, what made your men 'Skeedaddle' so." I told him that our men only wanted to show them that they could beat them at every game they tried, that they had beat them *fighting* so often, they wanted a little variety. Pa was out in the field soon after the skirmish took place & the Yankees on the hill in front of our house fired on him three times. One of the balls passed through his coat under his left arm, one by his ear, & the other through his hat—they *knew* he was an *unarmed* citizen too, Lou. I'll tell you what the *cowardly rascals* have no respect whatever, for age, nor sex.

The day the army came to Holly Springs & when the wagon trains were passing thirty & forty of the Yankees would rush in at a time, take every thing they wanted to eat they could lay their hands on, & break, destroy & steal every thing they wanted to—all of our mules, horses & wagons were taken, 42 wagons were loaded with corn at one time from our cribs, & a good many more after. I'll tell you that I thought we would certainly starve. One thousand *black republicans*, the 26th Ill., camped in our grove for two weeks—we did have such a beautiful grove & place too, but you ought to see it now, it looks like some "banquet hall deserted"—all the gates and railings are torn down & burnt & as for a rail it is a *curosity* up here. Col. [Robert A.] Gil[l]more was in command of the 26th. He made our house headquarters; he use to let his men go out foraging every day & one day while some of them were out stealing chickens & hogs about four miles from here at Thompson[']s place, a company of our *gurillas* overhauled them— killed two & wounded two. I never saw such enraged men in my life as they were when those that were taken prisoners & paroled came in camp with the news. The Col. took Pa's room for a hospital; when they were bringing the wounded in, you never heard men groan as they did in my life, *all* our sick & wounded in the hospital did not make as much noise as those *two* did. Sis Lucy said she was trying to look *serious* to keep them from knowing how much *delighted* she was, when she happened to look at me & that there was such a *placid smile* on my countenance, she had to bight her lips to keep from laughing. I did feel *so happy* when I looked on the sufferings & heard the groans of those *blue devils*. Gil[l]more searched our house for arms and found two swords & it has been searched again for *wines*. I wore my pistol (a very fine six shooter) all the time & I stood by my saratoga [and] would not permit them to search it. One said, "she's a trump." I met with an old school mate of Dabney's from Anapolis, his name was Meriman, a first cousin of Meriman, the jeweller, in Memphis. I liked him as well as I could a Yankee; & surprising to say he was a gentleman. I remarked to him one night that it seemed to be the policy of the Yankee government to send one or two gentlemen with every regiment to let it be known that there were some gentlemen in the north, & Col. Gilmore was present & he seemed to take it all to himself & commence to thank me for considering him one, when I turned to him & said you need not think that I consider that *fill* the *bill* atall Col. that remains to be seen hereafter. You ought to have seen how *blank* he looked all the officers laughed at him so much. They had a large flag waveing in our grove & you could not see anything but *blue* coats & *tents*. The Col. made the band come up & play Dixie for me. . . . The next set that camped on us was the 90th Ill. Irish Leagon. They treated us a great deal better than the black republicans did—the Irish were all democrats. One of the officer's wives, Mrs. Steward staid here. She was very nice lady, by the way, she was almost a Secesh, she was begging me to play for her & I told her I played nothing but *Rebel* songs. She said they were the very kind she wanted to hear—so I sung "My Maryland," Bonnie blue flag, "Mississippi Camp Song," "Cheer Boys Cheer," ["]Life on the tented field" & ["]Dixy." She said Oh! they are *beautiful*. I dont blame you for loving them. She made me write them off for her to take to Shacaugo [i.e. Chicago] with her. The next day Capt. Flynn came up he asked me if I knew what he came for I told him *no*, he then said it was to beg a great favor of me & he hoped I would be so kind as to grant it, that he wanted me to sing "My Maryland" for him. At first I thanked him & told him I did not play for Federal offercers but Pa said I must that Capt. Flynn had kept us from almost starving & had been so kind to us so I consented. He was so much pleased with it that he got me to write the words off for him. I put a little *Confederate flag* at the top of it & wrote under it "No northern hand shall rule this land, to the breeze give freedom's banner." He sent it on North to his wife. I wish you could have seen the parting between Capt. Flynn & myself, the Major & him & a good many officers came up to tell me goodbye & the Major was saying he was going to reduce the south to starvation & then send us north. I said to him I had rather *starve* to *death* in the South than be a beggar in the North, Major. Capt. Flynn jumped up, caught me by the hand & said "Miss Scales, you are a *bold soul[e]d* Rebel & I admire you so much for it. I do wish I could stay here & protect you while our army is retreating. I'd fight for you, God knows I would." That sounds strange for a *Yankee*, dont it? He called to me one day & wanted to know if I knew the name I went by in camp, I told him *no*, he said they called me the "right bower of the *Rebel* army"—The next we had were the "Grierson Th[i]eves["] & the next the 7th Kan. Jayhawkers. I cant write of these; it makes my blood boil to think of the outrages they committed. They tore the earrings out of the Ladys ears, pulled there rings & bre[a]st pins of[f], took them by the hair through them down & knocked them about. Capt Flynn & Col. Steward protected us, one of them sent me word that they shot ladies as well as men, & if I did not stop talking to them so & displaying my Confederate flag he'd blow my dam brains out. I sent word by the lady that I did not expect anything better from Yankees, but he must remember *two* could play at that game. . . .

MARTHA CRAGAN, 1863[11]

> Martha Cragan resided in north Mississippi. Her brief note to Governor Charles Clark testifies to the desperation that citizens experienced dealing with Confederate and state policies while trying to survive in the latter days of the war.

With the impression that citizens were allowed to take cotton to the lines to exchange for salt, [cotton] cards[12], and other necessaries of which we are in very great need, a few of my neighbors and myself started to the lines for that purpose; the pickets overtook us crossing the river, burned our cotton, confiscated our drivers, wagons and teams. I never would have attempted it if necessity *had not have* drove me to it, having been deprived of the necessaries of life for the last three years, with a large and helpless family of girls, with no husband or son to assist in making them a support, and but one old and decrepid [*sic*] servant, the one they confiscated. I appealed to Gen'l [James Ronald] Chalmers and he released my servant and replied he could do nothing more for me, and referred me to General [Joseph Eggleston] Johnston. I have written to Gen Johnston, but have not received an answer. I was advised to appeal to your generosity to give me back my wagon and team. It will do the Government no good, (for my team are oxen and too poor to eat for food, nor do they work them in Government wagons) while at the same time they will alleviate the sufferings of a poor widow and helpless family. I do not see where we are to get salt and cards but we could better do without them than our team. I do not know whether you will listen to my poor pleadings but if you will favor me this request you will be remembered in the prayers of many grateful hearts. My wagon and team are at Oxford Miss, Chalmers' Headquarters.

I remain yours respectfuly, and am in hopes of hearing from you soon.

CHARLES CLARK, 1863[13]

Charles Clark, one of Mississippi's two wartime governors, responded to Cragan. He was at once sympathetic to her plight but also insistent that citizens adhere to wartime policies.

Madam, I have rec'd your letter and will send it to Gen'l Johnston, and endeavor to procure the release of your team, which I have no doubt I will do as the military authorities have no right to detain it. Carrying cotton to the enemy is an offence against the law and cannot be permitted. Confiscating private property by military power is also without law and equally reprehensible.

Chapter 7

FREE LABOR AND VIOLENCE IN RECONSTRUCTION

 *debt peonage*

At the end of the Civil War, the Federal government sought to secure for emancipated slaves the full meaning of liberty. Through the Bureau of Refugees, Freedmen, and Abandoned Lands, the government worked to ensure that freedpeople received first wages then later a fair share of the crops they planted. As long as cotton prices remained high, the sharecropping system that begin to emerge soon after the war benefitted both freedpeople and landlords. Yet, when cotton prices began to fall in the late 1860s, sharecroppers, many of whom had borrowed money and supplies from local merchants, fell victim to the 1867 crop-lien law. The crop-lien law had been originally passed to protect money-lenders (generally merchants) from defaulting sharecroppers whose only asset might be the crop in the ground, but an unintended consequence of the law was that merchants were able to control the production of sharecroppers. Creditors insisted that indebted sharecroppers plant only cotton, a fact that caused farmers to become more dependent on merchants for their sustenance and thus caused them to fall ever deeper in debt. By 1875, the sharecropping system, which had once been regarded as a boon to freedpeople, had come to resemble another form of slavery.

On the political front, the first years after the war promised a new day of liberty for freedpeople. Between 1865 and 1868 the Thirteenth, Fourteenth, and Fifteenth amendments to the United States Constitution granted ex-slaves freedom from slavery and the rights of citizenship; freedmen also received the right to vote. In 1868, the first statewide, bi-racial election in Mississippi took place, and not surprisingly, the electorate chose a heavily-Republican body of delegates to write a new state constitution guaranteeing freed people their liberty. Over the next eight years, white Republican governors and legislators worked to reconstruct Mississippi's war-ravaged infrastructure and economy. They rebuilt levees and state institutions; they instituted a system of public schools; and they sought to protect the right of freed people to vote.

The extension of political, educational, and economic liberty to ex-slaves, not to mention ex- slaves's ability to achieve a measure of such liberties, troubled the great majority of white Mississippians. For nearly a decade after 1868, whites, acting independently and through the Democratic party, as well as the Ku Klux Klan, violently opposed the reconstruction of Mississippi. In 1868, the first Ku Klux Klan organizations appeared in northeast Mississippi, and they made public schools, Republicans, and "uppity" blacks the targets of their violence. The Democratic party engaged in violence, vote fraud, and intimidation at every election. In fact, the aims and tactics of the Klan and the Democratic party so closely coincided that victims had difficulty distinguishing which of the two committed particular acts of violence. In the late 1860s and into the early 1870s, the state and Federal governments responded effectively to the violence.

But, after the second inauguration of President Ulysses S. Grant in 1872, the Federal government, the Republican party, and the northern public lost interest in what were referred to as "autumnal outrages" and the congressional investigations that inevitably followed. Abandoned by their one-time northern allies, black Mississippians (and their white Republican allies) faced the full force of politically-motivated violence. By 1880, even the most optimistic observer understood that the day of black liberty was over. The selections that follow illustrate the fate of black free labor and Republicans in Reconstruction-era Mississippi.

A LABOR CONTRACT, 1866[1]

On January 5, 1866, W. R. Bath and Ned Littlepage signed the
following sharecropping contract. Bath was a landlord, and Littlepage
was a freedman. Although sharecropping contracts varied widely, the
document signed by Bath and Littlepage includes many features typically
found in such contracts.

Contract for cultivating land between W. R. Bath and freedman Ned
Littlepage for the year eighteen hundred & sixty six (beginning 8th of
Jan) the said Ned Littlepage agrees to cultivate a part of the farm of
said Bath on shares as follows, the said Bath agrees to give him one
half of the cotton raised by said Ned Littlepage and one half of
potatoes and one third of the corn & fodder, peas & [illegible] and
to gather & house [i.e. to store] the same. Said Bath is also to have
the smith work done necessary for the farm and furnish two mules or
horses to work on said farm during the cultivation of said crop. There
will be three horses or mules used for the purpose of cultivating the
said farm which the said Bath is to feed. The above named Ned
Littlepage agrees to furnish one mule and do all the wood work on the
plows[,] pay for one half of the cotton seeds planted also pay for one
half of the potatoe seed planted and one third of the pea seeds necessary to plant the corn crop the said Ned Littlepage agrees to feed &
clothe his own family and pay all Dr Bills and keep a respectable and
orderly house and further agrees to use all energy and industry to
make a good crop.

JULIA DIXON, 1869–1870

Julia Dixon was the wife of a Washington County planter. Her sons,
Harry St. John Dixon and Jimmy, left Mississippi for the San Joaquim
Valley rather attempt to live among free blacks. By 1869, Harry had
moved to Millerton in Fresno County, where he practiced law and held
several elected offices. Julia, who remained on the family's Washington

County plantation, wrote frequently to her son. Her letters describe plantation life after the war, her interest in fleeing Mississippi, and the impact of the crop-lien law on free labor.

The First Letter, 1869[2]

. . . The country is more prosperous than when you left. All have made good crops, & are in better spirits. The negroes have been slow in gathering it, but will finish picking cotton in a few days, but have (on this place) a good deal to gin yet, consequently we do not know yet what we have made. Your Father is anxious to cultivate the whole place. Wash has gone to Jackson after Jacob & his wife & others, of the old set. He thinks he and Nat can increase their "squad["] to ten first class hands. Alfred['s] Ohio family have come home to work this year. . . . All that worked here last year are well pleased with the proceeds of their crops, and say they will remain this year. . . . Where hands are able to furnish *every thing* the planters are offering them ¼ of the crop, & when they furnish half they give half of the crop. What an opportunity for the negro to make a fortune, at the present prices of cotton.

The Second Letter, 1869[3]

. . . I brought home [from Memphis] with me three servants: a cook[,] dinning room servant (man)& house girl. The man attends to the dining room & when Edmond leaves: he is to attend to the horses & do anything about the house & yard we choose to put him at—his wife is a pretty good cook. They say they will go to Cal[ifornia] with us. They suit us better than any we have had since the War, but I fear they will become demoralized, here where the negroes are so independent & are behaving so badly. (Wash & Fred have come out openly & are among the prominent members of the "Loyal League" society.[)] Last Saturday & the week before, a company dressed in uniform passed our gate, mounted on fat prancing horses, with an immense Flag (Yankee) floating at the head of the columns, with fife & drums playing "Yankee doddle." The feelings that scenes like those produce are anything, but pleasant to southerners. To pass the affair by as lightly as possible, Louly Mal' & myself walked out on the gallery to see the show, when to our surprise, we were loudly cheered. I dont think they really meant anything more than to imitate *whitefolks*, but it looked to me very much like "equality" & was of course very distasteful. On the next parade day: Your Father was at home, and after they returned (the negroes who live on this place) he told them that the whole thing was disagreeable to him & that he would not allow them to make this place head-quarters, & asked them who owned the flag. The reply was that it belonged to a man who lived [elsewhere], he told them give it to the owner, that he would not permit it to be hoisted on his premises. Greg (negro) radical speaker, a few days after, said in his speech in Greenville that the people in this county were not loyal that he had heard a man give an order to "take the U.S. flag off of his place that he was still at war with it.["] I am thoroughly disgusted with this country and hope before many months roll away that I will be with my dear boys, my children are all & all to me. . . .

The Third Letter, 1870[4]

. . . The [sharecropping] contracts that are being made with the negroes are, five acres of land for a bale of cotton. This is the only safe contract that can be made as the negroes are becoming more worthless every year—all the hands who worked our place last year will remain, except Joe's set. I am really very glad that we will have nothing more to do with the ungrateful creatures. They have passed through the Jews hands & have all come out largely in debt: no cash to buy fine horses & mules as they did last year. . . .

ALLEN P. HUGGINS, 1872[5]

Allen P. Huggins, a white Republican originally from the north, served as Assistant U.S. Revenue agent and superintendent of public schools in

Monroe County. The whipping that Huggins sustained at the hands of the Klan may be the most famous of the period. In a fiery Congressional speech, Benjamin F. Butler exhibited Huggins's blood-soaked shirt and in doing so created a metaphor for the rhetorical exercise in which northern politicians engaged when they denounced their Democratic rivals for permitting violence against blacks: they were said to be "waving the bloody shirt."

The selection of Huggins's testimony before a Congressional committee that follows begins after he has explained how a band of Klansmen awakened him while asleep at the home of a Mr. Ross. The Klan called for him to present himself in the yard so that he might receive the official warning prepared for him. Huggins stepped into the yard only after securing from the Klansmen a promise that he would not be harmed.

Answer. There were about twenty who came up afterward to the horses; there were one hundred and twenty in the crowd altogether, as I numbered them. The gate was closed, and I went down to the fence. The night was as bright as a moonlight night can well be. I looked at my watch, and I had no difficulty in telling the position of the hands of my watch. When I got down to the fence I asked the chief if he would now state my little bit of warning, that I wanted to hear it and be gone. He said the decree of the camp was that I should leave the country within ten days, and leave the State; that I could not stay there. He then gave me the decree, pronounced it out in a very pompous manner, and said it was given at a certain place, and registered in some corner of hell; I never did get the name exactly.

Question. The location of the registrar's office there you do not remember?

Answer. No, sir, I do not remember. He told me that the rule of the camp was, first, to give the warning; second, to enforce obedience to their laws by whipping; third, to kill by the Klan altogether; and, fourth, if that was not done, and if the one who was warned still refused to obey, then they were sworn to kill him, either privately, by assassination, or otherwise. I was then warned again that I would have to go, that I could not stay there, that there was no such thing as getting around one of their decrees; that if I undertook to stay there I certainly should die. They repeated again that I could not live there under any circumstances; they gave me ten days to go away. They said that during that time I must relieve them from all the taxes of the country. . . .

I reminded them that I could not possibly be held in any way responsible for any tax except the revenue tax and the school tax; that the State and county taxes really amounted to three times all the other taxes. They said I could take them off, and they knew it; that I had got to do it, and to promise them that I would do it. I asked them if the tax was my offense, or what my offense was. They said that I was collecting obnoxious taxes from southern gentlemen to keep damned old radicals in office; that they wanted me to understand that no laws should be enforced in that country that they did not make themselves; that they did not like my general radical ways a bit; that was the charge they gave against me. In fact, they treated me very courteously, except the beating they gave me; but otherwise I was not insulted or treated unkindly at all. . . .

[T]hey were civil. One of them commenced to curse; he began; "God damn," and was going to say something, when the captain stopped him and said that he should not do that; that all they wanted of me was to get me out of the country; they said they did not like my radical ways anyway. I asked them if their operations were against the radical party; they said they were; that they had suffered and endured the radical sway as long as they could; that the radicals had oppressed them with taxation; that they were oppressing them all the time, and that I was the instrument of collecting the taxes; that they had stood it just as long as they could, and that this was their way of getting rid of it; that they were bound to rid themselves of radicals or else kill them, or if it took the killing of them, or something to that effect. There was a colored school and a white school in the neighborhood. I knew most of the men there were from that neighborhood; I asked them with reference to Mr. Davis's school; that was the white school, where I supposed the most of their children were attending; I asked them if they were not satisfied with his school; they said, "No;" that they liked Davis well enough as a teacher, but that they were opposed to the free-school system entirely; that the whites could do as they had always done before; that they could educate their own children; that so far as the negroes were concerned, they did not need educating, only to work. They said they had no objection to Davis at all, but that they could manage their own affairs without the State or the United States sending such as I was there to educate their children, and at the same time to educate the negroes too. After the conversation on the school subject closed, one of them said, "Well, sir, what do you say to our warning? Will you leave?" I told them I should leave Monroe County at my pleasure, and not until I got ready. The captain then said to me, "Sir, you say you will not leave; you will not obey our warning." I said I would not obey; that I would leave when I got ready, and not before; that I would not be driven from any place. The gate was then thrown open, and the fence was climbed by twenty men in a moment. I was surrounded and disarmed; the pistol that I had had until that time was taken away. They then took me between an eighth and a quarter of a mile down the road, and came to a hill, where they stopped; they then asked me if I was still of the same opinion—that I would not leave the country; I told them I was; that I would not leave. I reasoned with them a little; I told them I was like every other man; that all I had was there; that this was a very sudden thing, and that I would rather die than say that; that I would not say it under any circumstances. They said they should hate very much to interfere with me; that they had made promises to Mr. Ross and myself; that I had really not been obnoxious to them only in the tax line, and that they would not like to interfere with me, for they counted me as a gentleman; that they did not want to interfere with me at all; that all they wanted was to get rid of me from the county and from the State; that I could not stay there. They then said, "you cannot stay at Jackson; you must leave the State." Mr. Ross saw that they really intended to treat me badly.

Question. Was Mr. Ross along?

Answer. He was along; he went with me. He said, "Remember your promise; you must not do anything to harm the man at all; your promise is out." After they had said that they remembered their promise, I warned them to beware what they did, and told them that I never would let go of them; that if they left me alive I would certainly do what I could; that I was a United States officer, and would not take any such treatment without doing what I could to get redress; that it was not safe for them to do what they were doing. They ordered me to take off my coat, which I refused to do; they then took it off by force. After that they asked if I consented to leave, and I still refused. They said that if I would promise them, I should go back to my bed and sleep quietly, and they would all go on home; they really urged in every way that it was possible for men to do to get me to promise to leave the county and the State without any violence. They then showed me a rope with a noose, and said that was for such as myself who were stubborn; that if did not consent to leave I should die, that dead men told no tales. At this time I saw a man coming from toward the horses, from where I then supposed, and where I afterward knew the horses were; he had a stirrup-strap some inch and a quarter in width, and at least an eighth of an inch thick; it was very stout leather; the stirrup was a wooden one. As he came up he threw down the wooden stirrup and came on toward me, and I saw that he was intending to hit me with the strap, that that was the weapon they intended to use first. He came on, and without further ceremony at all—I was in shirt sleeves—he struck me two blows, calling out, "one, two," and said, "Now, boys, count." They counted every lash they gave me. The first man gave me ten blows himself, standing on my left side, striking over my left arm and on my back; the next one gave me five blows. Then a fresh hand took it and gave me ten blows; that made twenty-five. They then stopped and asked me again if I would leave the county. I still refused, and told them that now they had commenced they would go just as far as they pleased; that all had been done that I cared for; that I would as soon die then as take what I had taken. They continued to strike their blows on my back in the same way until they had reached fifty. None of them struck more than ten blows, some of them only three, and some as low as two. They said they all wanted to get a chance at me; that I was stubborn, and just such a man as they liked to pound. When they had struck me fifty blows they stopped again and asked me if I would leave; I told them I would not. Then one of the strongest and most burly in the crowd took the strap himself and gave me twenty-five blows without stopping; that made seventy-five; I heard them say, "Seventy-five." At that time my strength gave way entirely; I grew dizzy and cold; I asked for my coat; that is the last I remember for several minutes. When I recovered myself they were still about me; I was standing; I do not think I had been down; they must have held me up all the time. I heard them say, "He is not dead yet; he is a live man yet; dead men tell no tales." But still they all seemed disposed as I thought to let me go; I heard no threatening, except what passed a few moments afterward. They all passed in front of me, or a great number of them—I will not say all— and drew their pistols and showed them to me; they told me that if was not gone within ten days they were all sworn in their camp, and sworn positively, that they would kill me, either privately or publicly. They then asked me where my office was; I told them my office was at the court-house in Aberdeen. They said they would kill me, either privately or publicly; that they would be sure to do it if I did not leave. . . . [B]efore they got through I had completely recovered my senses, and I noticed everything particularly, and saw that all had the same style of pistols, what appeared to be about six-inch revolvers. Their clothing I noticed especially; I was with them a long time; it was as light as the moon could make it. Their clothing was all of the same pattern and form; they were all cut and made garments. Their face-pieces were very defective; if I had known the men personally, I could have recognized nearly all of them. I did recognize several of them, and swore against some at the Oxford court. They were countrymen, men I had not had much to do with. If I had known them, I could have recognized twenty persons, at least, their face-pieces were so very defective. . . .

ISAAC BOURNE, 1874[6]

In 1874, writing to President Grant from Silver Creek in Lawrence
County, Isaac Bourne, a poorly-educated African American, called for
Federal assistance. The urgency of his request is most evident in the last
few lines of the letter.

Mr. Presadent Grant of the United State. I will Drope you a few lines
to let you know how We is in Posuppun [i.e. imposed upon] By the
White Peopel in Laurence County and in Lincoln County Miss. thar
tak up the Corldred Peopel and Haury thim By a subpecsin [suspicion]
and mak them tall antheng Whare it be so or not. We are press so We
Cant Stand it. if the law Waant Pertict ous We dont [know] What to
Do. We ask you for insistans [assistance] from you. Els not let ous
have the chace to Do that

HENRY B. WHITFIELD, 1875[7]

Henry Whitfield was the District Attorney of the Seventh Judicial District
in northeastern Mississippi. His letter to Attorney General Edward
Pierrepont describes the ways in which Democrats used vote fraud and
intimidation to carry the gubernatorial election of 1875.

. . . The laws both of the State of Mississippi, and of the United States,
have been flagrantly and defiantly violated both before and during the
late election in this state, held Nov. 2d. The grand jury for the Circuit
Court of this (Lowndes) county is now in session. It is proposed to
investigate all violations of laws touching this question in the coming
week. I am fearful it will prove utterly futile, for the following reasons.
During my term of office, I have seen such investigations made, and
from the political and race complexion of grand juries, nothing has
been done. Notorious violations of the election law have been
absolutely ignored by grand jurors who had direct and personal knowledge of their violation. It is impossible to get the witnesses, *who have*

personal knowledge of the facts, to tell the truth, or what they know, even in presence of the grand jury, for fear of their lives, or for considerations of policy, protection or personal friends, accomplishment of political and party purposes, etc. . . .

The only hope is now through the officers and Courts of the United States. If these fail, then a large mass of the people here are without remedy, or protection, *by reason of the political nullification of the Constitution and laws of the Country.* . . .

The most patent influence used by one party in the late canvass and election was *intimidation, or terrorism,* in manifold forms. The purchase and exhibition of fire arms was public and notorious. In three counties, to my personal knowledge, cannon were purchased, and used as the *loudest argument.* In Lowndes, Colfax[,][8] and Monroe, particularly these cannon were frequently fired by day and at night; were carried to different places in the county where there was to be public speaking, or gatherings, and often fired on the route. In a large part of this (Lowndes) county, . . . the boom of the cannon in the three counties could be heard. The effect of this kind of *argument* on the colored voters, who, as you may know, are naturally peaceable, timid and cowardly, as the results of slavery, can be more readily imagined and understood than described.

On Thursday, Oct. 28th, I was at West Point, in Colfax County, adjoining this, and in my judicial Circuit. There was a grand rally of the Democratic party. Some eight hundred to a thousand men were in the procession which I witnessed, on foot and on horseback. A notable feature was that *two cannon* were drawn along in the crowd; one said to be a six pounder, by white boys in uniform; the other, a large cannon drawn by horses, and managed by men in usual uniform of an Artillery Company. In addition to this, many of the men had what is called the large "Ku-Klux pistol," buckled around them . . .

As a consequence of such acts, with others equally as bad, or worse, with direct and positive threats, etc. that County (Colfax), which has always been largely Republican, is alleged to have gone Democratic by more than a thousand majority.

In order that you may understand the *modus operandi*, you will find enclosed two tickets, one genuine Republican, the other a fraud. My information is, that, at one precinct when over six hundred (600) votes were cast, and where a leading Democrat, after the polls were closed on election day, claimed only thirty seven (37) votes, when the ballots were counted the following day, *a night intervening*, the result was declared in favor of the Democrats, by a large majority, the fraudulent green tickets claimed to represent Republican votes!

In this (Lowndes) County, in addition to the other means spoken of there was a state of affairs on Monday night, Nov. 1st preceding the election on Tuesday, unparalleled for atrocity in the history of civilization.

To give an idea of how equality of rights was observed, I state, that on Saturday, Oct. 30th, the Democrats had appointed a public meeting and speaking at the Court-house, at 12 o'clock, M. To assemble the crowd, several men marched along the streets, which were crowded with people, wagons and teams, beating drums, blowing a fife, etc. The Cannon—a twenty four pounder—was brought in front of the Court-house, which is adjacent to the business part of the city, and fired three times, right in the public street, breaking and shattering the glass in the adjacent buildings. This was immediately under my office window, and before my own eyes.

On Monday night following, the Republicans were to have a meeting at a school house, in a quiet place, in the suburbs of the city. A few of the men started with drums and fife, to march to the place of meeting. They had gone but a short distance along the public street, when they were charged upon by a body of men, the heads cut out of their drums, the wood work stamped to pieces, and the men scattered in confusion.

On this same Monday night preceding the election next day, there was a terrible riot and reign of terror, caused by an alleged combination of the negroes to fire the city. I state the following facts, and you can draw your own inferences.

There was to be a torch light procession of the Democrats this (Monday[)] night: A large number of them assembled at a public place in the city. While supposed to be preparing for this procession, about 8 o'clock, when every body was awake and many in the streets, the alarm of fire was issued. It proved to be an old, open shed, in the southern part of the city, in which a quantity of pea-vines, hay, wood, etc. were stored, all worth not exceeding two hundred dollars. . . .

This old shed was, also, in less than a hundred yards of the house of Robert Gleed, a colored Republican and candidate for Sheriff, who was charged with inciting the negroes to fire the town, whose property, a neat dwelling house worth fifteen hundred dollars, was as much, or more, endangered by this fire as any other house in the neighborhood.

Soon after this first alarm of fire, there was another in the northern part of the town. This proved to be an old, dilapidated stable, worth no more than fifty dollars.

From this the excitement became intense. The streets were filled with armed men. The colored people generally fled to their houses, or the woods. Leading white Republicans were waited on, instantly by bodies of armed me, and notified, that if there was another fire in the town that night *They would be held personally responsible*.

The result was, four (4) negroes killed, whose bodies were found next day; several wounded; and many missing who not been heard from since that time.

You will find enclosed a slip cut from a Democratic newspaper. . . . Where the Republicans should have received fully twelve hundred (1200) votes, there were only *seventeen* (17) regular tickets voted on the day of election!!.

(The above was written at intervals of leisure during the session of the Circuit Court, where I was much engaged. The grand jury adjourned, after making a written report to the Court, saying substantially in regard to this question, that, they had examined forty six (46) witnesses touching the fires and homicides in Columbus on the night of Nov 1st but from the evidence adduced, were unable to connect any person with the crimes, as it seemed impossible to identify individuals on the night in question.)

This convinced me, more than ever, that the State Courts were and are utterly powerless to punish this class of offences. I have no disposition to say any thing more. . . .

In conclusion, I ask you to bear in mind that this communication is *private and confidential,* intended for your official information, and such action as you may deem expedient. It certainly cannot be expected, in the present condition of affairs, and state of feelings, existing here, that any man will become a martyr to his principles without some prospect of vindication, or protection.

WILLIAM FRAZEE, 1876[9]

In July 1876, the federal grand jury for the Northern District of Mississippi filed the following report with Judge R. A. Hill. The report closes with a poignant assessment of the status of political liberty in Mississippi. William Frazee was the grand jury foreman.

The U.S. Grand Jury for the Northern District of Miss. at Oxford, June Term 1876, beg leave to report that they have examined two hundred eighty one witnesses and found ninety true bills; a large majority of these bills were for violations of the Revenue laws.

Although we have had a protracted session we have only made a partial and cursory examination of the innumerable cases of violations of the election laws, that have come to our knowledge. We regret to report that from the examination had, we must say that the fraud in circulation and violence perpetrated at the late election is without parallel in the annals of history, and that time would fail us to take the testimony that could be easily introduced demonstrating the fact that there is sufficient grounds for the finding of thousands of indictments against persons who are grossly guilty of the above mentioned violations of the election laws.

From the facts elicited during this grand inquest, and from our own knowledge of the reign of terror that was inaugurated during the late election campaign we can only recommend to the citizens of Mississippi to make an earnest appeal to the strong arm of the U.S. government to give them that protection that is guaranteed to every American citizen, that is protection in freedom of speech in their person and property and the right of suffrage.

We do assert that all of these rights were openly violated and trampled in the dirt during the late election, and that there is no redress for these grievances under the present state government[,] and unless the U.S. government enforces that shield of protection that is guaranteed by the constitution to every American citizen however humble and obscure, then may the citizens of Mississippi exclaim farewell to liberty, farewell to the freedom of the ballot box. . . .

AN ANONYMOUS HOLMES COUNTY REPUBLICAN, 1876[10]

In late August 1876, an anonymous Republican living in Holmes County responded to a query by Ira Tarbell, a journalist who became famous for her exposé of the Standard Oil Company, about the failure of local Republicans to organize in central Mississippi. The response reveals the variety and consequences of Democratic party intimidation.

You ask, "cannot something be done to organize Republican clubs in our County?["] I answer it cannot be done except at Jackson, without imminent risk of life, or great private damage to participants, in consequence of the complete system of Democratic organization in all our heavy voting counties, in all of which are semi-military companies far better armed than at the inception of the Rebellion, and much more hostile to Republicans than then, and all practising upon the system inaugurated by Geo. W. Harper [editor] of the Raymond *Gazette*, of *superintending* with *armed* manifestations all known gatherings of

Republicans, with the avowed purpose of breaking them up; knowing that they cannot cope with armed invasion, Republicans give it up. I have reason to believe, though I have no direct proof, that as a Party the Democracy, by its leaders, has made a part of their tactics this year absolutely to frighten down all organizations of Republicans, and then to intimidate the weak, and timid (and this embraces the whole colored vote) into voting the Democratic ticket, after which as in Alabama, they will proclaim that their has been a *"peaceful"* election. . . . And if a Republican meeting were called to form a club at *Bolton, Edwards, Raymond, Clinton, Cayugeo, Auburn, Dry Grove, Byram,* or, *Brownsville,* they would be dispersed by bands of armed bandits before they could choose a chairman. There are Democratic Clubs everywhere in active operation. It cuts up Republicanism by the roots. Possibly, *at the Polls* there will be no open display of force, and violence as that might call [Federal] Judge [R. A.] Hill's, court into action. But the mischief will all have been done before hand. Republicans are whipped in Miss at the word *"go"* and you need have no Judges to settle the case which is all fixed in advance. The truth is . . . Congress has not given us the benefit of Federal Legislation, at all adequate to *squeeze* rebellion out of the backs of the adherents, and moreover over the *"lost cause."* That's the whole of it. The work of *Registration* and *Elections, both,* should be taken entirely in hand by the *nation.* At least, so far as *Federal* elections, are concerned. *I am ultra on this.* Judge Hill[']s court is open since the 17th inst. for election purposes, and as yet *nothing is done.* Only *Kemper, Washington, Copiah, Adams,* and Hinds, have applied for supervision, and in this county, the Chairman of the County Committee, though appealed to by us daily, since the 12th inst. to recommend supervisors for the different Beats, has done nothing yet, alleging that such is the state of things outside of Jackson, that he *cannot find* Republicans who will be willing to act. . . . If you see the Attorney General, you will have learned that I have now a case submitted to me as Comm[issione]r which brings squarely up the question, how far the *U.S. Courts* can give protection by law to the right of the people to organize themselves for elections by primary meetings and Clubs. A man[']s life was set upon by a lot of ruffians (*Democratic supervision*) in Holmes Co. and *he was told that the Democracy were resolved he should not form a Republican Club in that county*. He *persisted* and was trying to hold a meeting to instruct the voters of a particular precinct, whose bounds had been recently so changed as to *fuddle* the negroes as to what district they belonged to, when they set upon him, deceived him into going out with them, when a crowd previously in waiting set upon him with arms and tried to take his life, shooting at him several times, and being hotly pursued, he shot once back at them, and made his escape. They then got out a State Warrant against him, and sent it here to Genl [James Z.] George[11], who had him arrested and put in Jail—on charge of "*assault with intent to kill*." This you know is the regular Democratic refuge with which to cover their own outrages on the persons, and rights of negroes. It prevails in all these southern states, so that it has become one of their most ready excuses to kill negroes. Well, [Luke] Lea, was sent for to see him in Jail, and after great delay and attempts, refusal to let him confer with the prisoner, he drew up a formal affidavit against the several parties who outraged him, then the negro swore to it, and I referred the affidavit, under the rules, to the District Attorney, for advice as to issuing a Warrant upon it, and Lea, has sent the whole case up to the Atty General, to *know if the case can be prosecuted under 5520 U.S. Statues*, which section, Lea, states the case ably and fully to Genl Taft, and presents him the *pro's and con's* and submits the whole question, and this may decide the whole result of this years Election in Mississippi, for without practical intervention by the U.S. Courts, in time to checkmate their everlasting outrages on the freedom of Elections by *effective* Judicial proceedings this whole election is a farce!

I trust the Atty. General, will be found equal to the occasion for if the Grant [P]arish cases[12], is held by the Department, to keep the Federal hand off in such a case as this, then, insurrection in Mississippi, against the US laws, is *supreme and cannot be reached*. Each

Republican in such cases ought just to choose his Democratic master and go scripture fashion, and have his ear nailed to the Doorpost of the [house] in which he is to remain a *slave* forever!

"A NEGRO"

In early 1879, an African American, writing anonymously to Governor John Marshall Stone, chastised Mississippi's white Democrats in no uncertain terms. In his two missives, the letter-writer, apparently a one-time Mississippi resident who then lived in the area of Washington, D.C., taunted Stone. The letters are powerful and violent ones that attack, if under the cover of obscurity, extant myths that portrayed black men as desiring white women, acquiescent in the loss of their citizenship, and timid about repaying violence with violence. No documents better capture the anger that black Mississippians reserved for those most directly responsible for stealing from them the promise of Reconstruction.

The First Letter, 1878[13]

Infamous Scoundrel! You Democratic devil; you unjust cowardly dog, well may such a rascal as you be chosen to be the governor of such a godforsaken, murderous, drunken people as they are in Mississippi, a people so wicked that they are not fit to be loose upon the earth and God's rod is wiping them off by thousands.[14] Oh Miss Chisholm is avenged, the wrath of God is now let loose upon the South for all their wickedness. You yourself will soon be in hell where you will have to drink all the time, the blood of the Chisholm family, [Charles] Caldwell and all the negroes that were killed by those infernal hell-hounds called Democrats.[15] Memphis is desolate, Glory to God for his avenging rod, the Solid South will soon be a Solid Wilderness and better people will go to inhabit it and all the murderous Mississippi devils will be in hell driven by negroes whom they murdered upon the earth. In a short time those proud ignorant ugly Southern white girls will go about with their buttocks uncovered. Negroes will scorn them. Your wife and daughter will be desolate; those ugly, snuff dipping, whisky drinking, toddy loving Mississippi white hussies will soon all be naked unless they repent and leave off their wickedness and pride. All this will come upon the South for killing negroes and northern men. The Southern people are a Whisky-drinking, tobacco-chewing, Constant-spitting, Negro-hating, Negro-killing, red-handed, ignorant uneducated, uncivilized set of devils.

This is the Song they sing

> *"I want to be a Democrat and with the Democrats stand,*
> *A pistol in my pocket and shotgun in my hand*
> *Then right behind the negro so closely I will stand,*
> *And if he does not vote for me I'll blow out all his brains[."]*

You hate Northern men because they are your superior in everything.

Now I leave you to your own reflections you scoundrel. I will soon come to Jackson to kick your ass. You thief.

The Second Letter, 1879 [?][16]

. . . I hope you will some of these days find yourself in the Penitentiary or in hell. You good for nothing nasty, stinking, Southern Son of a Solid South. That infamous [Winfield S.] Featherstone[17] is already[?] in hell drinking Negro blood to cool his tongue. Caldwell, Chisholm and all the murdered victims of Democratic hate will rise in judgement against you and all of your infernal hellhounds. All the Southern people are Barbarians, a Whisky drinking, Tobacco-chewing, Constant-Spitting, nasty, dirty, Corn Bread eating, molasses-licking, Fat-back swallowing, Negro hating, negro-killing, negro-women ravishing, lousy set. The Northern people are your superiors and that is the reason you hate them. Tell one arm [Reuben] Reynolds[18] from Aberdeen I will write him soon. I send a kick in this letter for him and you. Mississippi is hell and Aberdeen is hell's dark door. The Yellow fever failed to correct you Southern devils and so in 1880 you will all be totally annihilated and not only defeated. I am coming to Jackson in a few days to spit in your face and to kick your backside and to show you how I abominate, abhor, and detest a Southerner.

I remain

Your master & superior

A Negro

Your master [James G.] Blain[e][19] will make you all come to your senses in 1880.

The negroes of the South are now going to emigrate West and then into whose blood will you Southern Barbarians dip your foul hands? Say!

What will you all do for victims to murder? Say!

It will not be a Solid South any more, but a *hollow* South, no more negroes to kill no more Cotton to feed your infernal lazy set. Oh! You drinking set of devils. Oh you detestable set of nasty lousy white beasts. Your wife is a nasty *wench*.

Answer this letter you beast. You ought to have a millstone tied to your neck and cast into the Pearl River[.]

Chapter 8

REFORMING MISSISSIPPI

During Reconstruction, Republican legislators and governors passed legislation that led Mississippi toward economic diversification; throughout the remainder of the nineteenth century, the Democratic politicians who followed them in office continued the march toward industrialization. Between the early 1870s and the late 1880s, legislation favorable to railroad companies allowed rail line builders tax breaks, access to state convict labor, and cheap or free land. Government efforts to attract railroad investors paid off: in 1870, 990 miles of railroad lines crisscrossed the state; in 1890, the total number of miles reached 2,397, and in 1910, 4,342 miles of track traversed Mississippi. The arrival of railroads in Mississippi encouraged other industries to locate in the state. Across Mississippi, local business and government leaders believed a manufacturing facility would usher in an age of prosperity for their village; and consequently, cotton seed mills, brick works, and textile mills soon dotted the landscape. In the Piney Woods and the Delta, large-scale timber cutters and sawmill operators made fortunes from the forests of the regions. Between 1880 and 1900, the value of products manufactured in Mississippi increased by 150 percent, and investors poured 350 percent more money into Mississippi manufacturing facilities in 1900 than they had in 1880.

The advent of a diversifying economy in Mississippi had consequences. New cities were created along railroad lines, and along with the state's old cities, they quickly became overcrowded and unhealthy. In late nineteenth-century cities, diseases, such as tuberculosis and malaria, ran rampant. The effects of poor nutrition, immature or nonexistent sanitation services, and heavy alcohol, even cocaine, consumption seemed like new and startling phenomena, if only because the clustering of so many people in small places made certain of the phenomena visible. While some of the folk who filled Mississippi cities arrived from the north or Europe, many were country boys and girls who fled their family farms to seek a better life. That farmers should suffer especially during Mississippi's rush to enter the New South might hardly seem surprising. Producing commodities in a period of deflation and confronting discrimination at the hands of the state legislature and Federal government—both of which preferred encouraging industrialization rather than sustaining agriculture—left farmers with a sense of second-class citizenship. Once the bone and sinew of the United States, they believed that the age in which farmers held the key to national economic success and political power had passed.

In the late nineteenth and early twentieth centuries, both farmers and middle-class reformers, though their motives differed, sought to change the new economic order. Mississippi farmers, particularly small-scale operators in north Mississippi, wished to turn back the clock to a time when power resided with country folk. They longed to be as they imagined their forefathers: independent, self-sufficient, market producers. To accomplish their goals, they joined the Patrons of Husbandry or the Grange. The Grange sought through cooperative buying and selling to restore farmers to their once exalted position of power, wealth, and prestige. In Mississippi, the Grange reached the peak of its membership in the mid 1870s and began steadily to decline afterwards. Nonetheless, the Grange strove to educate farmers about crop diversification, build cooperative stores, and create more visibility in the marketplace for Mississippi produce. As the Grange began to wither, another organization, the Farmers' Alliance, emerged. The Farmers' Alliance shared many objectives with the Grange, though in Mississippi, the Alliance more aggressively sought systemic reform through trust busting and effective railroad regulation. By the early 1890s, the national Farmers' Alliance determined to enter the realm of politics by transforming itself into the Populist party so that it might effect economic and political changes for farmers. In Mississippi, however, Alliance men anguished over the decision. Many members feared breaking with the Democratic party, and unfortunately, Mississippi's Populist party refused to ally itself with black farmers.

Middle-class reformers also sought to end the social, economic, and political ills that besieged Mississippi during the late nineteenth and early twentieth centuries. Temperance reformers wanted to curtail or eliminate alcohol consumption. In the early 1880s, a state chapter of the Women's Christian Temperance Union formed, and by 1888, membership had grown sufficiently to justify the publication of a WCTU newspaper. The campaign to end the sale of alcohol produced a statewide local option law in 1886 and a statewide prohibition law in 1908. Changing the lives of Mississippi children ensnared by the evils associated with industrialization occupied the energy of other middle-class reformers. Their efforts eventually led to the creation of a juvenile reformatory and child labor laws. Physicians and other professionals also sought to create a healthier and wiser Mississippi.

PATRONS OF HUSBANDRY, 1884[1]

When the meetings of the Holmes County Grange described below were held, the statewide Patrons of Husbandry was nearly extinct. Few chapters existed outside of Holmes County. But despite the collapse of the organization, Holmes County Grangers continued to work toward reforming the behavior of farmers, both individually and collectively, hoping to reverse the flow of power and wealth out of the countryside.

Holmes County Grange No. 7 met in regular session with Oak Grove Grange No. 578, July 10th 1884, and was opened in due form by worthy master J. G. Hamilton. . . . Committee on Cooperation reported as follows: "Your Committee on Cooperation would respectfully report that there is now only one Grange Store in this county, and it is not conducted on the Rochdale plan. From the last report that we have had of it, however, it is doing well. There are other features of cooperation that we regard as very important for the good of the Order.

We think it would not be amiss to have cooperation between this committee and your Committee on Education so that cooperation in the matter of education our members in their duties, rights and responsibilities may be brought about and then your Committee on Dormant Granges can cooperate with these two committees, and all of us can act together, pull together, and at all times, and in every community work together for the uniting of all farmers, and all working men, and bring unto them the Grange secrets, and teach them that our 'declaration of purposes' does not inculcate anything that would injure any country, but would certainly do the greatest good to the greatest number of the citizens of this country. Therefore we would urge all our members to cooperate with each other in doing all that they can to get all farmers to join the Grange, or find for use, some other order, which will suit the agricultural people of this country better." F. A. Howell, Chman.

The report was discussed by Bros. McCaleb, Howell, Wilson, Christmas, Wright and Hamilton & adopted.

The Committee on Agriculture, Commerce and Immigration made a report which was discussed by Bros Christmas, Wright, Hamilton, and Wilson, and adopted. The report is as follows: "Your committee on Agriculture and Commerce beg leave to make the following report: The acreage in cotton, so far as our observation extends is somewhat greater than last year, but we think the plant about twenty days later, there being yet but few blooms. There are large fields that do not at this time afford a bloom; showing to us most conclusively that the plant is unusually late and small. The growth of the cotton has been very rapid in the last 10 days when it has been well worked. Some fields still remain grassy from which we cannot expect much of a yield. We are sorry to have to report the corn crop as not being good. From the many inquiries we have made of our brother farmers comes the answer, the crop is spotted, and we think if there is not rain in a very few days that large portions of the spots will be very sorry indeed. This was written yesterday. It rained last night. Still we urge all other upon every patron and farmer to look well after all other food and hay crops. Peas could yet be planted and should be on every available spot of land that is not already in cultivation. The sweet potatoe crops looks well when it has been well worked. The gardins [*sic*] are good, but need rain. At this time fruit crop good. Work stock not doing well as the old corn is getting scarce, and the plowing has been very heavy. Hogs have died recently to an alarming extent with cholera, and those alive look badly. The Spring oats yielded a fair crop and many farmers are laying by their crops feeding their plow stock with them." F. W. Eakin Chmn.

"Resolved that if, the faculty of the A & M College can hold a Farmer's Institute in Holmes Co. this summer, that we, the members of Holmes County Grange No. 7 insist that one be held in our county at Lexington at as early a time as may be convenient; if not, then some time during the next vacation. . . ."

July 11th 1884, Grange was called to order by Wm. J. G. Hamilton and proceeded to select the place to hold the next regular meeting of this Grange, and Bowling Green was elected. "Resolved that the action of our Board of Supervisors in refusing the request of the Patrons of Husbandry, to make an appropriation authorized by an Act of the Legislature of Miss for the purpose of exhibiting the resources of Holmes County at the Cotton Centennial to be held in the City of New Orleans[,] L[ouisian]a is to be regretted from the fact that it is an evidence that we are not abreast with the progressive spirit of our common country; and a disregard of the wishes of the farmers who bear the burden of taxes, and resolved that we commend F. W. Eakin and Wm. Irish for votes in favor of an appropriation." . . .

TRUST BUSTING, 1888[2]

In 1888, the state Farmers' Alliance called on members of the new organization to pool their resources in order to defeat the recently-formed jute-bagging trust. The trust was formed by established jute-bag manufacturers who agreed to set prices for their product. Jute is a bamboo-like plant that was processed into crude fabric, which was used to wrap bales of cotton.

The Executive Committee of the State Farmers Alliance take this method of addressing you through your various County and Subordinate organizations upon a matter which we deem of vital importance to you individually and collectively. For the first time since our organization you are called upon to exhibit your valor in doing battle against our avowed enemy—monopoly—to prove your devotion to the principles upon which our organization is founded. In every warfare, especially in those in which defeat means slavery, or even weakened powers for future resistance to an enemy whose ulterior object is reduction to a state but little removed from serfdom, and must finally culminate in abject dependence. It is expected of every soldier that he will gird himself with the whole armor necessary to successful resistance and manfully battle for that which secures to him the enjoyment of the right and for the discomfiture of the enemy which denies him this inalienable privilege.

It is, we presume, well known to the members of our organization that there has been formed during the present year a trust whose object is to destroy competition, limit production and increase the price of what is usually known as jute bagging, an article which has been almost exclusively used by the producers of cotton for years past in wrapping and making marketable the product. . . .

To accomplish the defeat of this trust which if successfully done we believe will greatly lessen the danger of encroachments of similar combines in the future, and give to our people confidence in their own strength and to inspire them with reasonable assurance that deliverance may be obtained and independence secured, united effort must be employed. We must feel that this work of deliverance from existing and threatened evils and placing ourselves in an attitude of independence is one in which every member of our organization should contribute his part. It is proposed and specially requested that this letter be carefully read and considered at the first meeting of your Alliance, and if you have no regular meeting before your County Alliance assembles that your President call a meeting to consider this matter, that a book be procured and that every member be urged to subscribe the amount he feels he can and ought for the immediate establishment of this enterprise. . . .

An enterprise of this kind cannot be established without money and while we fully realize the fact that our people are generally poor and hard pressed, yet we do confidently believe when you properly consider this matter, its importance for the present, and the good results which in future must flow from such a measure, that you will respond to the extent of your ability and even practice self-denial in order to aid an enterprise so praise worthy. This business will be conducted upon a plain, simple, co-operative plan, clear of complications, and which can be readily understood.

As a business enterprise, we fell assured that it will be a safe one, and in support of this we will state that no difficulty would be experienced in getting up the requisite amount of stock to commence operations from parties outside of our order, but all recognize the importance of having the business controlled by the Farmers Alliance.

We take pleasure in stating to you that a substitute, or even substitutes, have been found for jute bagging.

Much attention has lately been directed to a covering made of cotton and we are pleased to say to you that this article has been subjected to all required tests, water, hooks, compress, etc., and is declared to be a success.

We earnestly recommend to you to use a substitute for Jute when it is possible to procure it even though it should cost more and you should be loser thereby. . . .

Remember that every bale which you cover with cotton bagging weakens the Trust, and when jute bagging is used the trust is strengthened and the better prepared to fight you in the future. We need not to remind you that when cotton is used the demand is increased and by this means the probability of an increased price is better. We counsel you to be firm in your hostility to trusts of every kind. Be not seduced by fair promises and specious reasonings. Be true to the principles of our order and keep your organization intact, when we believe that we can assure you that the sun of prosperity will soon make bright the places now obscured by the gloom of adversity.

FRANK BURKITT, 1892[3]

Frank Burkitt, a politician from northeastern Mississippi and editor of the *Chickasaw (County) Messenger*, became Mississippi's leading Populist. For his defection from the Democratic party, he was incessantly hounded and his newspaper office burned. Burkitt's leadership of the Populist party, however heartfelt, never produced significant victories for his party. His 1892 letter to Walter Barker is perhaps the only extant explanation of Burkitt's decision to join the Populist party.

I regret as much as you that circumstances compelled my resignation as a Democratic elector, but I could not retain the position after what has so recently transpired at home; in the State, and at Washington, and be honest and Consistent. I cannot defend the [Democratic party's] Chicago platform, nor the recent acts of Congress ignoring the demands of the industrial classes. I was born a plebeian and I prefer to suffer with my people than eat from the flesh pots of Egypt. Every impulse of my nature revolts at the treatment the money power has visited upon the labouring people of this country for the past twenty five years[,] and every beat of my heart is in sympathy with the wealth providers of the land. The Democratic party has ceased to hear their cry for relief and I cannot follow it farther. . . . For you personally[,] permit me to express what I have always felt ever since our first acquaintance—the kindest regards.

HARRIET B. KELLS, 1890[4]

Middle-class reformers pursued reform in a variety of areas. Harriet Kells was the editor of the *Mississippi White Ribbon*, the state newspaper of the

Women's Christian Temperance Union, which sought to eliminate the influence of alcohol in society. The newspaper began publication at Meridian in 1888.

What is the remedy to prevent intemperance? We reply, Prohibition. To a very large extent the legislation of our State in regard to the drink traffic has always been prohibitory. The usual phraseology of our laws is, "it shall not be lawful." The right to sell as I understand, is always exceptional, and is granted on explicit conditions being necessary as a part of the contract for all in whose favor the exception is made. There is a law prohibiting the sale on Sunday. That absolutely prohibits the sale for one-seventh of the year. We also have a law prohibiting the sale on election days. Why prohibit the sale on election days? This is the answer given: That it is because the right of suffrage is a very high privilege, and it is not only right but essential that a man should have a clear brain and steady nerves when he steps up to the polls to exercise this important right. But is it not just as important that a man should have clear brain and steady nerves through all the rest of the year when he performs all the other high duties of citizenship, as well as his own business in providing for his own support and that of his family? CONSTITUTIONAL PROHIBITION will extend the safeguards of the people, deemed essential on election days, to all days in the year, on none of which a man is relieved from the duties of citizenship, and would make clear-brained citizens a permanency for the State.

FIGHTING HOOKWORM, 1910[5]

In 1910, the State Board of Health issued the following pamphlet as part of its effort to eradicate hookworm disease in Mississippi. The Board distributed the pamphlet to public school teachers and arranged information about hookworm disease in a question and answer format to encourage discussion. The need for such seemingly elementary information about the importance of outdoor toilets was great. In 1911, a survey of 20,979 households in forty-three Mississippi counties revealed 60 percent did not have outdoor privies. Among school children, infection rates were as high as 91 percent.

SOIL POLLUTION AS CAUSE OF GROUND-ITCH, HOOK-WORM DISEASE (GROUND- ANEMIA), AND DIRT-EATING

All children should learn these four rules for preventing disease, namely:

Rule 1. *Do not spit on the floor, for to do so may spread disease.* Both "Consumption" and diphtheria are spread in this way.

Rule 2. *Protect against mosquitoes.* Mosquitoes spread malaria ("chills and fever" or "ague"), yellow fever, dengue fever (also known as "break-bone fever"), and elephant foot.

Rule 3. *Do not pollute the soil.* Hookworm disease is spread only by soil pollution. Typhoid, dysentery and other intestinal diseases are usually spread by soil pollution.

Rule 4. *Protect against flies.* These carry filth and germs to the food and thus spread typhoid fever. They may spread other diseases also, such as consumption, inflammation of the eyes, etc. Flies are filthy creatures and should be kept out of the house.

There are many other important points in protecting against disease, but these four rules are of greatest importance, especially for the Southern States. . . .

QUESTION 2. WHAT ARE THE COMMON METHODS OF POLLUTING THE SOIL?

Suppose that a person has consumption, and that, instead of spitting into a cuspidor or spittoon, he spits on the ground? His spit or expectoration contains little germs, which are so small that they cannot be seen by the naked eye. These little germs are scattered on the ground, and, of course, they render the soil impure and are likely to spread consumption to healthy people. It is chiefly because of this danger of spreading consumption that we see so many signs with the words, "Do not spit on the floor."

Or suppose that a person has some disease of the kidneys or of the bladder, and the excretion from these organs is disposed of carelessly? He pollutes or contaminates the ground or water into which the waste containing the germs may pass, and in this way sickness may be spread to other people.

Or suppose that a person has disease germs in the bowels, and that, instead of disposing of the waste in a sanitary manner, he allows the soil to become polluted, and may thus spread his sickness to other people?

In to-day's lesson we are to study this last method of soil pollution.

QUESTION 3. DOES THE BIBLE WARN AGAINST SOIL POLLUTION?

Yes. See Deuteronomy xxiii., 12 and 13:

"12. Thou shalt have a place also without the camp, whither thou shalt go forth abroad;

13. And thou shalt have a paddle upon thy weapon; and it shall be, when thou wilt ease thyself abroad, thou shalt dig therewith, and shalt turn back and cover that which cometh from thee." . . .

QUESTION 5. HOW IS HOOKWORM DISEASE SPREAD?

A person who has hookworm disease spreads it by polluting the soil. The worms cannot multiply in the bowels, but they lay hundreds of minute eggs . . ., which are passed in the discharges. . . .

QUESTION 7. HOW DOES THIS WORM ENTER PEOPLE?

The young worm enters the body in two ways:

a. If there is a heavy dew, or if it rains, or if the worm is living in a moist, shady place, the young worm is very active; when a person walks barefooted over the ground which is polluted by the presence of this young worm, the hookworm crawls into the skin . . . . Or,

b. The young worms may be swallowed, either in drinking water or with some salad or other food upon which they have crawled. . . .

QUESTION 8. IF THE WORM ENTERS THE SKIN, WHAT DOES IT CAUSE?

When this young worm enters the skin, it causes "ground-itch," also known as "toe-itch," "foot-itch," "cow-itch," "dew-itch" or "dew-poison." Thus "ground itch" results from soil pollution and is the beginning of hookworm disease. On this account hookworm disease may be called "ground-itch anemia," which means that a person is pale and has pale, watery blood, caused by the hookworms which entered his skin. . . .

QUESTION 18. WHY IS GROUND-ITCH MORE COMMON IN THE COUNTRY DISTRICTS, AS ON FARMS, THAN IN THE CITIES?

Ground-itch is more common in the country districts than in the cities because there is less care taken in the country to prevent soil pollution than there is in the cities. In large cities the city government places long pipes under the ground; from these large pipes smaller pipes run into the houses, and water closets are built in the houses and connected with these smaller pipes. All of these pipes together form what is called the "sewer system," and the discharges from the body are carried far away from the house, so that the ground around the houses is not polluted. In smaller cities and towns the houses have privies in the back yards, and when these privies are properly built, and cleaned regularly every week, as they should be, the soil does not become polluted. But on the farms and in the very small towns people are not so careful to prevent soil pollution, so that ground-itch is more common. Only about sixty per cent (or six out of ten) of five hundred and eighty-one farm houses, recently examined in five Southern States, had privies. On account of this lack of privies, ground-itch is very common on the farm. . . .

QUESTION 22. HOW DOES A PERSON FEEL WHEN HE HAS HOOKWORM DISEASE?

A person with hookworm disease usually says he has headaches, dizziness, buzzing in the ears, palpitation of the heart and soreness in the pit of the stomach when you press on it; he may be very weak, and not able to work hard, walk far or study much; he gets tired easily; sometimes he complains that it is hard for him to breathe; usually he does not sweat much.

QUESTION 23. DOES HOOKWORM DISEASE MAKE IT HARDER TO STUDY?

Yes. Although some pupils with hookworm disease are able to learn their lessons and to stand well in school, many others are too sick to study, and they fail in their examinations and become "repeaters." . . .

QUESTION 26. CAN A DOCTOR TELL WHETHER A PERSON HAS HOOKWORMS SIMPLY BY LOOKING AT HIM?

Yes, in case the person has a great many hookworms and it is clearly sick from the disease. If the person is not sick enough so that the doctor can be sure whether the patient has hookworms, it is necessary to give to the doctor a specimen (about half an ounce) of the fresh passage from the bowels; this is sent by the doctor to the State Board of Health or to the State laboratory, where it is examined to see whether it contains hookworm eggs. . . . If these eggs are found, the person should be treated for hookworms. . . .

QUESTION 33. IS IT A GOOD PLANT TO TAKE "PATENT" OR SECRET MEDICINES FOR HOOKWORMS?

NO. Much harm may be done by taking secret and "patent" medicines, especially those advertised as "sure cures." It is always best to go to the family physician, who can study the patient and can decide what medicine and how much of it should be used. . . .

QUESTION 36. IF HOOKWORM DISEASE REMAINS UNTREATED, WHAT MAY RESULT?

A person with severe hookworm disease may become a "dirt-eater" in case he is not treated. Many persons die as a result of the infection. Some persons remain weak and sickly for years without knowing the cause; their strength (vitality) is reduced, and if they are taken sick from some other disease, such as consumption or pneumonia, they are more liable to die than if they were not weakened by the hookworms. Some persons do not suffer any, but they may spread the disease to other people; such persons are called "carriers." . . .

QUESTION 44. HOW CAN HOOKWORM DISEASE BE PREVENTED?

By building good privies and keeping them clean. No only should every house have a good privy or closet, but churches and schools also should be provided with them. . . .

QUESTION 48. HOW SHOULD A PRIVY BE BUILT?

There should be a pail, or a barrel, or a tub, or a water-tight box under the seat. . . , and the privy should be closed in back so that chickens, hogs, and dogs cannot reach the discharges.

QUESTION 49. HOW CAN FLIES BE KEPT AWAY FROM THE TUB?

By pouring some fluid known as disinfectant into the tub. Or some water may be placed in the tub and a cupful of crude oil may be poured on the water.

QUESTION 50. WHY IS IT SO DANGEROUS FOR FLIES TO VISIT PRIVIES?

Because flies may go from the privy to the house and carry filth and the germs of disease to the sugar, butter, bread, meat,and other food. . . .

EMILY BUTT, 1911[6]

Emily Butt, chair of a committee devoted to creating a juvenile reformatory, apparently wrote the pamphlet from which the following text was drawn. Interest in reforming the penitentiary system appeared initially in the 1880s. Soon reformers like Butt extended the call for reform to a plea for building a separate facility for youthful offenders. In 1896, the governor vetoed a Juvenile Reformatory bill; a similar bill died in the legislature in 1908; and in 1910, the house killed the bill.

In order to disprove this assertion [i.e. that boy criminals could not be reformed], a Jackson High School teacher, Miss Emily Butt, heartily seconded by Governor Noel and the prison officials, volunteered in the summer of 1909 to spend two months in the Rankin State Farm, where the white men and boys are kept, instructing the seventeen boys there at the time. One of these was fourteen years old. He served his term and went out, still in short trousers. The ages of the others varied from fifteen to twenty-one; their sentences from six months to life. One was there for murder, one for manslaughter, two for assault and battery, the others for burglary and grad larceny. . . .

The causes which led to the crimes would be interesting to a student of penology. Some boys of excellent parentage are there, and one stops to wonder where lies the fault in their bringing up. Stories of escapades at night when trustful parents thought them safe in bed, and of over-indulgent mothers who stood between them and merited punishment, furnish a clue. As a rule, they are under developed, especially from an intellectual standpoint, though by no means stupid or dull. Generally speaking, they belong to that class familiar to every teacher, the boy who on account of health, lack of interest or opportunity, a desire to go to work, or any one of a dozen reasons, is behind the average boy of the same age. The obstacle removed, boys of this class frequently develop with amazing rapidity. The north and east, with their hordes of foreigners, and city slums, have to deal with the opposite type of juvenile criminals, those young in years, but old in crime. For this reason, our efforts to train and teach promise a greater measure of success.

During the months of July and August, these seventeen boys went to work about sunrise, came in about half past eleven, and spent the hours from half past one to six in the school room. Most of them showed a lack of early training in every particular, five of them never having been to school a day in their lives. Some scarcely know their letters. Two or three would be classed in the eighth or ninth grade. At first it seemed incredible that there were seventeen-year-old boys of average intelligence in the State of Mississippi who could neither read nor write, and their statements were received with doubt, but close supervision revealed the fact that it was too true. In the two months all of this class had read well into the second reader, mastered the four rules in arithmetic, including the tables, and all save one wrote clearly and legibly. . . .

They seemed to be as responsive to moral training as to intellectual, though this is harder to estimate. Gambling, swearing and excessive cigarette smoking are three of the evils that were conspicuous. Strong efforts were made by the boys themselves to overcome these, and those in a position to know, say that the improvement was remarkable. From the beginning, lessons in morals were given precedence over all others and the fact was impressed upon them that education should mean the making of character. . . .

The hardest problem, the one that during that summer seemed almost impossible of solution, was the question of association. It is rather surprising to those who have never given the matter thought to learn that there are class distinctions in the penitentiary just as on the outside, but the lines are rather more distinctly drawn. Men of gentle birth and breeding are there, men, who in a moment of frenzy, have committed deeds from which their very souls recoil in horror now; others, who, while technically guilty, are victims of circumstances rather than of their own evil intentions. Needless to say, these two classes form a very small part of the prison population. Then there is the illiterate, but well meaning fellow, whose crime was chiefly the result of ignorance, or, perhaps, of a false standard. And so on down the line until we come to the demon in human form, whose every thought reeks with vileness, the bare presence of whom is pollution, whose chief delight is to pour tales of crime into the ears of the unsophisticated, and whose idea of bliss seems to be the contamination of youths. These are the ones with whom every inch of ground had to be contested. These are the ones whose efforts were directed to the tearing down at night of the teaching done in the day; these are the ones who ridiculed the boys and tried to make them believe that behind the work being done for them lay some sinister motive. As the forces of evil are always eventually overcome by good, steady progress was made, but what might have been accomplished had the boys been separated from bad influences! . . .

So ended the work of the summer of 1909. Little in the way of actual results on the lives of these boys was expected by the promoters of this brief summer school, two short months of care as opposed to the long years preceding, surely if one "made good" by reason of the work, it was justified.

All of the seventeen except two have either finished their terms or been pardoned. No definite effort has been made to keep up with them, but their letters are frequent, telling of battles fought and victories won; sometimes of temptation that was too strong for them, asking advice on matters material and spiritual, financial and moral. They never ask for aid other than advice. One is at West Point, N.Y., having joined the Army; another is a fireman on a railroad; another working in an overall factory; two are employed by farmers; one is at work in a sawmill; others are at home with their parents. . . .

Since June, 1909, to the present time, a period of less than two years, fifty white boys under twenty-one, have been on the Rankin State Farm. Approximately a hundred others have been in the county jails and on the county farms.

What are you going to do about it? Are you going to help in the campaign that stands from giving every boy in the State of Mississippi a chance to make a man of himself? If so, study the question, see that your neighbor is informed; ask your papers to take it up; above all, send men to the Legislature who have correct views on this subject.

THE SEAFOOD INDUSTRY AND IMMIGRANT CHILDREN, 1912[7]

In 1912, Rene Baché wrote the following report on child labor at Gulf Coast seafood packing plants. He drew his information about the industry from reports filed by representatives of the National Child Labor Committee, including Dr. A. J. McKelway and photographer Lewis W. Hine. The essay points out that however far Mississippi lagged behind in its industrial development, the state's economic advance came at a high price for young children. In 1912, Mississippi passed its first child labor laws, protecting children under the age of 8 from the worst abuses.

Two questions—one of them relating to child labor, and the other having to do with shrimps—have combined to make a puzzling problem for the wise men.

Along the Gulf coast—at Biloxi, at Pass Christian, and other points favorably located with reference to the fishery—there are great shrimp canneries, in which children by the hundreds, many of them very little ones, are employed. The work they do consists chiefly in picking the shrimps out of their shells.

It is not only very arduous labor, but attended with an incidental hardship of no ordinary kind, inasmuch as the shrimps contain a chemical substance of a corrosive nature which attacks the hands, causing the skin to peel off. So powerful is this corrosive that the clothes of the children, and even their shoes, as they stand amid accumulations of the shells, are eaten and destroyed by it.

In order to keep on at their work, the children are obliged to harden their hands by dipping them from time to time into a solution of alum. They suffer severely. But the distress they have to undergo has had nothing to do with an investigation recently undertaken by the government Bureau of Chemistry, the object of which was purely commercial. The sufferings of the children might be ignored, but the chemical substance in question eats the tins in which the shrimps are packed, causing perforations.

So much loss has been occasioned in this way that appeal was made by the shrimp packers to the Bureau of Chemistry for definite information as to the nature of the chemic substance, and for a remedy for the mischief, if obtainable. In response, the government experts have made an elaborate series of experiments with consignments of the long-whiskered crustaceans shipped for the purpose from Biloxi, Miss. They have succeeded in isolating the mysterious corrosive, and in reducing it to the form of crystals. It is a somewhat complex compound, to which the name "monmethylamin" has been given.

One fact ascertained long ago by the packers was that the corrosive substance seems to disappear when the shrimps have been preserved

for a while with ice. If they are caught at some distance form the packing houses, they are commonly iced in the boats; or, if taken near by,
they are sometimes laid down in ice for a day or two, during which
time they appear to lose the peculiar chemic property described. This
(say the experts) is because the substance concerned is volatile, and
much of it evaporates and passes off while the shrimps are on ice. But
it is evident that a good deal remains, for, even when the shrimps are
thus treated, the cans containing them will rapidly corrode unless
lined in some way—preferably with parchment paper.

So much having been said for the commercial side of the question,
which is all that interests the packers, it is almost equally worth while
perhaps to consider the unfortunate situation of the children employed
in the canneries. But, inasmuch as the conditions in their case are in
no way different from those governing child workers in the oyster
canneries, it may be as well to bunch them all together in a discussion
of the subject. . . .

As a matter of fact, children of more tender age are employed in the
shrimp and oyster canneries than in any of the cotton mills of the
South, some of them being only four or five years old. The method of
handling the oysters consists in piling them into small cars and running
them into big "steam-chests," out of which they come with their shells
open, so that, when spread on long tables, it is an easy matter to take
out the "meats." This is the task allotted to the children, who, under
the stern eye of a "shucking boss," cut the meats out of the shells and
transfer them to tin buckets, ready for canning.

This is an immense industry in the Gulf States. At Pass Christian,
Miss., and other points great numbers of children are employed to
shuck oysters in the canneries. Nearly all of them are of foreign
parentage, and largely they are Poles. They are often housed under
the most squalid and insanitary conditions, and it is beyond question
that many of them die from the hardships they are obliged to endure.

Most of these children come from Maryland and Delaware. They
are employed during the summer and early fall in the vegetable and

fruit canneries of those States, and are shipped to the South in flocks to shuck oysters and pick shrimps through the winter and spring. When autumn arrives, agents for the shrimp and oyster packers visit Baltimore and other large towns in that part of the country, and pick up as many poor immigrants as they need, especially among the Poles—the Italians having become wary through experience. Such families, usually provided with plenty of children, are persuaded to go by the promise of free transportation and of the payment of their return passage—the latter expectation being nearly always unfulfilled. Very ignorant and commonly unacquainted with any language except their own, they are helpless to protect themselves, and, once herded on board steamers, they have no chance to escape.

Filled with the hope of going to a warm latitude—where, they are told, they can pick oranges off the trees—they are carried to Biloxi, Appalachicola, Pass Christian, and other places where the shrimp and oyster canneries are located. While at work, they commonly live under such conditions of squalor as would not be tolerated in the most poverty-stricken quarter of any Northern city. The pay is small, and for the children often not more than ten cents a day; but a good deal of Northern capital is most profitably invested in the canneries, and the big dividends they yield are largely derived from the labor of mere infants. . . .

At Bay St. Louis, Miss., many of the children engaged in picking shrimps were found suffering from bleeding fingers. They said it was an acid in the head of the shrimps that made the trouble. One cannery manager explained that six hours was about all the most practiced hands could stand of this sort of work in a day. Then their fingers were so sore that they had to stop, soaking them in alum to harden them for a renewal of the toil the following morning. The mother of one three-year-old girl said: "She really does help considerable." So likewise did a five-year-old sister.

Indeed, the shrimp packers say that unless the pickers begin at a very early age, they never attain high proficiency. Mr. [Lewis] Hine[s][8] found one eleven-year-old who said that she earned a dollar a day when shrimps were big. They vary more or less in size. A fisherman told him that last year, on good days, his seven-year-old girl and nine-year-old boy each made ninety cents a day.

In a cannery at Biloxi, on an occasion when an agent [of the National Child Labor Committee] visited it, shrimps happened to be scarce for the time being, and the management decided not to start work until daylight. For over an hour 100 women and children—about twenty of them under twelve, and some only five or six years of age—sat or stood about in the darkness, enveloped by a fog that drenched their clothing, simply to hold places at the picking tables. . . .

One of the worst features of the system described is that it deprives the children of the opportunity of education. Many families continue to work at late crops until Christmas, and meanwhile the boys and girls are kept away from school. . . .

Negro slavery has been abolished in this country, but child slavery has taken its place to a very large extent. . . .

Chapter 9

SUFFRAGE FOR SOME

White resentment of the Mississippi Constitution of 1868, the first to recognize black citizenship and to grant ex-slaves the right to vote, reached its apex in 1890 when the state legislature convened a constitutional convention. The most frequent objection to the constitution, one that had been heard since 1868, was that it had been written by "black Republicans." For many years, politicians had stalled the convening of a constitutional convention, but by the late 1880s, it had become increasingly difficult to do so. Both agrarian and middle-class reformers had begun clamoring for a new constitution. Middle-class reformers wanted the new constitution to include restrictions on the sale of alcohol, amendments outlawing gambling and the lottery, an end to the leasing of state convicts, and the codification and extension of laws that encouraged industrial development. Farmers, on the other hand, sought a change in the apportionment of legislative seats and the appropriation of state funds to shift from favoring predominately African-American counties in the Delta to the eastern counties where more whites lived. Their argument was that blacks did not enjoy the benefits of public schools or representative democracy, so they should not be counted when determining apportionment or appropriations. Farmers also advocated the popular election of judges and the restriction of statewide elected officials to one term in office.

Although their objectives differed, white Mississippians agreed that the new state constitution must disfranchise black voters. Yet, they knew that the

*Fourteenth and Fifteenth amendments to the United States constitution for-
bade discrimination against African Americans as a named class. In order to
disfranchise blacks, then, two strategies were broached: First, some proposed
that black voters be eliminated from the polls through property, education, or
other qualifications (including J. A. P. Campbell's plural voting scheme for
land owners). All understood that such qualifications would exclude certain
whites, generally poor whites, and some Mississippians thought the removal of
those whites from politics would have a salutary effect on elections and legislation. Second, some Mississippians believed that to discount the influence of blacks
at the polls women should be allowed to vote. They hoped that white women
would turn out in larger numbers than black women and thus help cancel the
impact of black voters. Although the faint effort to enfranchise women in 1890
failed, women continued to press for the right to vote, achieving their objective
only with the passage of the Nineteenth amendment to the U.S. constitution. If
in a reactionary manner, the constitutional convention, dedicated as it was primarily to the disfranchisement of African-American voters, represented
another expression of the reform impulse that gripped Mississippi in the late
nineteenth century.*

FRANK H. FOOTE, 1890[1]

Frank Foote was a commissioner of elections in Claiborne County.
After informing Charles K. Regan of his election as a delegate to the
constitutional convention—by a vote of 148-0—he added the postscript
that follows. His sardonic plan was not the only one uttered by
Mississippians making fun of J. A. P. Campbell's scheme of assigning
multiple votes to individuals based on the amount of property they
owned. Other Mississippians offered equally facetious plans: one plan
would have allowed citizens who had fathered no illegitimate children
to have multiple votes; another awarded the citizen without dogs more
votes than the owner of multiple dogs.

. . . I wish you would advocate the fat mans plan for the restriction of
vote & increase theirs also. "Every man who weighs 200 has 2 votes &

if his wife weighs 200 he is entitled to cast her 2 votes." This plan suits me as I weigh 220 & my frow [i.e. *frau*] 200—so you see I will have 4 votes whereas by Mr. Campbell['s] plan I am forlorn in one only—as I am not a landed proprietor except the traditional one of 4 × 6 in the cemetery.

IRVIN MILLER, 1890[2]

Irvin Miller was a minister from Leake County, who was elected a delegate to the state constitutional convention. Once at the convention, he was placed on the education committee. His August 1890 letters to the Carthage *Carthaginian* reveal, among other things, the interest of some delegates in extending to women the right to vote.

. . . It is believed that this committee [the Suffrage Committee] will report on Wednesday next, but no one knows definitely, as the committee sits with closed doors and its members are bound to secresy [*sic*]. Still a little will leak out despite all precautions to the contrary, and enough has become known to excite the curiosity and interest of members and others to a high pitch, and the report is awaited with intense anxiety. This interest is in no wise lessened by the rumor that one feature of the report will deal with the question of woman's suffrage, and there are not wanting many members of the Convention who declare that placing the ballot in the hands of woman furnishes the true and only available solution of the great problem with which we have now to deal.

Those who favor this plan are more numerous in the Convention than I had supposed, and their numbers are increasing every day. In my judgment the vote on this question will be very close, but at this the advocates of the plan are hardly numerous enough to carry it. I have not committed myself on this question yet, because I am not fully apprised [*sic*] of the sentiment of my feminine constituents as regards the question. I guess I had best confer with Mrs. Miller before I cast my vote. . . .

J. B. CHRISMAN, 1890[3]

Judge J. B. Chrisman of Lincoln County was a prominent advocate of the prohibition movement in Mississippi. As proven by the speech he delivered upon seeing a draft of the Suffrage Committee's proposal, his object at the constitutional conventional was to end voting by African Americans and "white ignoramuses."

The effect of my amendment is to substitute a property or educational qualification for the poll tax prerequisite of the Franchise Committee. A man must have, or his wife must have, a homestead, or other real or personal property of the value of $250.00, or he must be able to read and write the English language. If he has a homestead, he is a voter without reference to its value. If he has not a homestead, but owns $250.00 real or personal property, he still may vote. If he has neither, he must read and write the English language or he is debarred from the privilege of voting.

In my opinion nearly all the white people in the State would be able to vote under the rule this amendment makes. A great many colored people would also vote, but it is no part of my plan to make a rule for the whites that does not equally apply to the blacks, and under the operation of this substitute, for the Committee's recommendation white supremacy will be secured to the State for many years. We cannot foresee that it will for a hundred years, but it meets the emergency upon us. . . .

What was the shadow that hung over us—that darkened our future and alarmed our people? Sir, it is no secret that there has not been a full vote and a fair count in Mississippi since 1875—that we have been preserving the ascendency of the white people by revolutionary methods. In plain words, we have been stuffing ballot-boxes, committing perjury and here and there in the State carrying the elections by fraud and violence until the whole machinery for elections was about to rot down. The public conscience revolted. That which had a beginning in dispair [*sic*] at the situation, and

133 white
1 black

which seemed to justify any means for public preservation, was becoming a chronic ulcer upon the body politic—and threatened to disintegrate the morals of the people. Thoughtful men every where foresaw that there was disaster some where along the line of such a policy as certainly as there is a righteous judgment for nations as well as men.

And I say, Mr. President, no man can be in favor of perpetuating the election methods, which have prevailed in Mississippi since 1875, who is not a moral idiot, and no statesman believes that a government can be perpetuated by violence and fraud. The dullest intellect must see that it leads to political convulsions of some sort dangerous to life, liberty and property.

Men of observation and men who read books know that a republican government rests mainly on the virtue and intelligence of the people, and the ballot—a pure and untrammeled ballot, is its main reliance. Shorn of this instrumentality it will surely begin to die. It requires no Solomon to see that the ballot-box stuffer cannot be always relied on to elect the best men to office.

Now sir, what has this Committee offered us as a remedy? A two dollar poll tax!—the Australian Ballot and an apportionment.

And right here I stop to say that the proposition that in 1895 a man shall be able to read the Constitution, or be able to understand any clause of it when read to him, stamps the whole scheme of the Committee with disfavor. It don't look honest, straightforward and manly. It looks like a farce to make a registration officer decide whether a voter rightly interprets a clause of the Constitution. If the registrar decides that the voter rightly interprets the clause, he is a qualified voter. If he does not understand it, he cannot register. . . .

It looks as if it was intended that if the register wanted the man to vote he would read him some such clause as: Slavery, except as a punishment for crime shall be forever prohibited. "Do you understand that?" "Oh, yes." But if he did not want him to vote he would read him the interstate clause or the section forbidding the Legislature to pass *ex post facto* laws and demand a construction.

But let us look a little closer at this remedy in the shape of a poll tax, the Australian ballot and apportionment.

In the first place we are to look at the fact that we have 70,000 more colored voters than whites. I honestly believe that at home and abroad the colored man will be appealed to pay his poll tax as a religious duty and as a measure of safety for some great emergency, and that as great a number will this tax in proportion to their population as will whites. We have no guarantee that this will not be the result, and if it should be[,] the Australian ballot will give them the State. I say this, on the assumption that the law is to be administered in good faith, and we are to have a fair election. Of course if we are to go on carrying the election with Winchesters or by stuffing the ballot boxes, we do not need the Australian or the poll tax qualification. But if we mean to meet and remedy what I regard as the mischief—the temptation to violence and fraud by securing the right of the citizen to vote, then the committee's plan is a delusion and a snare. The Australian ballot is not the equivalent of an educational qualification. A man of ordinary capacity can soon learn the difference in the appearance upon the ticket of the names of Muldrow and Chrisman, and so without education and without property the ignorant, irresponsible vagabond voter will control the destiny and shape the public policy of the State. . . .

Sir, the tendency of political thought is to agrarianism, and communism, and there is a perfect rage at the idea of recognizing property as a qualification for voting. Yet it is property that supports the paupers, builds the bridges, and court-houses and jails of the counties. It is the property of the State, sir, that is called on to educate the rising generation, and to support all the ele[e]mosynary institutions of the State, to sustain the government in peace and in war, but the recognition of its right to protection is regarded as an outrage; and to avoid the disfranchisement of a lot of white ignoramuses we can't have an educational qualification, and to pander to the prejudices of those who have no property we cannot have a property qualification. All admit that this amendment to the right of franchise will solve the whole difficulty—will give us a clean ballot and white supremacy in subordination to the laws of the land and the Constitution of the United States.

I confess that for myself I would prefer both, though my amendment proposes a property or educational qualification. I put it so, because I hope the Convention will give us one or the other. I would put the knife in deep if I could, knowing you cannot cut off a rotting limb without taking with it some sound flesh.

Mr. President, I do not believe there is that antipathy among the people to a property and education qualification which it asserted exists. We have been educated to believe in manhood suffrage. The necessity for the limitation of the franchise has come upon us suddenly. The average citizen distrusted the proposition; he feared abuse of the scheme. Humble men who could read and write, imagined that they would not come up to the standard. The farmer with his humble homestead scarcely regarded himself as a man of property, but when they come to consider how moderate is the requirement and how effective it will prove as a rule of exclusion against the danger that threatens, they will be satisfied. Nor do I believe that men who are disfranchised will complain if it saves our civilization from barbarism. It is not the man who cannot read and write who is objecting, but in some cases at least it is the man who wants to write his vote.

Let us be honest and brave. Here is a plan that is practicable, constitutional, effective. Here is a plan without tricks, founded on reason and conscience. It is after the pattern of the fathers. More than half the colonies that formed the Constitution of the United [States] had a property or educational qualification, one or both.

They abandoned the policy because every man in that day was compelled to render military service every year. They were beleaguered by blood-thirsty tribes of Indians and with constant threats from hostile governments upon our border. Struggling against these fearful odds—every man a soldier—it was thought proper that he should have a voice in electing the officers that commanded him and the government that rested on his strong right arm.

Times have changed. Conditions require a return to the model of the fathers. It is a question of public preservation and the public safety is the supreme law. . . .

Give us a remedy as effectual in the government of the counties as in elections for State officers. Retire the bull-dozer and the ballot-box stuffer and bring to the people while the opportunity is afforded tranquility and peace. The two dollar poll tax will not do all this. I predict it will fail.

IRVIN MILLER, 1890[4]

Irvin Miller, whose letter describing the constitutional convention appears above, responded to J. B. Chrisman's attack on poor and uneducated voters.

MR. PRESIDENT. I have not afflicted this body with long speeches, and I do not design on this occasion to address this Convention at any great length, but I cannot refrain, in justice to my own feelings, from saying something of the able report of the Franchise Committee, and against the amendment offered by the distinguished gentleman from Lincoln county, Judge Chrisman. Mr. President and gentlemen of the Convention, you will pardon me for referring to myself. Thirty-five years ago, I left my native State, Kentucky and came to the sunny south in search of health and made my home in Mississippi, and I love my adopted State, and am interested in her welfare, her peace and prosperity, her soil contains the dust of my sainted mother and one of my brothers, and I expect it to be the receptacle of this body of mine when it returns to dust. When *I* came here I found the people in the main, poor, and education neglected in a large degree and while the State has made rapid progress both in wealth and education, many of the descendants of these pioneers are still among us, poor and uneducated, but they are good citizens nevertheless, and they are also true patriots, and I am not willing, by my vote, or my voice, to say, because they are poor they shall have no voice in the affairs of the government, which this amendment does virtually say. I have stood by their side in the late war; they assisted in carrying me from the field of battle when my body was mingled amid the terrible carnage.

I am bound to them by the dearest ties, and though they are few in number now, I cannot consent to give my vote to disfranchise them by a property qualification; for they are still poor and can't read. I have no prejudice against wealth or education, I wish everybody had wealth, I wish everybody had education, but they have not, and we must deal with facts. These poor soldiers came out of the war penniless. They have been industrious, they have labored hard, but for the most part they have had large and increasing families, and it is no easy matter for a man with eight or ten children, or more, to support them entirely by his own labor, hence they have not been able to accumulate wealth. I have in my mind now a few cases of this kind—I know a man in my section of the country who would be disfranchised under this amendment. He is a good citizen; he is honest; he is truthful; he is a christian, we worship at the same altar; we belong to the same church, and I cannot vote for him to be disfranchised. *share croppers*

Mr. President, as dearly as I prize the exercise of my own franchise, and this is about all I have ever had to do with politics, I say, sire, rather than see such men as the man of whom I speak, deprived of voting, I had rather give up my own franchise, and never cast another vote. You may call this sentimentality or you may call it prodigality, or whatever else you please. I am speaking the sentiment of my own heart. The calling of these men "white ignoramuses" as my friend, Judge Chrisman, calls them, does not change my mind upon the subject, he said "to avoid the disfranchisement of a lot of white ignoramuses we cannot have an educational qualification, and to pander to the prejudices of those who have no property, we cannot have a property qualification." I agree with my friend, Col. Boyd, from Tippah, when he said in his speech just a while ago, "that we were treading upon dangerous grounds" by such utterances as these, and like him,

I say we are not mistaken in the sentiment of the people we represent. I know I am no mistaken as to the people of my own county—they are opposed to property qualifications—and if I am not mistaken the State Farmer's Alliance declared against it. I believe they are right. I am in accord with them on this subject. I am not a member of the order, I am kept out by my occupation, but I heartily endorse it in its laudable undertaking, and wise fundamental principles that seek the elevation and the encouragement of the agricultural interests of our country. I say, Mr. President, I am in accord with them in these things and as I heard a distinguished gentleman say who is a member of this convention, I think they have as much right to organize for their mutual protection and advancement, as the merchants, the lawyers, the doctors, the bankers, or any body else, more than that, sir, I am here by the vote of the conservative, liberal minded men who belong to the Alliance in my county, for no man could be elected there to any office, without a part of the vote of that order. I am sure that the members of this order as a body in this State, are opposed to any property qualification being inserted in our Constitution. It is not the amount of property involved—the sum of two hundred and fifty dollars is comparatively an insignificant sum. No sir, it is not this; but it is the principle that underlies this, the principle, sir, that disfranchises a man because he has no property; a principle, sir, that in my humble judgment will cause a division in the ranks of the white people of our State.

I will now conclude my remarks by advocating the adoption of the report of this Committee on Franchise.

Sir, when I was canvassing my county, and told the people I was opposed to a property or educational qualification, they asked me if I had any other plan. I told them no, that I did not assume to be wise enough or statesman enough to solve this difficult problem, but I had faith enough in the intelligence and statesmanship, that would be in this Convention to believe, that they could in a measure at least, solve the question, and when, in my judgment, they have done so, I would stand by them. Now, Mr. President, I believe this committee has done that.

... They have not succeeded in doing so on their individual ideas as to what ought to be done, for as I understood it, the chairman of this committee stated in presenting this report that it was not what each member wanted in his individual capacity, but that it was a mutual concession and the result of a compromise. In this I agree, for I think we all ought to be willing to make some compromise for the general good of the State—in this report the white counties have not got what they demanded, the black counties have not got what they demanded, but the committee tell us this was the very best they could do under all the circumstance, and I believe what they say—hence I appeal to my brethren and representatives of the white counties to stand by the report of the committee and let us have the questionable and shameful methods of controlling the ballot box stopped; these methods are demoralizing to our young men, and ther[e] is a general outcry that they must cease. I believe the plan as reported by the Committee will effect this great reform. The Committee say they believe it will do so, and still leave the State under the control of the whites. . . . Let us not begin to tear it to pieces with amendments; for if we do this we are all at sea again for where is the man or men who can give something better. Something that will come nearer satisfying the people in all parts of the State.

Mr. President: We have no trouble with the colored people in my county, and we have quite a number of them there; they are quiet, industrious and humble—why is this? I will tell you why; because no white unprincipled emissary ever comes there among them to inflame their passions and to impose upon their ignorance, and Mr. President if the shot gun has to be used at all, to which I am opposed, I say it had better be used upon the white scoundrels who go among this race and inflame their passions and stir them up to violence.

THE LAW OF THE LAND, 1890[5]

The Constitution of 1890 included restrictions on the right to vote. Despite Chrisman's amendment and efforts to grant women the right, the original report of the Suffrage Committee was incorporated into the new constitution. Restrictions on the suffrage are outlined in the following sections of the constitution.

SEC. 240. All elections by the people shall be by ballot.

SEC. 241. Every male inhabitant of the State, except idiots, insane persons and Indians not taxed, who is a citizen of the United States, twenty-one years old and upwards, who has resided in this State two years, and one year in the election district, or in the incorporated city or town, in which he offers to vote, and who is duly registered as provided in this article, and who has never been convicted of bribery, burglary, theft, arson, obtaining money or goods under false pretenses, perjury, forgery, embezzlement or bigamy, and who has paid, on or before the first day of February of the year in which shall offer to vote, all taxes which may have been legally required of him, and which he has had an opportunity of paying according to law, for the two preceding years, and who shall produce to the officers holding the election satisfactory evidence that he has paid said taxes, is declared to be a qualified elector; but any minister of the gospel in charge of an organized church shall be entitled to vote after six months residence in the election district, if otherwise qualified.

SEC. 242. The Legislature shall provide by law for the registration of all persons entitled to vote at any election, and all persons offering to register shall take the following oath or affirmation: "I _____, do solemnly swear (or affirm) that I am twenty-one years old, (or I will be before the next election in this county) and that I will have resided in this State two years, and _____ election district of _____ county one year next preceding the ensuing election or (if it be stated in the oath that the person proposing to register is a minister of the gospel in charge of an organized church, then it will be sufficient to aver therein, two years residence in the State and six months in said election district), and am now in good faith a resident of the same, and that I am not disqualified from voting by reason of having been convicted of any crime named in the Constitution of this State as a disqualification to be an elector; that I will truly answer all questions propounded to me concerning my antecedents so far as they relate to my right to vote, and also as to my residence before my citizenship in this district; that I will faithfully support the Constitution of the United States and of the State of Mississippi, and will bear true faith and allegiance to the same. So help me God." . . . Any wilful and corrupt false statement in said affidavit, or in answer to any material question propounded as herein authorized, shall be perjury.

SEC. 243. A uniform poll tax of two dollars, to be used in aid of the common schools, and for no other purpose, is hereby imposed on every male inhabitant of this State between the ages of twenty-one and sixty years, except persons who are deaf and dumb or blind, or who are maimed by loss of hand or foot; said tax to be a lien only upon taxable property. The Board of Supervisors of any county may, for the purpose of aiding the common schools int hat county, increase the poll tax in said county, but in no case shall the entire poll tax exceed in any one year three dollars on each poll. No criminal proceedings shall be allowed to enforce the collection of the poll tax.

SEC. 244. On and after the first day of January, A.D., 1892, every elector shall, in addition to the foregoing qualifications, be able to read any section of the Constitution of this State; or he shall be able to understand the same when read to him, or give a reasonable interpretation thereof. A new registration shall be made before the next ensuing election after January the first, A.D., 1892. . . .

ANNIE C. PEYTON, 1886

In 1886, Annie C. Peyton, a resident of Hazelhurst, delivered the following address before the students at the Mississippi Industrial Institute, now the Mississippi University for Women. Peyton, a temperance activist, reflected the opinion of a sizeable number of Mississippians: they did not support the extension of suffrage rights to women because they feared that the franchise might undermine the place assigned them by society as saintly keepers of hearth and home. Peyton's speech testifies that the Victorian "cult of true womanhood" continued even in the late nineteenth-century to influence notions of women's roles in society.

It is proposed to add to the Constitution of the United States a sixteenth amendment, granting the right of suffrage to women. For eighteen years the advocates of this measure have urged its consideration upon Congress, and there is now pending a joint resolution to submit the proposed amendment to the Legislatures of the several States for adoption.

Those who favor this sixteenth amendment claim it as the grandest stride our nation can take toward universal freedom. They claim that the principle for which our forefathers contended in the revolution is violated, when women are taxed without being allowed to vote—or in other words, it is "taxation without representation." They appeal for the ballot as a matter of justice and equality to the women of this nation, and inquire by what right one half of humanity arrogates to itself the prerogative of governing the other half. . . .

This agitation for woman suffrage is widespread. Twenty-six States and territories were represented by women before the Committee of the Forty-eighth Congress, and should the now pending resolution be adopted, this question, which some of us have never seriously considered, will be presented to our Legislature for consideration and action. What, then will be our attitude in regard to woman suffrage?

IT IS ALWAYS SAFE TO DO RIGHT.

Then let us inquire, is it right—is it for the best interests of the State, the nation and humanity, that the burdens of government should be laid upon woman?

God created the sexes for different spheres in life. He fitted each for the duties each is designed to perform. He created one man and one woman and placed them in the garden of Eden in the family relation. Man was endowed with greater physical strength and was designed to be the head, or ruler, of the family, for after the curse was pronounced that a woman's sorrow should be greatly multiplied, we read: "And her desire shall be toward her husband, and he shall rule over her." This duty of obedience of wives to husbands is clearly taught and emphasized in the New Testament, showing that God designed that in the family government there should be one head, and that one, the man. And this duty of obedience of wives to husbands carries with it no humiliation to the true wife. The true wife loves and honors her husband, and cherishing these feelings, obedience becomes to her a chief delight. Not indeed the servile obedience rendered by a slave to a master, but obedience and deference growing out of that "love, which is the fulfilling of the law." . . .

Their destinies are henceforth united, their interests are one and inseparable. This is the scriptural view of marriage, and it follows, since the greater includes the less, if a woman marries a man, if she can trust to his keeping her hand and heart, the protection, and as God designed, the government, of their home—she can safely trust him on election day to cast the ballot in their mutual interests. Woman Suffrage, then, is not necessary for the protection of women.

Again, woman was designed to be the

MOTHER OF THE HUMAN RACE.

As mother she is the custodian of sacred interests, and with softened nature and less of physical strength, was fitted for the retirement of home, and the bearing and rearing of her children. There are times in the life of every mother when she could not got to the polls to deposit her ballot, even if the safety of the republic depended on her vote. For such times as these, and because of her very helplessness, God has wisely designed that she should have a protector—one to represent their united interests in the outside world. This is the plan of God, our Maker, a Being who is too wise to err, and too good to be unjust. . . . The wise man tells us to "train up a child in the way he should go, and when he is old he will not depart from it." The lessons learned at the mother's knees are the most lasting lessons of life. The sons that we rear in the nursery become the voters, the law-makers, the governors of this nation. As mothers, then, what need have we of the ballot, when we have the higher privilege of moulding the voter? The best way to provide for the prevention of crime, is to put a good mother in every home. Every crime originates in the human heart. If, therefore, during the twenty-one years of minority, the most impressible years of life, we mothers would instill lessons of truth and virtue, there would be no need of women in legislative halls to provide for the prevention of crime. What this country needs is

NOT STATESWOMEN,

but mothers—earnest, Christian women, who read the Bible, and are guided by it—who loves home, and take care of it and who train their children in the "nurture and admonition of the Lord." . . . God raise us up faithful mothers and teachers for the sons and daughters of this nation, and we will never feel our need of stateswomen. In the "Woman's Journal" (Nov 7, 1885) published at Boston, notice is given of suffrage meetings to be held on sundry times and places, among others, one "at Leominster, Sunday, November 8. Sunday, November 15 at South Hanson, at 10 a.m., 2:30 and 7:30 p.m. Sunday, November 22, at Holyoke." Who is to train the rising generation when mothers profane God's Sabbath attending suffrage meetings all day long?

As a Southern woman, a native of Mississippi, I protest against this USELESS AND GODLESS AGITATION. . . .

The majority of the Senate Committee of the Forty-ninth Congress, in their report speak of this petition as "woman's prayer to be free." Free from the law of her being? Free from her God assigned duties? Woman must have some place in the Universe, and who so competent to decide that place as the God who made her? They speak of woman suffrage as a "fundamental right"—as a long withheld.

"NATURAL RIGHT."

There can be no natural right to do that which is wrong. There is no fundamental right to transgress the law of God. The law of nature and of revelation both negative the idea that the duties of men and women are interchangeable. Sir William Blackstone says: "Upon these two foundations, the law of nature, and the law of revelation, depend all human laws; that is to say, no human laws should be suffered to contradict these."

AS TO TAXATION.

Women pay taxes on property, and in return receive protection of property equally with men. Women pay no poll tax and the rougher duties of citizenship are not required of them. They are very properly exempt from work on the public roads, from jury duty and are not required to serve in the army. Now it follows, if women must be full-fledged citizens, and put on an equality with men, all these things should be required of them. Think of our delicate daughters working the roads—of women locked night and day in a jury-room—and if by the votes of women this nation should be involved in war, it would be just and right that they should shoulder arms in defense of their country! These absurdities show some of the legitimate results of woman suffrage and convince us that women have *physical disabilities* that cannot be removed. God Almighty placed his fiat against woman suffrage when he made women to be mothers. . . .

I am proud that

NO WOMAN FROM MISSISSIPPI

went before Congress with a list of grievances—with a litany for wrongs to be righted. There were women from New York clamoring for suffrage, and there is enough legitimate woman's work in New York City alone to engage the time and effort of all her philanthropists. . . .

In Mississippi, God's plan for the sexes is recognized. We realize that in every woman's life there comes

AN ELECTION DAY.

On that day she is enthroned the queen of one man's heart and home; and on that day, she crowns her king. Into his faithful keeping, as a loving trust, she commits her life, liberty and happiness. He, henceforth, is to shield her from the ruder storms of life, and she is to make his home the very vestibule of Heaven. In the State government, we can safely trust our interests to the noble and knightly men of the

State. Every man is a mother's son, and what Southern son would betray his mother!

THIS COLLEGE,

the grandest of all our institutions, is evidence that the women of Mississippi have but to ask and they shall receive. In all parts of the State—in farmers' meetings, in legislative halls, in editorial chairs, the bravest and best have championed its interests. We asked for this institution that our daughters might be the better prepared for womanhood, and woman's duties. We do not complain that we are fettered, save by ignorance and poverty, and honest education will break these chains. No educated woman need complain that her sphere is restricted. There was never such a demand for strong souled, earnest, educated, Christian women as now. There is a Macedonian cry for these workers from the Atlantic to the Pacific, from Maine to Mexico—in fact, from all parts of the world.

Any true woman, whether married or single, realizes that even without the ballot, there is work enough to engage the hand, the head, and the heart—that woman's proper sphere is broad as the earth and infinitely high.

NELLIE NUGENT SOMERVILLE[6]

In 1897, Nellie Nugent Somerville became the first president of the Mississippi branch of the National American Woman Suffrage Association. She remained a tireless advocate for securing women's suffrage. In 1925, she was the first woman elected to the Mississippi House of Representatives.

... There is an old saying in holy writ, "if the blind lead the blind both shall fall into the ditch." This refers to moral leadership and moral blindness.

De Tocqueville assigned as the great cause of the French revolution, the lack of moral leadership. Said he of the social revolution that had been developing in France, "the most powerful, the most intelligent and the most moral classes of the nation had never attempted to connect themselves with it in order to guide it." When that revolution reached its culmination it broke in a storm of moral destruction. Dr. George Adam Smith says, "a people's own morals have more influence upon their destiny than despots or legislators."

We hear much of leaders and leadership; political leaders, commercial leaders; among women, social leaders. Men have been slow to concede any form of leadership to women: this exalted function of social leadership is generally allowed to be for ladies only. Of moral leaders, most important of all, little is heard, and yet, unless there are moral leaders, and unless they can assert their supremacy, our national development is moving in a dangerous direction.

The evidences of moral leadership must surely be found in the general prevailing moral standard of people in the visible results of that standard and in the direction which their development is taking. The standard set up by our religion is moral perfection but how has that been worked out in its practical application to life? We have not yet reached the point of denying moral perfection as a tenet of belief, but have we not reached the point of denying it as a practical possibility, still less as a necessity? The subtle form of unbelief which threatens the moral life of this nation is exemplified in the term "necessary evil." Formerly this applied to one evil only, but we seem to be adding to the list. Whenever some moral sharpshooter levels his gun against outrage, vice or oppression, he is told to come down from his perch, since that is only a "necessary evil."

Some evils, it appears, may be fought, but "necessary evil" must be held immune. Captains of industry say that child labor is a necessary evil. Thousands of children wearing their lives out in a treadmill of toil. Modern luxury says occupational disease is a necessary evil. Match factories causing phosphorus poison, "phossy jaw," now prevented by a recent federal act. Lead poison in tile factories. A few years ago the Glass Blowers Association presented statistics showing that 31 per cent of glass workers die of tuberculosis, half of them under 35 years of age.

But the most God-defying "necessary evil" is the double standard of morals, which calls for a standing army of women devoted body and soul to destruction. This thing has been tolerated and winked at until its effects have permeated and vitiated our whole social system. In regard to this a curious development has taken place. Men have claimed the right to do as they please that is to do wrong, but they have said to women, stand thou on the other side and do right.

About 50 years ago, or earlier, the educated Christian women of this nation began to do some vigorous independent thinking, ceased to accept second-hand opinions, and began to investigate for themselves.

The result of all this, the curious development which as at last "arrived," is that the double standard of morals, put under the search-light by the intellectual emancipation of women, has produced a double standard of conscience, one for men, and another for women.

Where, think you, shall we look for moral leadership, among the moral or the immoral class? Moral leadership is not the birthright of any man; it is the gift of God, and it depends upon character.

Shall it be said that moral leadership has been taken away from man? No, that need not be said, but this can be said clearly, undeniably, Divine Providence has opened the domain of moral leadership to the Christian women of this nation. This is the reason political power is being given and must be given to women; because, if the blessing of God is upon this nation, moral power and political power must be together.

Why does the editor of a leading church paper say, "the South is trembling at the thought of the approach of woman suffrage?" Because he knows in his very soul that the moral power in women must be recognized and ought to be recognized by enfranchising them.

Nearly 2000 years ago it was said to a class of men who claimed to be moral leaders, "you have taken away the key of knowledge." These 2000 years have witnessed a struggle on the part of the human race to regain that key of knowledge and place it in the hands of all men. What then is that key of knowledge? I assume it to be this: the opportunity to seek the truth in all things, without prejudice in regard to all human relations, facts and conditions.

Truth is not created by any man; it is merely discovered. In every age there have been men or classes of men who would cover up the truth with artifice and invention, and restrain other men from finding it. When at last men gained freedom to seek the truth, to do their own thinking, women were still restrained. But at last women, too, have won that freedom. The politicians have a slogan. "Let the people rule." There might be another slogan, "Let the women think."

But this key of knowledge at last, as never before, men and women have taken this matter into their own hands; they are saying, "we will have the truth, the whole truth, and nothing but the truth," in regard to all human relations, facts and conditions.

Great organizations are formed, great meetings held for nothing but this: to find the truth, and having found it, to legalize it. Assuredly moral leadership is with those who are determined to see facts as they are and to tell the truth about them.

The final test is the recognition of leadership. Is Christian America stoning her prophets or honoring them? The statue of Frances Willard is in the capitol at Washington. When Mrs. Sarah Platt Decker, of Denver, died, public honors were accorded her. When Mrs. Stevens, president of the National W. C. T. U., died, the Governor of Maine ordered flags to be placed at half mast, saying, "no citizen of Maine had ever rendered more distinguished service." Miss Jane Addams has been called the "first citizen" of the United States. Dr. Anna Shaw has won for herself a position of moral leadership which few, if any, can equal.

Moral leadership is asserting itself, combating that vicious complacent theory of "necessary evil." There are strong men and women who have set up the standard of moral perfection, not as a remote theory, but as a present necessity.

De Tocqueville said, "A new science of politics is indispensable to a new world."

The demand for political freedom will inevitably follow the consciousness of moral and intellectual freedom. Political freedom in this new world means the right of suffrage. Shall men deny political freedom when God has given to women moral freedom and moral leadership?

Chapter 10

THE JIM CROW WORLD

The institution of slavery placed black and white Mississippians in close prox-
imity to each other. During the long years of slavery, the law and common
practice provided for different treatment of the two races, but fear of rebellion
and distrust of enslaved labor made it necessary for slaves and masters to live,
work, and often to worship together. The abolition of slavery and the establish-
ment of citizenship for African Americans presented to white Mississippians
committed to maintaining black subordination a peculiar question: How could
blacks be kept in "their place" when the Federal government insisted that they
be treated equitably before the law? White Mississippians answered the ques-
tion by insisting on the rigid division of the world into black and white spheres,
thereby defying the intent of the Fourteenth and Fifteenth amendments, as
well as the spirit of true citizenship promised by Reconstruction. In some
instances, the segregation of blacks was maintained by law; in other instances,
"customs" were quickly crafted to assert and maintain segregation.

Perhaps the first facilities to experience segregation were railroad cars. As
early as the 1870s, Ham Carter, a black Republican, sued the Mississippi
Central Railroad Company for selling his wife a first-class ticket and forcing
her to sit in the second-class compartment. His suit was not successful, and the
practice of segregation continued unabated. In fact, in the famous 1896 Plessy
v. Ferguson decision handed down by the Supreme Court, the U.S. govern-
ment supported white southerners in their effort to establish segregation.

189

The court ruled that separate facilities for blacks and whites were constitu-
tional, as long as the facilities were of equal quality. Bolstered by the Supreme
Court ruling, municipalities and other entities insisted that blacks use separate
entrances to gain access to theaters, drink only from water fountains marked
"colored," and use restrooms reserved for their race only. Blacks were also pro-
hibited from using public libraries, swimming pools and beaches, and many
other facilities operated with tax dollars. The state of Mississippi most notably
entered the arena of segregation by mandating the maintenance of separate
and supposedly equal facilities for the education of black and white students.

African Americans responded to the reign of Jim Crow (segregation) in
numerous ways, and black Mississippians advocated the full range of responses
to Jim Crow laws and customs. Some embraced the accommodationist position
of Booker T. Washington, who encouraged blacks to become carpenters,
plumbers, and brick masons, thereby proving to whites their essential value to
society. A small handful of black Mississippians in the early twentieth century
joined the N.A.A.C.P. and embraced the philosophy of W. E. B. Du Bois, who
argued that blacks should resist Jim Crow at every turn. Others still fled
Mississippi. Regardless of their reaction to Jim Crow, the severity of segrega-
tion's restrictions and the constant threat of violence made Mississippi a
challenging place to live. Yet, despite the difficulties, black Mississippians, par-
ticularly those living in urban areas, created a largely autonomous world. In
their world, black physicians, lawyers, bankers, and business owners served their
needs. At the same time, however, the great majority of black Mississippians did
not live in urban centers. For them, the existence of an urban, black middle-
class provided no comfort as they confronted the harsh realities of Jim Crow.

CHARLES BANKS[1]

In 1903, Charles Banks, a businessman in Clarksdale, moved to Mound
Bayou to become a banker. Although he did not own the bank, he was
the cashier and prime mover at the institution. From Mound Bayou, he
became closely associated with Booker T. Washington, corresponding
frequently with him, traveling with him, and serving as an officer in the

National Negro Business League. In the letter that follows, Banks, like
Washington and other middle-class blacks in the Jim Crow south,
advocated support for the accommodationist position.

In keeping with your suggestion of sometime ago for the Negroes
throughout the country to take up the matter of better accommodations by the railroads for our people, I am writing to advise, that this
was pretty generally done throughout Mississippi.

At Jackson, Miss., a committee headed by Mr. P. W. Howard[2] of
that city, took the matter up with the officials, were courteously
received and promised full consideration on the matters set forth to
them. In this connection however, I am glad to state that in the matter of accommodations for our people on the Yazoo & Mississippi
Valley Railroad which is owned and operated by the Illinois Central
and on which Mound Bayou is located, we fell inclined to commend,
rather than condemn their attitude towards us as a race in the matter
of accommodation and general service. The writer has on more than
one occasion, taken up matters with them along this line, and in each
case they have manifested their willingness to grant any and every
request that was in any degree practicable. I have ridden on most of
the roads in the south as well as the northeast and west, and it is my
deliberate opinion that the accommodations for the Negroes on the
line of the Yazoo & Mississippi Valley between Memphis and
Vicksburg is equal to that of the whites so far as day coaches are concerned, and as good as can be found anywhere. I regret however, that
I cannot make such a statement for the rest of the lines operating in
Mississippi, and I am trusting with you, that the concerted action in
having our people call upon the representatives of the railroads, and
soliciting their favorable consideration of our claims for better accommodation will have the desired results.

I am not sure that it is good judgement for me to embrace in this
letter another matter that has given me some little concern, but I will
do so anyway. There is a great tendency on the part of some our people to institute suits against railroads for every little imaginary thing

to say nothing of real causes. In a large measure the desire does not originate with them to pursue such a course, but they serve as the instrument. In my opinion we could hardly expect the highest and most favorable consideration from those whom we desire to reach when it is understood that we perniciously and indiscriminately harass the companies with law suits without merit or foundation, and I am hoping that we can in some way discourage those parties.

MOVING NORTH[3]

In 1919, Emmett Scott published two collections of letters in the Journal of Negro History. He collected the letters from a variety of sources, many from the office of the *Chicago Defender*, the most widely distributed black newspaper of the period. Since the letters were contemporary to their publication, Scott in editing them, unfortunately though understandably, removed the names of the letter writers. Nonetheless, the letters evince a spirit of despair about living in Mississippi.

Letter From Natchez[4]

Dear Sir: I thought that you might help me in Some way either personally or through you influence, is why I am worrying you for which I beg pardon.

I am a married man having wife and mother to support, (I mention this in order to properly convey my plight) conditions here are not altogether good and living expenses growing while wages are small. My greatest desire is to leave for a better place but am unable to raise the money.

I can write short stories all of which po[r]tr[a]y negro characters but no burlesque can also write poems, have a gift for cartooning but have never learned the technicalities of comic drawing. These things will never profit me anything here in Natchez. Would like to know if you could use one or two of my short stories in serial form in your great paper they are very interesting and would furnish good reading matter.

By this means I could probably leave here in short and thus come in possession of better employment enabling me to take up my drawing which I like best.

Kindly let me hear from you and if you cannot favor me could you refer me to any Negro publication buying fiction from their race.

Letter from Lexington[5]

My Dear Mr. H _____: I am writing to you for some information and assistance if you can give it.

I am a young man and am disable, in a very great degree, to do hard manual labor. I was educated at Alcorn College and have been teaching a few years: but ah: me the Superintendent under whom we poor colored teachers have to teach cares less for a colored man than he does for the vilest beast. I am compelled to teach 150 children without any assistance and receives only $27.00 a month, the white with 30 get $100.

I am so sick I am so tired of such conditions that I sometime think that life for me is not worth while and most eminently believe with Patrick Henry "Give me liberty or give me death." If I was a strong able bodied man I would have gone from here long ago, but this handicaps me and, I must make inquiries before I leap.

Mr. H _____, do you think you can assist me to a position I am good at stenography typewriting and bookkeeping or any kind of work not to[o] rough or heavy. I am 4 feet 6 in high and weigh 104 pounds.

I will gladly give any other information you my desire and will greatly appreciate any assistance you may render me.

Letter from Greenville[6]

Dear Sir: This letter is a letter of information of which you will find stamp envelop for reply. I want to come north some time soon but I do not want to leve here looking for a job wher I would be in dorse all winter. Now the work I am doing here is running a gauge edger in a saw mill. I know all about the grading of lumber. I have been working in lumber about 25 or 27 years My wedges [*sic*] here is $3.00 a day 11 hours a day. I want to come north where I can educate my 3 little children also my wife. Now if you cannot fit me up at what I am doing down here I can learn anything any one els can. also there is a great deal of good women cooks here would leave any time all they want is to know where to go and some way to go. please write me at once just how I can get my people where they can get something for their work. there are women here cooking for $1.50 and $2.00 a week. I would like to live in Chicago or Ohio or Philadelphia. Tell Mr. [R. S.] Abbott [editor of the *Chicago Defender*] that our pepel are being snatched off the trains here in Greenville and a rested but in spite of all this, they are leaving every day and every night 100 or more is expecting to leave this week. Let me here from you at once.

P. K. MESCHACK, 1895[7]

Although historians generally associate the back-to-Africa movement with the post-World War I activities of the Negro Improvement Association led by Marcus Garvey, African Americans since the antebellum period had dreamed of returning to Africa to escape discrimination and violence. In 1895, P. K. Meschack, a resident of Ellisville asked former governor John M. Stone if he and his neighbors could flee to Africa without recrimination.

the opinion I have of your abilities as scholar, Your behavior as a gentleman, Your pity as a Christian encourages me to solicit your kind assistance in a very important affair. Hon[.] sir the question to whitch I am about to put before you is this, thes[e] Goodly number of pore negros, who wants to go to Africia, but not having no protection Down heare they is under the opinion that thes[e] white peopil will try to prevent them from Leaving, and they are wishing to find out from you Do the Law compell them to stay heare in the USA, or can they Go to Eany outher country. the Whole Reason for thes negros wants to leave is because theare is so much mobing[.] Lynching are among them Till it forces the Negros to wants to Go some wheare to prevent such things as mention above, pray hoping to heare from our Ex Gov of Mississippi.

TEXT BOOKS IN MISSISSIPPI, 1940[8]

The N.A.A.C.P.'s journal *Opportunity* published the following brief article about new textbook regulations in Mississippi. The taunting first line in the article speaks loudly for the desire of African Americans to challenge Jim Crow and achieve for themselves and the nation the promise of American democracy.

Down in Mississippi they are afraid of Democracy. The legislature of that sovereign state has invited universal ridicule by passing a text book law for Negro schools. In the future, according to this law, text books furnished Negro schools shall be different from those furnished to white schools. In the text books for Negroes all reference to voting, elections, civic responsibilities and democracy will be excluded. Thus Negro children will not be informed as to their theoretical rights or duties under the democratic system of government.

Mississippi and most of the states in the South have always been afraid of Democracy. It has never existed in most of these common-wealths either for the Negro or the poor white. The iniquitous meas-ures adopted to deprive the Negro of the franchise, such as the poll tax, have served to constrict the democratic process and to limit the exercise of the franchise among whites. The history of the South has demonstrated that social injustice and labor exploitation have not been, nor can they ever be confined to the Negro, although compar-atively he suffers most.

The action of the Mississippi legislature would be a cause for general laughter if it did not indicate the sinister character of the mental out-look of the elected representatives of that state, an outlook little short of depraved as regards the Negro. In a world that sees Democracy wag-ing a bitter fight to survive the onslaughts of authoritarian principles of government, Mississippi, a component part of the great Democracy of the West, moves toward repudiation of its basic principles. It is not surprising considering the general backwardness of that commonwealth, but it is important in indicating again how quickly even the pretense of Democracy may be abandoned by those who have always sought to evade its responsibilities.

A TRIPLE LYNCHING IN DUCK HILL, 1937[9]

Hundreds of lynchings were reported in Mississippi during the early twentieth century, and undoubtedly, many more went unnoticed by newspapers. The great majority of victims were African Americans accused of crimes (serious ones and petty ones) or of offenses against social conventions. The 1937 lynching of Roosevelt Townes, "Bootjack" McDaniels, and "Shorty" Durham was a gruesome case, as the following Associated Press story indicates, that ended in the murder of two of the men.

1937
Communal
Violence

Winona, April 13(AP)—While women, and even little children, looked upon the gruesome scene, two negroes accused of murdering a white merchant, were tortured with fire and lynched by a frenzied mob of nearly 500 persons near Duck Hill, this afternoon.

A third negro suspected by the mob in the slaying of George Windham, a county storekeeper, was severely whipped and run out of the county after narrowly escaping the mob's vicious vengeance.

Roosevelt Townes, who had confessed, Sheriff E. E. Wright said, that he shot Windham, was tied to a stake, tortured slowly to death by flames from a blow torch.

A negro identified only as "Bootjack" McDaniels, indicted with Townes in the Windham slaying, was shot by members of the mob, and his body burned.

Townes and McDaniels were taken from Sheriff E. E. Wright and two deputies early this afternoon as they were being led from the courtroom to be returned to the jail to await trial Thursday.

The negroes were handcuffed, and placed in a waiting school bus. Members of the mob piled into the bus, and others into automobiles.

The caravan sped northward toward Duck Hill and to the site of George Windham's small store, where the white man was fatally shot through a window last December.

Governor Hugh White hastily wired Chairman Summers[10] of the house judiciary committee that he regretted the occurrence and that a full investigation would be made of the lynching.

"This terrible thing will be immediately investigated by the grand jury," said Circuit Judge John F. Allen, of Kosciusko, who was presiding at the regular criminal term of circuit court here when the negroes were arraigned.

Judge Allen said he would hold a conference with the district attorney, and that plans for investigating the double lynching would be made immediately.

Governor Hugh White, who had just boasted to a farm Chermurgic conference in Jackson that Mississippi had not had a lynching in 15 months, was outraged at reports of the lynching. . . .

"It was all done quickly, quietly and orderly," said Deputy Sheriff A. J. Curtis, one of the officers overpowered by the mob.

Curtis said that when the prisoners were led out of the courthouse door a group of men milling about the courtyard closed in on the sheriff, his two deputies and the prisoners.

"Two men grabbed my arms and pinned them behind me," he said. "The other officers were overpowered in the same way. There was no other form of violence, and no effort was made at shooting," the officer said.

Curtis said the men were not masked, but said he did not recognize any of the men.

The negro prisoners were seized, he said, and hustled into the waiting school bus. Members of the mob jumped in waiting automobiles and followed the bus rapidly out of town.

As the caravan proceeded along the highway, the line of cars lengthened. One Winona citizen who would not permit the use of his name said "there must have been 500 men there before it was all over."

Reaching a wooded spot about 1 mile from the store where George Windham was murderded, the negroes were stripped to the waist, and chained to two trees. One member of the mob brought forth a blow torch, and turned on the searing flame.

On Bared Breasts

The torch flames were turned on the negroes' bared breasts, and they were commanded to "tell all you know," one source reported.

Townes, it was said, readily confessed that he shot Windham through a window of the white man's small store. McDaniels, who was arrested about ten days ago, was quoted as confessing, after being tortured, that he was inside the store when Windham was shot, and robbed the place after the white man was killed.

From statements made by the screaming negroes, "Shorty" Durham, a negro who lived near the scene of the lynching, was implicated.

Several members of the mob hurried to Durham's home and brought him before the mob. Crying and protesting his innocence, Durham persuaded the mob that he had not actively participated in the Windham slaying, and he was freed after being beaten severely, and warned to get out of the county.

Townes, it was said, died under the severe torture of the torch. McDaniels was shot through the head, being given a more merciful death by the mob. . . .

HARRIS DICKSON, 1937[11]

Harris Dickson, while employed by a New Deal agency, composed the following verse as a collection of street corner chatter heard in Jim Crow Vicksburg. The banter is a collection of put-downs, defenses, and folklore that suggests the means by which African Americans confronted segregated Mississippi. Dickson was born in 1868 at Yazoo City. Educated at George Washington University, he opened a law practice at Vicksburg in 1896 and served a two-year term as municipal judge. In 1917, *Collier's Weekly* employed him as a war correspondent in France. Among his publications were nearly two dozen books, including

The Story of King Cotton (1937) and countless fiction and non-fiction in national magazines.

Put yo' brains in a jaybird's head an' he'd fly backwards.

Jump down your throat an' gallop your insides out.

Yessuh, my little boy he's tol'able honest for his age.

Dat road got littler an' littler til it jest run up a tree.

Been ponderin' so hard I ain't had time to think.

Got de hookworm hustle.

Mouth's so wide ef 'twarn't for his ears de top of his head would be an island.

Steppin' high like a rooster in deep mud.

When dat preacher leaves my house I steps out in de backyard an' counts my chickens.

> *Nigger heaven*
> *Easy made*
> *Quart, a gal*
> *An' plenty shade*

I gave him thunder an' lightning stewed down to a fine pizen.

Dat white cussed me from de birth o' Saul an' Silas to de death o' de devil, an' called me ev'ything 'cept a child o' God.

Cunnel, dat nigger sprinkled dis here peedee root an' love powders over me, an' dat's what fust injuced me to commit love.

So lazy yo' vittles don't taste good.

Water's so low dat de garfishes is gittin' freckle-faced.

Got tuk down drunk.

A fool's tongue is long enough to cut his throat.

Money thinks I'm dead.

You ain't got enough sense to deliver a chaw of tobacco in a spittoon.

The bosom of his trousers.

> *De Lord, he made a nigger, made 'im in de night*
> *Made 'im in a hurry an' forgot to make him white*
> *Naught's a naught, figger's a figger*
> *All for de white man, none for de nigger*

All folks was born black, an' demn what's turnt white, dey jest had more sense. Angel o' de Lord come down an' told de ontire bunch to meet on de f'oth Friday at de dark o' de moon an' wash deyselves in Jordan. He oxplained to 'em dat dey'd all turn white an' straighten de kinks outen deir hair. Angel kept preachin' an' preachin', but dem fool niggers didn't pay him no mind. Angel can't teach a nigger nothin'. When we f'oth Friday come a mightly little sprinklin' of 'em went down to de river an' commenced to scrub. Water was mighty low. 'Twarn't like Old Missip'—'scusin' de Lord's river—'twarn't no more'n a creek. You jest oughter seed dat crowd o' niggers settin' on de fence snickerin' at dem what went in washing'. Snickerin' an' throwin' slams. More niggers dan you ever see in Vicksburg on circus day.

Dem what went in de river kept scrubbin' and washin', special deir hair to git de kinks out. Ole Aunt Grinny Granny—great-grandmanny of all dem niggers—she sot on a log all day long, eatin' cheese and crackers and lowratin' dem what was washin'. When fust dark come, she jumped up and clapped her hands: "'Fore Gawd, dem niggers is gittin' white!" Grinny Granny jerked off her head hand-kercher an' went tumblin' down de bank to wash her hair, an' all dem fool niggers followed her. But de water was all used up, jest a tiny drap in de bottom, no more'n enough to moisten de palms o' deir hands and de soles o' deir feet. So dat's why a nigger is white in dem places.

Make your face look like a dime's wuth o' dog meat.
Jaybird jabber. [Gabble of women.]
Ef you wants to see how much folks is goin' to miss you, jest stick yo' finger in de pond den pull it out an' look at de hole.
Cavortin' like a fat pony in high oats.
Make a straight coattail. [Scared man running.]
Grinn' like a baked 'possum.
Lean hound for a long race and a poor man for chillun.
So hongry my belly thinks my throat's cut.

Cluttered with trouble.

Dat nigger ain't skeered o' work; he'll lie down beside de biggest kind o' job an' go to sleep.

> *Name's Sam*
> *Don't give a damn*
> *Rather be a nigger*
> *Dan a po' white man*

Enjoyin' poor health.

Swamp's so dry dere's four million bullfrogs ain't never learned how to swim.

Dat ooman's nine years old'n God.

A mighty miration. [Make a to-do.]

De devil gits up when de sun goes down, an' comes to plow his field.

Life is short an' full o'blisters.

Wish I was at home sick in bed.

"How is you today?" "Po'ly, thank God!"

Heap o' stir an' no biskits.

Busy as a bumblebee in a bucket of tar.

Don't remember yo' name, but I knows yo' favor.

Why don't you put sugar in yo' shoes to coax yo' breeches down?

Rather tell a lie on credit dan de truth for cash.

Yo head's a-blossomin' fer de grave.

Overspoke myself.

Got a runnin' off at de mouth.

Honest farmer puts straight wood on de outside his load.

On dat day seven women shall take hold of one man.

Dey 'scused me wrongful. [False charge of crime.]

A dunghill gentleman.

Beat him into doll rags.

It's agin nature and can't be did.

Afterclaps can go to the devil.

In a turkey dream.

Handful o' the dockyments. [Playing cards.]

Wake, snakes, day's a-breakin'.

Busted in flinderjigs.

See him deep in hell as a pigeon can fly in a week.

Rich as mud.

A dog will cry if you beat him with a bone.

Tread in my footsteps ef you can spraddle far enough.

Full of wrath and cabbage.

Manhood distended his hide.

Whip you from the point of a dagger to the anchor of a ship.

RICHARD WRIGHT, 1937[12]

Richard Wright was born near Natchez. At the age of fifteen, Wright fled
Mississippi for Memphis and then left the south for Chicago. In Chicago,
he pursued his interests in the publication of fiction and non-fiction and
in socialist politics, serving at one time as the secretary of the John Reed
Club. The account that follows is taken from an autobiographical essay
and portrays the day-to-day horror of being black and living in Jim Crow
Mississippi.

. . . We moved from Arkansas to Mississippi. Here we had the good
fortune not to live behind the railroad tracks, or close to white neigh-
borhoods. We lived in the very heart of the local Black Belt. There
were black churches and black preachers; there were black schools and
black teachers; black groceries and black clerks. In fact, everything was
so solidly black that for a long time I did not even think of white folks,
save in remote and vague terms. But this could not last forever. As one
grows older one eats more. One's clothing costs more. When I finished grammar school I had to go to work. My mother could no
longer feed and clothe me on her cooking job.

There is but one place where a black boy who knows no trade can
get a job. And that's where the houses and faces are white, where the
trees, lawns, and hedges are green. My first job was with an optical
company in Jackson, Mississippi. The morning I applied I stood

straight and neat before the boss, answering all his questions with sharp yessirs and nosirs. I was very careful to pronounce my *sirs* distinctly, in order that he might know that I was polite, that I knew where I was, and that I knew he was a *white* man. I wanted that job badly.

He looked me over as though he were examining a prize poodle. He questioned me closely about my schooling, being particularly insistent about how much mathematics I had had. He seemed very pleased when I told him I had had two years of algebra.

"Boy, how would you like to try to learn something around here?" he asked me.

"I'd like it fine, sir," I said, happy. I had visions of "working my way up." Even Negroes have those visions.

"All right," he said. "Come on."

I followed him to the small factory.

"Pease," he said to a white man of about thirty-five, "this is Richard. He's going to work for us."

Pease looked at me and nodded.

I was then taken to a white boy of about seventeen.

"Morrie, this is Richard, who's going to work for us."

"What yuh sayin' there, boy!" Morrie boomed at me.

"Fine!" I answered.

The boss instructed these two to help me, teach me, give me jobs to do, and let me learn what I could in my spare time.

My wages were five dollars a week.

I worked hard, trying to please. For the first month I got along O.K. Both Pease and Morrie seemed to like me. But one thing was missing. And I kept thinking about it. I was not learning anything, and nobody was volunteering to help me. Thinking they had forgotten that I was to learn something about the mechanics of grinding lenses, I asked Morrie one day to tell me about the work. He grew red.

"What yuh tryin' t'do, nigger, git smart?" he asked.

"Naw; I ain't tryin' t'git smart," I said.

"Well, don't, if yuh know whut's good for yuh!"

I was puzzled. Maybe he just doesn't want to help me, I thought. I went to Pease.

"Say, are you crazy, you black bastard?" Pease asked me, his gray eyes growing hard.

I spoke out, reminding him that the boss had said I was to be given a chance to learn something.

"Nigger, you think you're *white*, don't you?"

"Naw, sir!"

"Well, you're acting mighty like it!"

"But, Mr. Pease, the boss said . . ."

Pease shook his fist in my face.

"This is a *white* man's work around here, and you better watch yourself!"

From then on they changed toward me. They said good-morning no more. When I was just a bit slow in performing some duty, I was called a lazy black son-of-a-bitch.

Once I thought of reporting all this to the boss. But the mere idea of what would happen to me if Pease and Morrie should learn that I had "snitched" stopped me. And after all, the boss was a white man, too. What was the use?

The climax came at noon one summer day. Pease called me to his work-bench. To get to him I had to go between two narrow benches and stand with my back against a wall.

"Yes, sir," I said.

"Richard, I want to ask you something," Pease began pleasantly, not looking up from his work.

"Yes, sir," I said again.

Morrie came over, blocking the narrow passage between the benches. He folded his arms, staring at me solemnly.

I looked from one to the other, sensing that something was coming.

"Yes, sir," I said for the third time.

Pease looked up and spoke very slowly.

"Richard, *Mr.* Morrie here tells me you called me *Pease*."

I stiffened. A void seemed to open up in me. I knew this was the show-down.

He meant that I had failed to call him *Mr.* Pease. I looked at Morrie. He was gripping a steel bar in his hands. I opened my mouth to speak, to protest, to assure Pease that I had never called him simply *Pease*, and that I had never had any intentions of doing so, when Morrie grabbed me by the collar, ramming my head against the wall.

"Now, be careful, nigger!" snarled Morrie, baring his teeth. "*I heard yuh call 'im Pease!* 'N' if yuh say yuh didn't, yuh're callin' me a *lie*, see?" He waved the steel bar threateningly.

If I had said: No, sire, Mr. Pease, I never called you *Pease*, I would have been automatically calling Morrie a liar. And if I had said: Yes, sir, Mr. Pease, I called you *Pease*, I would have been pleading guilty to having uttered the worst insult that a Negro can utter to a southern white man. I stood hesitating, trying to frame a neutral reply.

"Richard, I asked you a question!" said Pease. Anger was creeping into his voice.

"I don't remember calling you *Pease*, Mr. Pease," I said cautiously. "And if I did, I sure didn't mean . . ."

"You black son-of-a-bitch! You called me *Pease*, then!" he sapt, slapping me till I bent sideways over a bench. Morrie was on top of me demanding:

"Didn't yuh call 'im *Pease*? If yuh say yuh, didn't, I'll rip yo' gut string loose with this f—kin'bar, yuh black granny dodger! You can't call a white man a lie 'n' git erway with it, you black son-of-a-bitch!"

I wilted. I begged them not to bother me. I knew what they wanted. They wanted me to leave.

"I'll leave," I promised. "I'll leave right *now*."

They gave me a minute to get out of the factory. I was warned not to show up again, or tell the boss.

I went.

When I told the folks at home what had happened, they called me a fool. They told me that I must never again attempt to exceed my boundaries. When you are working for white folks, they said, you got to "stay in your place" if you want to keep working.

My Jim Crow education continued on my next job, which was portering in a clothing store. One morning, while polishing brass out front, the boss and his twenty-year son got out of their car and half dragged and half kicked a Negro woman into the store. A policeman standing at the corner looked on, twirling his nightstick. I watched out of the corner of my eye, never slackening the strokes of my chamois upon the brass. After a few minutes, I heard shrill screams coming from the rear of the store. Later the woman stumbled out, bleeding, crying, and holding her stomach. When she reached the end of the block, the policeman grabbed her and accused her of being drunk. Silently I watched him throw her into a patrol wagon.

When I went to the rear of the store, the boss and his son were washing their hands at the sink. They were chuckling. The floor was bloody, and strewn with wisps of hair and clothing. No doubt I must have appeared pretty shocked, for the boss slapped me reassuringly on the back.

"Boy, that's what we do to niggers when they don't want to pay their bills," he said, laughing.

His son looked at me and grinned.

"Here, have a cigarette," he said.

Not knowing what to do, I took it. He lit his and held the match for me. This was a gesture of kidness, indicating that even if they had beaten the poor old woman, they would not beat me if I knew enough to keep my mouth shut.

"Yes, sir," I said, and asked no questions.

After they had gone, I sat on the edge of a packing box and stared at the bloody floor till the cigarette went out.

That day at noon, while eating in a hamburger joint, I told my fellow Negro porters what had happened. No one seemed surprised. One fellow, after swallowing a huge bite, turned to me and asked:

"Huh. Is tha' all they did t' her?"

"Yeah. Wasn't tha' enough?" I asked.

"Shucks! Man, she's a lucky bitch!" he said, burying his lips deep into a juicy hamburger. "Hell, it's a wonder they didn't lay her when they got through."

. . . My next job was as hall-boy in a hotel. Here my Jim Crow education broadened and deepened. When the bell-boys were busy, I was often called to assit them. As many of the rooms in the hotel were occupied by prostitutes, I was constantly called to carry them liqour and cigarettes. These women were nude most of the time. They did not bother about clothing even for bell-boys. When you went into their rooms, you were supposed to take their nakedness for granted, as though it startled you no more than a blue vase or a red rug. Your presence awake in them no sense of shame, for you were not regarded as human. If they were alone, you could steal sidelong glimpses at them. But if they were receiving men, not a flicker of your eyelids must show. . . .

One of the bell-boys was caught in bed with a white prostitute. He was castrated, and run out of town. Immediately after this all the bell-boys and hall-boys were called togther and warned. We were given to understand that they boy who had been castrated was a "mighty, mighty lucky bastard." We were impressed with the fact that next time the management of the hotel would not be responsible for the lives of "trouble-makin' niggers."

One night, just as I was about to go home, I met one of the Negro maids. She lived in my direction, and we fell in to walk part of the way home together. As we passed the white nightwatchman, he slapped the maid on her buttock. I turned around, amazed. The watchman looked at me with a long, hard, fixed-under stare. Suddenly he pulled his gun, and asked:

"Nigger, don't yuh like it?"

I hesitated.

"I asked yuh don't yuh like it?" he asked again, stepping forward.

"Yes, sir," I mumbled.

"Talk like it, then!"

"Oh, yes, sir!" I said with as much heartiness as I could muster.

Outside, I walked ahead of the girl, ashamed to face her. She caught up with me and said:

"Don't be a fool; yuh couldn't help it!"

This watchman boasted of having killed two Negroes in self-defense.

Yet, in spite of all this, the life of the hotel ran with an amazing smoothness. It would have been impossible for a stranger to detect anything. The maids, the hall-boys, and the bell-boys were all smiles. They had to be. . . .

Chapter 11

THE GREAT DEPRESSION AND NEW DEAL

In the popular imagination, the 1920s is regarded as a decade of plenty: during the decade, Americans manufactured and purchased automobiles, radios, and scores of new consumer products at a pace never before seen. The American economy was strong, and its strength seemed inexhaustible. Yet, late in the 1920s, growth of the consumer economy began to slow. By 1929, the economy had retracted: factories closed and countless Americans stood in breadlines to receive their meals. For those who doubted that the economy had collapsed, the October 1929 crash of the stock market served as a clear sign that the nation languished in the doldrums of a severe economic depression. The Great Depression was so severe that by 1933, it is estimated that one-third of the population was out of work, and entire sectors of the economy, for example, the New England textile industry, shut. Although Mississippians were aware of the nationwide 1920s boom and some benefitted from it, the vast majority of Mississippians, particularly farmers, never fully tasted the economic bonanza of the decade. By the early 1930s, however, the depression had become so deep that even the agricultural economy of Mississippi keenly felt the strain. Finished products were in short supply, and the price paid for Mississippi's chief product—cotton—hovered at the 5 cent level, down by more than 50 percent from its previous peak in the twentieth century.

Yet, in 1932, the presidential campaign of Franklin Deleano Roosevelt gave hope to many Americans. Roosevelt promised to provide relief for the nation's suffering citizens, to reform government institutions, and to stimulate the economy with programs designed to put the unemployed to work. Of the programs created under the auspices of Roosevelt's New Deal, several merit particular attention. The Agricultural Adjustment Administration (AAA), which was created in 1933, awarded a parity payment (a subsidy) to farmers who volunteered for the program. In exchange for reducing the number of acres planted in crops like cotton, farmers would receive money for the crop they did not plant. Even though the U.S. Supreme Court overturned the AAA, Congress, through other legislation, kept alive the acreage reduction and subsidy portions of the AAA. The Civilian Conservation Corps, another program inaugurated in 1933, put young men to work replanting the forests of Mississippi that timber companies had denuded since the 1880s; and the Civil Works Administration put thousands of Mississippians back to work. The Tennessee Valley Authority, which harnessed the energy of rivers in the upland south, supplied rural residents and businesses with electricity and led to the creation of Rural Electric Associations—consumer-owned electrical cooperatives that supplied Mississippians with electric lights. The documents that follow attest to the impact of the Great Depression and New Deal legislation on Mississippians.

DOWN AND OUT DURING THE DEPRESSION

The four letters that appear below were written to president-elect Franklin Delano Roosevelt. Each of the letter writers discusses the impact of the Great Depression on their lives. G. T. Grove of Beauregard in Copiah County describes the plight of farmers. J. F. Craig of Indianoloa complains of the high taxes, heavy debts, and low prices that farmers must bear. He advocates reforms that New Deal legislation eventually embraced, but he denies that increased government spending can restore the nation's economy. Writing from Jackson, G. E. Rivers describes the plight of the unemployed and encourages Roosevelt to support legislation to institute a six-hour workday. Finally, Will Danis, an

African-American living in Jackson speaks for those who felt most
severely the effects of the depression.

G. T. Grove, 1932[1]

I appreciate your letter of September first.

I wish to assure you that officially and personally you have my sincere and loyal support.

Of course there is no doubt as to how Mississippi will vote in the
coming election. It will be my endeavor to get out as large a vote as is
possible, a thing we do not always do under our system. This year we
should make a better showing.

My district is strictly agricultural. Cotton, Trucking and Dairying
engage most of our people.

The principal thing we hear now is low prices for our products and
high taxes. Even with lower prices for most things we buy, we are not
able to pay our debts or break even.

Cotton is bringing the farmer on our local market today six cents
while raw milk is bringing 5 cents per gallon delivered at the cream-
ery. The same milk is retailing to the consumer in New Orleans from
36 to 50 cents per gallon. Our people think there is too much spread
between what we get and what the consumer pays.

Very few of our people here believe the Government can help any
by any price fixing scheme but do believe we can be helped by a better marketing system.

I know your programme will help us and for that reason we are
working for you and our Party. . . .

J. F. Craig, 1933[2]

I am enclosing Clippings, from Commercial Appeal Which i hope you
will find time to read. This will give you first hand information, why
it is impossible under present form of Government for any Farmer
big or little, to even exist, and pay from $2.00 to $3.00 per acre Taxes.
Our Banking laws allowes the Banks to close and rob us, of all our lifes

saveings. States and Government takes our Land, and Homes for Taxes. Rents it to Loafers for $1.00 per acre Then loan them what Taxes we have paid, to those same people without securety. This labor have only paid about 25% from last years Loan, Cotton at 9 to 12c per lb. when the Government would not buy a Bale from a real Farmer, who owns his place, and pays his labor on his Loan account.

In the beginning of your Campaign, I heard you say, it was impossible for a man to lift his self from the mire by his boot straps, or get him out of [debt] by loaning him more money. You are certainly right. This same rule applies to Government, I am only a Committee of one private Citizen, Own lots of land, bought at a big price, am out of debt so far. All My money tied up in closed Banks, $7000.00 Taxes, last week, which leaves Me less than $500. in actual cash. My land not worth taxes, i have 80 families of Labor and Mules to feed, Farming at a loss of over $20,000 per year, This land and my Home, is all i have left, and is worthless under present conditions.

However we are in the hands of a just God, and i have pinned all my faith in your ability to guide us out of this trouble.

However i cannot refrain from giveing you a little first hand information, and a few suggestions, the way i see things do not buy Silver or anything else, and issue Bonds for them. Work up Uncle Sam['s], Cotton, in Greenbacks, and pay back the Taxes, that has been wrongly collected from everybody, Give the real home owners, who spent their lives their homes back. Pay every deposits in closed Banks, in real Money, that he is entitled to receive with interest. Put Uncle Sammy, in the banking business, but get him out of all private business. Pay them all with paper money, and the prices will take of them selves. Lincoln did this, it worked then it will work again.

G. E. Rivers, 1932[3]

I am writing to you in the interest of the unemployed of which I am one. I was working for the Illinois Central Railroad when they reduced their forces from seventy thousand men and women to thirty five thousand, a 50 per cent reduction and I lost my job.

The Illinois Central has been ruined by the Barge Lines and we in turn have been ruined by being cut off. Some of my unemployed friends have asked me to write to some of our United States Senators and Congressmen and ask them if they cannot give us a six hour day and a five day week. Very few of the unemployed belong to their Brotherhoods now, not being able to keep their dues paid up and therefore have no one to represent them. I have written to Senators Pat Harrison and Hubert D. Stevens and Congressman J. W. Collier of Mississippi and declared that I would also write to you.

It is estimated that there are 12,000,000 men and women in the United States who are out of employment and for every bread winner there are at least three dependents making 48,000,000 million people who are out of a job or depending on someone who is not employed. Our Congressmen have spent about two weeks lately debating on an independence bill for 13,000,000 Philipinos to be given them twelve years hence, who would probably be better off without independence, but not one word have I heard in the interest of the unemployed 12,000,000 and their dependents except to give them flour to eat and cotton to make clothes which is a great help to be sure, and I have no doubt is appreciated by those who are accepting it, but work is what we want—not a dole. Give us a six hour day and a five day week as asked for by the American Federation of Labor and thereby spread out the work so as to give everyone employment. This is an awful condition which we face and while my advice isn't worth anything, I can't see how the Democratic party can survive it without quick and speedy action. If nothing is done to relieve this situation before you are inaugurated our Congressmen, if they would put as much energy behind the six hour laws as they have the Philipino law, and the Beer Bill, the majority of our unemployed would be at work in thirty days after they pass the law and then prosperity will have returned. The railroads will have something to haul, the manufacturers will be busy and the farmers will have a market for what they produce.

Speaking for myself, I would not expect to be paid as much for a six hour day as for an eight hour day. If we ask for something unreasonable we will not get anything. I cannot see how an employer or corporation could object to a law which would not cost them a cent but which would convert 12,000,000 unemployed, and their dependents and in some cases a menace to society into an asset to their business. I anticipate that a six hour law will meet some objection where seniority rules; by only a few however who want the earth, but any individual or corporation who are so selfish or so unmindful of the welfare of his fellowman as to place himself as a bar to the relief of 48,000,000 people who constitute almost half of this Republic, would be unpatriotic and a bad citizen, unworthy of any man's respect or consideration. . . .

Will Danis, 1932[4]

I am writing you these few lines to let you hear from me. I am very glad to know that you have this office. This is one of your old darkies that used to be with you.

I prayed and I groan when I heard that you were running for the office that you would get it. I did everything to help you get this office that a Negro could do. I am so glad until I don't know what I do. I am an ex-soldier and I am wounded and I can't get anyone to fix me up. I haven't drawn anything since I cam[e] from the army and I really need it. Mr. Roosevelt, I am naked and have been hungry for three days. Send me overalls and underwear and send and get me out of Miss. because it is the worst place that I ever been in all my life. My size 150 lbs., 5/6' tall, 32' waist wear #9 shoe.

A NEW DEAL FOR MISSISSIPPI FARMERS

In 1931, Jones County farmers forwarded a petition to Governor Theodore Bilbo proposing a state-sponsored acreage reduction. Their hope was that by removing acres from production, the supply of cotton and other farm products would rise. Mississippi never sponsored such a program, but in 1933, the Federal government, through the Agricultural Adjustment Administration paid farmers a subsidy to reduce the number of acres they cultivated. The editorial that appeared in the Holly Springs South Reporter pleads with farmers to enroll in the AAA plan. But not everyone benefitted from crop reductions. R. L. Musgrove, writing to Secretary of Agriculture Henry Wallace, complained that the AAA treated farm families as static, injuring those who whose families grew. G. B. Mayberry's letter indicates another complaint with the operation of the AAA. Mayberry, a Noxubee County organizer for the Southern Tenant Farmers' Union, a predominately African-American union, was beaten and temporarily chased out of Mississippi when he tried to determine when sharecroppers could elect representatives to the county-level Agricultural Conservation Association, which set quotas for farmers and thus determined parity payments for participating farmers.

Jones County Farmers, 1931[5]

Whereas, the present cotton situation is deplorable, with certain bankruptcy in immediate prospect for farmers, merchants and others dependent upon cotton, not alone in this county, but in every section of the cotton growing south; and,

Whereas, in our opinion, the drastic situation can be met only by drastic action, and,

Whereas, in our opinion, the only effective remedy is the total prohibition of all cotton growing in this and other states in 1933; therefore be it

Resolved, by the farmers of Jones County, Mississippi, in mass meeting assembled, that we endorse the [Huey P.] Long plan of entirely prohibiting, by state legislative action, the planting, growing or ginning of cotton during the year 1932. And be it further

Resolved, that we urge upon Governor Theo. G. Bilbo, of Mississippi and Governor Ross S. Sterling of Texas the immediate calling of their respective legislatures, for the purpose of enacting laws, prohibiting cotton planting, growing or ginning in the year 1932. And be it further

Resolved, that we call upon our state senator and representative in the state legislature to urge upon Governor Bilbo the need for immediate legislative action, and to pledge to him that if called together they will consider this legislation and no other.

Resolved, that Governor Elect Mike Sennett Connor, if no action is taken by the present governor, to convene the legislature, be requested to secure from members of the house and senate-elect pledges to put the Long plan into effect when they convene. And be it further

Resolved, that copies of these resolutions be at once wired to Governor Theodore G. Bilbo of Mississippi and Governor Ross Sterling of Texas.

Done by the farmers of Jones County, Mississippi in mass meeting assembled, this the fifth day of September 1931.

The Agricultural Adjustment Administration, 1933[6]

The Roosevelt plan to effect a cut of 25 to 50 percent in cotton production is conspicuously unique and well thought out. It is hoped that it will be put through unanimously, and if so, it will be of great benefit to all Southern cotton planters and tenant farmers, and, in turn, to the entire country.

Supposing the signatures obtained to the plan, through unresponsiveness of the growers or through their over estimates of production per acre, make it successful only to the extent of half what is hoped for, or less. What will be the result?

We believe the government will accept the curtailed offer on the ground that half a slice is better than none at all. If that should be the case, who is going to benefit?

The only man who is going to benefit in that case is the man who signed up, and gets his money now for the portion of the crop he has agreed to plow under.

The point is this—if all sign up, there is going to be a much higher price paid for all of this year's crop, while if only half of the farmers sign up the price will probably drop from present levels considerably. A signing-up of only half the farmers would be taken generally as a failure of the plan—even though it would do some good. That's what would make the price of cotton fall.

But, take the man—one of the half who sign up—he gets present prices (and more) for the cotton he plowed under—a great deal more than he would get for his remaining crop. The others will get the lower price for their entire crop.

R. L. Musgrove, 1935[7]

I am writing you in regard to the plight myself and thousands of others who have large families and are rather heavy in debt are in under the agricultural adjustment administration.

So far, I have been loyal to the new farm deal and I believe you are trying to be fair to all farmers, so far as you can, but thousands of farmers in my situation are ruined and will lose our homes if there isn't some change made.

For instance, take my situation for 1934. I was cut and re-cut on my allotment until I was allowed a few bales of cotton for a family of nine and a three-horse farm. The gross income from my farm for 1934 was $555.00. I paid a $285.00 crop production loan[,] $45.00 taxes[,] $25.00 cotton exemption tax, $25.00 farm building repairs, and $75.00 for drug and doctor bills for my family and live stock. The sum of these items from the gross income leaves $100.00 with which to buy school books and clothing for a large family and live through the winter. My indebtedness to the Federal Land Bank is $2300.00. The 1934 installment on this was $115.00, and is yet unpaid, and I don't see any chance to pay under existing circumstances.

Here is what has my hands tied: During the base acreage period, 1928 to 1932, my family was small. Consequently, my cotton acreage was small. Since that time my help has grown up to the extent that I could grow much more cotton now than during the base acreage period. Yet I have to grow less and at a price about equal to cost of production.

. . . If there can be anything done for those of us in such straits, I think it will not only help us, but everybody in general.

G. B. Mayberry, 1939[8]

I am writing you these lines to let you know what happened to me. Listen, I went on Monday the 20th Day of November to get the date and place from the County Agent [C. W. Gary], and he asked me do I belong in this union, and I told him, Yes, sir, and he ask me would I take his advice it would be better for me to join the Farm Bureau. I told him that I was a member of that, and he said that he hand't got the date. Then I asked him when I could get it, and he told me about the first of December, and I told him all right, I will come back, and he asked me for my name. And on the 22nd, listen to me, in came Mr. C. V. Addam, the Chancery Clerk to my house and Mr. Anderson Linzy came to my house and hand-cuffed me and shoved the pistol on me and hand-cuffed me and put me in the car and carried me away from my house. When I was handcuffed I gave my sign, and Mr. Linzy hit me in the head two times, and when they got me to the other four men, then Mr. Leon Perkins hit me 5 times right in the head and stamp me twice with his feet, and put me in the car and carried me to Macon River Bridge, and put me on hiway 45, and told me to go to the water mill before I turn out, and don't come back no more, and gave my family one day to get out of the county. It is so bad. I want some help. They taken my box from my wife and my membership card and organizers credentials, and going to get after all they can. They can't have no meeting, and told me they better not hear from me, and I better not tell you all about it that they would spend money to find me and kill me, so what am I to do?

Mr. Anderson Linzy hit me 2 times side the head. Mr. L. Perkins hit me 4 times side the head and stamp me 2 times. Mr. C. V. Adams, the County Clerk, he got me for these men. Mr. H. [G.] Land, Mr. Chas. Jackson and Mr. Sturd [Steward] Adams, these other men I did not know, all from Macon, Miss., and I got one of my brothers word and he came to me. I was in the woods when he found me, and he gave me what money he had, and I am trying to get to the train for here, but I can't get my clothes, but I am coming like I is. Look for me, I am in the woods and my wife and children all got to get out, and I can't go home. Please let me hear from you and write the letter to Y. C. Cotton, Macon, Mississippi, Rt.3, Box 81 and he will get it to me.

RELIEF FOR URBAN WOMEN, 1934[9]

In March 1934, Hyacinth Yerger, an employee of the Civil Works Administration office in Biloxi, wrote Congressman William Colmer. While relaying the status of efforts by the CWA to provide women with clothing, she asks Colmer about the fate of women when the CWA would cease to exist in May 1934.

The Federal project of National Parks is one to be continued in Mississippi. It occurs to me there should be another one in Mississippi, and since the Coast was the first settlement, I am wondering if there is a way by which we could establish one? Will you look into the matter and see what the prospect is? We are using every means possible to put our women to work, especially on Federal Projects. We also hope some provision will be made for Directors of Woman[']s Work when the CWA goes out May 1, 1934. The need is by no means over. Of 1400 women registered on CWA (women who are in absolute need, but pride has kept them from going on Relief) only about 5 have been put to work. Since order went out "not to purchase any materials," sewing has had to be eliminated. Clothing given out last October by Relief office is about worn out and Welfare Worker tells me that she has 3500 on *her* rolls. They need a new supply of clothing, you know that two or three garments made of cheap materials do not last over six months and no one was given more than that. What people are *going* to do after May 1st, 1934, is a matter of interest and surmise, among those who know conditions here. I am sure that Our President and Mr. [Harry] Hopkins [Director of the Federal Emergency Relief Administration] realize conditions as well as we do, and will make provision to care for situation. . . .

THE TVA IN TUPELO, 1933[10]

Begun in 1933, the Tennessee Valley Authority damned rivers in three southern states to supply electricity to homes and business. By providing the rural south with electricity, the TVA hoped to stimulate the local economy and convert southerners into more voracious consumers. The following report of TVA's impact on Tupelo written by Lorena Hickok in 1934 suggests that the TVA may have been succeeding.

. . . Down in Tupelo everybody seems to be feeling grand. Garment factories and a textile mill are going peacefully along under the [National Industrial Recovery Administration] code, the Chamber of Commerce is getting inquiries from industries attracted there by the low power rate, and the proprietor of a 38-room hotel relates with satisfaction how she operates her hotel, with lights, fans in all rooms, two vacuum cleaners, two electric irons, refrigerator, and radio with an electric bill of around $20 a month.

Incidentally there are now in Tupelo six companies selling electric equipment, including both the expensive kinds and the new, cheaper models put out by the manufactures in agreement with TVA. They say that in 17 days, after the new models were brought in, 137 refrigerators were sold and 17 ranges—that one dealer sold in one week 21 units, i.e. stoves or refrigerators.

Differences in prices between the regular equipment, and the new models, not quite so de luxe, run something like this: electric refrigerators, top standard price $137, new price $80; hot water heaters, top standard price around $95, new top price $60; ranges, top standard price $137, new top price $80.

When I was in Tupelo they had no figures to show just how much electric equipment had been sold, but I was impressed with the figures of one dealer, who handles only the high priced stuff. In less than a month he had sold ten refrigerators and five ranges. And Tupelo is only a small town, about 6,000 population.

It is still a little early to see what the new electric rate is going to do for householders and farmers in and around Corinth and Tupelo. I went down there thinking perhaps I could see some urban housewives and farm wives actually using the electric refrigerators and stoves that they'd never have had in their lives if it hadn't been for TVA. But it hasn't reached that class yet. New wiring is just being begun—10 miles of it in Tupelo! But it's going along. Dealers say they are taking orders from farmers right along. One thing they are doing is to cut down greatly the cost of wiring a house. For instance, in Tupelo it used to cost as high as $60 to have an electric stove installed in your house. It now costs $5.

Even though I was disappointed in not being able to find in Tupelo and the surrounding country housewives using electric equipment that they had never expected to have, I felt that my trip was not in vain. Private industry, to a large extent, in Tupelo has actually tried out the subsistence homestead idea! And it seems to work!

It began back in 1923 with one garment factory, the management of which adopted a policy of hiring only workers who lived out in the country, on their own little farms. The movement spread. There are in Tupelo two garment factories and a textile mill that employ a total of around 2,000 people, and of these, I was told, only 700 or 800 live in town. Busses collect the workers from their farms, averaging around 15 acres each, every morning and bring them to work. And each evening take them home. As a matter of fact, they are school busses. They bring the workers into town first, then take the children to school, and in the afternoon they take the children home and then come after the workers.

People generally around Tupelo are pretty keen about the idea after having seen it in operation for several years. Relief workers told me that very, very few of the workers who lived that way had appeared on the relief rolls. One young man, a clerical worker in one of the garment factories, told me how it works out for him. He has a 10-acre farm, about three miles from town. Has a cow, some pigs and chickens, garden, some pasturage, a good comfortable house, Raises practically everything he eats.

["]As a matter of fact," he said, "except for what I pay out for clothes and the upkeep on my car, the salary I earn here in the factory is just about all net profit! And I've got the place, all clear of debt, to go to if anything happens to my job."

They are setting up near Tupelo a subsistence homestead unit to which no one will be admitted who hasn't a job. Most of them are employed in the garment factories. Well, at least those people have a reasonably good chance of being able to pay their way out. . . .

THE WAGE AND HOUR ACT

Even though the Supreme Court declared the National Industrial Recovery Administration to be unconstitutional in 1935 and thereby killed the application of a minimum wage law, laborers and labor unions continued to insist that Congress establish a minimum wage. In 1938, Congress passed the Wage and Hour Act. The bill drew praise from workers and loathing from employers. In differing degrees, F. M. Tatum and R. H. Crosby, both owners of major lumber mills in south Mississippi, wrote Congressman William Colmer to complain about passage of the Wage and Hour Act and otherwise to attack the New Deal. The reservations about the Act and other New Deal legislation expressed by Tatum and Crosby do not appear in the petitions signed by Tatum employees and the one signed by union members affiliated with the American Federation of Labor. E. I. Bateman's letter to Colmer plainly describes the tension between labor and employees during the 1930s.

F. M. Tatum, 1938[11]

This letter is written to tell you that most of our people, both the working class and the business men, feel that the defeat of the reorganization bill and the President's attempt to stuff the Supreme Court are the only two helpful and sound things that have come out of Washington since 1934. They also feel that Senator Harrison's stand on the tax bill is what the country needs. What we need is a simple form of government without extravagance, waste and the numerous bureaus employing hundreds of thousands of people that have been formed by the present administration, and in which you have had a part. It is a great pity that the representatives of our people are not interested in the welfare of our Nation, and as statesmen do their duty regardless of politics or their own personal interest.

We all know that the present foolish program just advocated by the President is nothing in the world but a political gesture to perpetuate the New Dealers in office.

We all know that our country grew to what it is by economy and be exporting over 60% of all its manufactured goods, a large part of its agricultural products—especially cotton—and competing on foreign markets, and we did not do this with such foolish strangulation and regulation as the Wagner Bill, the National Labor Board, the TVA, etc. . . .

We all know that to get out of the present depression, both personal and from a governmental standpoint, that we cannot foolishly spend our way out but must have hard work, long hours and small pay, get on a competitive basis and work our way back to prosperity. This enormous task can be accomplished if and when the pork barrels are stopped, personal interests are no longer served and the welfare of the Nation gets first consideration.

We are very much in hopes that you will take a definite stand to help save South Mississippi and America by helping organize and leading a Crusade, if you please, against further waste and extravagance and the return to reasonable, simple government that does not strangle or compete against its people.

R. H. Crosby, 1938[12]

There has been quite a bit of criticism about your vote on the Wage and Hour bill, and I understand several of your friends around Picayune have wired you some pretty stiff telegrams. I did not wire you for the reason I believe in the Wage and Hour bill, on a fair basis, as the salvation of some of our industrial problems in this country.

Furthermore notwithstanding the fact that some of the criticism leveled at you is that you were influenced by the labor vote from Gulfport, I do not believe this is true, but that you voted your convictions, regardless of consequences, which a representative elected by his people should do.

I believe we should have a minimum wage, and that 25c is a fair basis to start with. I do not believe, however, that the south can stand the same wage basis as the North and East have established in some industries until freight rates, which give the North and East preference, are straightened out, and there is an equalization that would put the South on an equal basis. . . .

Also, can you explain to me why it is that our Southern representatives string along with our President after five years of endeavoring to balance employment? We have a situation today where we have as many unemployed as in 1933, when he went into office, with commodities practically as low. We have doubled our indebtedness, and the only thing I see that we have secure is that every one who has had his finger in the Government pie seems to have lost his self respect; they think they are entitled to live on the Federal Government, regardless of their qualifications. We have farmers in Pearl River County who are receiving assistance from the Government and living off this assistance, instead of endeavoring to make a living on their farms. I was out at our Cybur store the other day and there was a crate of celery to be distributed among the relief class, from in front of our store; the negroes did not know how to use celery, and it was left right there. These negroes are being furnished beans and rice by the relief agencies, and they have practically quit endeavoring to farm. I am not in favor of cutting off relief for those who deserve it, but I am firmly convinced that the relief program in our portion of the state is breeding a class of people that eventually will have no regard for property rights, no thought of endeavoring to better themselves, and with an entire lack of respect for the Government of this country.

I cannot see how our representatives can continue to follow the President, knowing that money is being spent in the doubtful states through W.P.A. projects, such as is being spent in Pennsylvania and in New York state, with the sole idea of keeping these two states in the Democratic party. You well know there is as much money being spent in Pennsylvania [a]lone as there is in the entire South. Some people tell us it is on account of the wealth of Pennsylvania. Do they take into consideration such corporations as Aluminum Corporation and Gulf Oil Company, who make practically all of their earnings in the South, but pay Federal taxes in the state of Pennsylvania?

This is the first letter I have ever written you, and perhaps it will be the last, but I just wanted you to know that there are some of us who feel there should be some start to help our conditions in this country, but that we do expect our representatives to quit playing politics, and get down to the business of getting our country back to where it should be.

Tatum Employees, 1938[13]

We, the employe[e]s of Tatum Lumber company, do hereby beg the corporation [i.e. cooperation] of your power in congressional leadership of the South in helping to bring better wages and shorter work hours to the Southern laboring class.

We are hardly being paid a living wage now for the 10 (ten) hours we ar[e] struggling through that being 4 (four) days a week. We have our Doctor bills to raise above our living to take care of our sick children, leaving us to exist on the barest necessities of life. So please don't give the rich man all the breaks. Take a family of five or six and see how far $2.18 per day four days in a week will carry them, with the high cost of living.

It is absolutely a shame sin and disgrace to humanity. God Almighty is not going to stand for so much more. The day is coming when we are going to have a Judgement and we are going to be judged for what we have done. We don't look down on one man for the way we are having to budget through life to keep the bare necessities of life for our children and sick ones.

Please if this has any bearing at all pass it around as we are not able to enclose a check to have our bidding done as our Employers can do. But remember there will be an election before so very long and the few hundred dollars you receive from them wont keep you there so long as so many of our good votes will.

Again we beg of you to consider our living conditions here in the South (of which we are proud (South)[)] before you cast your vote when the bill comes up for furthur Study.

Gulfport Central Labor Union, 1938[14]

WHEREAS, numerous industrialists, of the South have assembled in conference at New Orleans for the purpose of waging war on the Wage and Hour Bill now before Congress, and

WHEREAS, the said Southern industrialists, with their usual hypocrisy and deception pretend to base their opposition to the Wage and Hour Bill on the alleged ground that it will cripple and retard industrial activity and development in the South, but in reality are opposing it because they are determined to do all in their power to keep the workers of the South chained to the chariot-wheel of starvation wages and degrading conditions of work in order to extract still more profits from the sweat, blood and tears of Southern workers, who are rebelling as never against industrial despots and oligarchs of the South, and

WHEREAS, the obvious purpose of the Wage and Hour Bill is not to hamper industry at all but to eliminate the sweat-shop factories that infest the South, to curb the unfair competition of industries which are robbing their workers, and to mitigate the Hellish horrors of wage-slavery which make life for the Southern masses a torment and a night-mare while it enriches a handful of Southern capitalists and landlords, Therefore,

BE IT RESOLVED that we, the representatives of organized labor . . . in the State of Mississippi, feel it our stern duty to raise our voices in behalf of all Southern workers, the organized or unorganized, and to promote with every means at our command the speedy passage of the Wage and Hour Bill during the present session of Congress; and to condemn and denounce as hypocritical and false the prophesies of calamity to Southern industry made by the Southern Industrialists who conferred and conspired against the said Bill in New Orleans, and

BE IT RESOLVED that in our opinion, the Wage and Hour Bill, if passed and enforced will put in the hands of the oppressed workers of the South another weapon with which to whip and drive all sweat-shops and their greedy owners and parasitic supporters from Southern soil and thereby make a place and ample opportunity for an industrial development and activity which will permit the masses of the South a civilized and decent standard of living and their share of good and higher things in American civilization today: and

BE IT RESOLVED that the Southern industrialists and all others of a like mind who oppose the Wage and Hour Bill, are the avowed enemies of the Southern working class, and are a stumbling block to the development of the South toward a higher and fairer civilization, in that the said industrialists are willing for the millions of the Southern masses to remain crucified on the CROSS OF EXPLOITATION AND GREED erected by the hands of those self same industrials: and we denounce them as our enemies, we denounce the system of wage slavery they represent and seek to perpetuate at the expense of the workers as outrageous, disgraceful and infamous, and we here and now announce ourselves and the workers we represent as determined to employ every means at our command to promote the passage of the Wage and Hour Bill; and we pledge ourselves and proclaim to all the workers of the South and their friends, that regardless of the fate of the Wage and Hour Bill, whether it passes or is defeated by Southern industrialists, we have declared war and shall wage it unceasingly on all industries and industrialists that deny a decent wage and decent working conditions to Southern workers, until the masses of the South have achieved a standard of living which is theirs by right and until the last industrial pirate is driven in haste from the last sweat-shop on Southern soil.

E. I. Bateman, 1938[15]

This morning[']s [New Orleans] Times Picayune carried the list of names of L[ouisiana]a and Miss[issippi] representatives and how they voted yesterday on the Wage & hour bill—I note with pleasure, satisfaction and admiration that you voted for this bill—congratulations to you.

I have a good force of men working under my supervision, long hours 10–12–14–16 hours a day for 1.50 to 2.25 per day—no overtime under any consideration.

I have heard my men say that they will vote for you for any office you desire to run for.

When you are ready for the Senate we are ready to send you there and Power to you.

on back

Dear mr Colmer

I inadvert[ant]ly left this letter on my desk over night and my boss Dr. [Richard] Cox of Gulf Park College[16] where I am employed as Supt or Chief Engineer saw it and I have been fired as a result. Which goes to show you just how bitterly big business hates the idea of giving labor an existance. I am not sorry to be separated from such an organization or such an employer even if I have to join the bread lines.

Chapter 12

REACTIONS TO <u>BROWN</u>

By 1954, when the U.S. Supreme Court handed down its Brown v. Board of Education *decision, Mississippians—white and black—had long antici-pated that the court would overturn the 1898* Plessy v. Ferguson *decision, which had sanctioned the creation of separate but equal public facilities. Although the Supreme Court failed to dictate how and when desegregation should occur, the court's follow-up decision in 1955 ordered desegregation to take place with "all deliberate speed." In Mississippi, desegregation proceeded at a painfully slow pace. Between 1954 and 1970, local school districts stymied efforts to end the dual-race public school system. The tactics of massive resistence used to undermine the court decision included so-called "freedom-of-choice" plans and the creation of elaborate and slow processes for desegregating one grade at a time. In 1969, however, the time for foot dragging ended. The Supreme Court, through its* Alexander *decision, ordered Mississippi to dis-mantle its dual-race system immediately.*

The reaction of white Mississippians to the Brown *decision might have been predicted. For more than two decades, whites had denounced every effort to end Jim Crow and desegregation. Wartime measures like the Fair Employment Practices Commission, as well as congressional efforts to pass anti-poll tax and anti-lynching laws, earned the particular wrath of white Mississippians.* To Secure These Rights, *a 1948 report that called for the Federal government to eradicate all vestiges of Jim Crow, garnered the antipathy of postwar whites, causing many to question their loyalty to the national Democratic party. Federal court decisions ordering the integration of professional schools and the military and another ending the white-only primary served as additional warnings to white Mississippians: the end of the Age of Jim Crow rapidly approached. But most, though certainly not all, white Mississippians refused to accept desegregation.*

When the Supreme Court rendered its Brown *decision, white Mississippians, who for so long had felt besieged by the Federal government, initiated a campaign of massive resistence. The Citizens Council, an organization of middle-class businessmen and professionals, spearheaded the effort to block desegregation. The ideology of the Citizens Council was perhaps most famously articulated in Tom Brady's pamphlet titled* Black Monday. *Most white Mississippians shared Brady's belief that desegregation represented an attack on American values. Yet, at the same, other white Mississippians sought ways to give meaning to the Supreme Court decision.*

Mississippi's African American community likewise was divided over how to respond to the Brown *decision. In 1954, courageous blacks began petitioning local school boards to eliminate Jim Crow educational facilities. But, for their courage, they often paid a dear price: whites fired petitioners from their jobs and cut off credit at businesses and banks. Six weeks after the May 1954* Brown *decision, Governor Hugh White invited black leaders to attend a meeting of the newly-created Legal Education Advisory Committee. Although conservative black leaders had convinced White to call the meeting, the citizens who attended determined to resist efforts by White and black conservatives to create a coalition of blacks who would cooperate in Mississippi's effort to stymie enforcement of the* Brown *decision.*

BLACK MONDAY, 1955[1]

Thomas Pickens Brady, who was born in New Orleans in 1903, graduated from Yale University and the law school at the University of Mississippi. After establishing a successful law practice in Brookhaven, Brady became a Circuit Judge and fierce critic of the national Democratic party's embrace of civil rights reform. In 1948, he chaired the speaker's bureau of the States' Rights Democratic Party (the Dixiecrats). Soon after the Supreme Court rendered its *Brown* decision, Brady delivered his "*Black Monday*" address before the Greenwood chapter of the Sons of the American Revolution. He published an expanded version of the address in pamphlet form. Among the ideas espoused by Brady were the creation of a separate state for blacks, the abolition of school taxes and public schools, the popular election of the U.S. Attorney General, and the raising of standards for appointment to the Supreme Court. Brady based his defense of Jim Crow on his concepts of ethnology and his fear of communism.

"If we could first know where we are and whither we are tending, we could better judge what to do and how to do it."[2]

Any man who professes to completely understand whither we are going "on this bank and shoal of time" is either a pompous hypocrite or a madman.

As Stalin, "the master of confusion,"[3] long desired, the people of America have finally been driven into a quandary. Torn between conflicting ideals and misled by deceptive half-truths, they know not what to believe and are lost in a morass of indecision. They are an easy prey for the siren voices of communism.

There is, however, one segment of our populace which is not confused. It knows what it wants, and whither it wants to go. It is the communized and socialized minority groups. These groups are not disjointed. Though there may not be any formal "fundamental law of the union"[4] of these minority groups, they are nevertheless bound together, they are united in principle and purpose. They may quarrel among themselves but they are united against any opposition. They are energetic and patient. They are cunning and intelligent. When circumstances permit, they are ruthless and cruel. They have a legislative and economic program which they are determined to realize at any cost.

The end always justifies the means. That program, in spite of its complexity, is the communizing of America. Step by step, slowly but surely, gradually but completely, they strive toward this ultimate goal.

Now hear this, oh, Sovereign States of America! You sovereign states in which the negro, the Fillipino, the Puerto Rican and other minority racial groups constitute, at best, but one to five per cent of your total population. You who are not concerned with the "*Black Monday*" decision. Do not suppose for one foolish second that you are not affected by it.

Before the school there is the municipality, its organizations, its clubs, its hotels, its buses, its restaurants, its swimming pools, its churches, its hospitals and its homes. Irrespective of the wishes and customs of the majority, of ninety-six per cent of the population, the desires of the organized four per cent can decide and control any issue. Where now is the majority rule in America?

Is it where it is, in Russia, in the hands of the select and designated few, the minorities of the ruling class? . . . Do not erroneously suppose that the segregation ruling by the Supreme Court will satiate the inordinate hunger for power of these minority groups. Each one of their foresworn aims will be relentlessly prosecuted. Though the other three civil rights measures of the Roosevelt and Truman administrations, to wit: the Anti-Poll tax, the Anti-Lynch and the FEPC bills, have not been written into the law of our land, they are on the way to become an integral part of our legislative and judicial structure, as is now the case with the spurious Anti-Segregation decision.

Sovereign States, the realization of these goals will but whet their ravenous appetites. . . .

There will be more FHA's and more corruption, more TVA's, et ceteras. The Government will first control and then usurp the banking business, then it will manage and socialize transportation, agriculture and any other private enterprises where the totalitarian state will be advanced. We will all become socialized Federal workers, working for the glory of the State.

This is but a part of what lies ahead of "*Black Monday*." Sovereign States, do you know what lies behind it? The communists of America have been trying since 1936 to destroy the South.[5] The bait which attracts them is the negro population. Hate campaigns against the Southern States were conducted in the North. Abuse and falsehoods were flagrantly utilized. Counsel and advice were given the negro leaders. A bloodless revolution was planned.

The negro was to be placed in office and in control, while the whites were to be driven out. A black empire was to be established in the Southern States of this nation, ruled by negroes. All public offices were to be held by negroes. The most fantastic and preposterous promises were made. The good will which had for eighty years existed between the races has been disturbed. Pilgrimages for the South to the North were encouraged where indoctrinization of the negroes took place. The new converts were returned to the South to disseminate their "new, glorious knowledge," and begin the creation of this fine socialistic Eden. Back of all this was but one motive, not the welfare of the negro, but the splitting away and controlling of a fine section of this nation, the segment which gave to democracy Thomas Jefferson, Washington, Madison, Monroe and Andrew Jackson. It was and is being done in behalf of Communist Russia. If the South, the stronghold of democracy, could be destroyed, then the nation could be destroyed.

This plan failed. The economic superiority of the white man or the innate loyalty of the Southern negro to this country, or both probably, caused the abandonment of the plan by the Communists. Then, too, it was prematurely conceived.

The plan to abolish segregation in the seventeen States, thirteen of which are Southern, was substituted. The medium through which this was to be accomplished was the National Association for the Advancement of Colored People, its affiliate organizations, together with the CIO [i.e. the Congress of Industrial Organizations]. . . .

The Communist masses of Russia and Red China must have howled with glee on "Black Monday." They know the unanimous decision of the Supreme Court abolishing segregation in the four Districts and States involved was an illegal usurpation of the legislative prerogative of those State Legislatures and of Congress. The hoards of Russia and Red China know that another deadly blow has been dealt our Constitution, that outmoded, effete document which still precariously stands in the way of a new, brave communistic order in this country. They know that the South was struck below the belt, that the long governing principle of *stare decisis* is no longer operative in this country; that sociological criteria have supplanted laws in the deciding of cases in this country by our supreme judiciary. . . .

The honor and glory, the courage and patriotism, the learning and wisdom of the highest judicial tribunal ever produced on this earth has been socialized and psychologized. Yes, the unanimous decision of the U.S. Supreme Court was to the constitutional rights of the sovereign states what the kiss of Iscariot in Gethsemane was to the Master.

Let us face the facts. As every honest lawyer with only average experience knows, the selection of the personnel of the Supreme Court is the result of partisan politics. The designation of Governor [Earl] Warren as Chief Justice was a grievous mistake. The past record of this man, who has not even presided as a police justice, proclaims it. The furibund communism of California, verifies it. . . . Though ex-Governor Warren is an honorable, distinguished, favorite son of California, yet his appointment was a judicial mistake—a political, executive error.

AMALGAMATION THE GOAL

Let's get one thing unmistakably clear. There cannot be the slightest doubt that the leaders of the three million block-voting negroes of the North and East and of California, together with segments of the Communist-front organizations of our population, have set as their goal the "passing" of the negro in these United States. Only the most stupid or gullible would dare to dispute this fact. These new deal, square deal, liberated, black qualified electors are determined to indoctrinate the Southern negro with this ideal, and arouse him to follow them in their social program for amalgamation of the two races. . . .

The great barrier to the integration of the races has been segregation. It is also the greatest factor for peace and harmony between the races. The NAACP realizes that until the barrier is removed in the schools, churches and in housing districts, integration of the races will be extremely difficult. For this reason, education on the grammar school level was the center of the target. You cannot place little white and negro children together in classrooms and not have integration. They will sing together, dance together, eat together and play together. They will grow up together and the sensitivity of the white children will be dulled. Constantly the negro will be endeavoring to usurp every right and privilege which will lead to intermarriage. This is the way it has worked out in the North. This is the way the NAACP wants it to work out in the South, and that is what Russia wants. . . .

The racial question, which is squarely presented by the *"Black Monday"* decision of the Supreme Court, is but one vital part of this problem. **The great threat to this Nation is that of creeping Socialism and Communism. The inter-racial angle is but a means to an end, in the overall effort to socialize and communize our Government. The grading down of the intelligence quotient of one-third of the people of this country through amalgamation of the white and negro race would be a great asset in the communizing of Our Government. . . .**

This is no time to be calm. We have been as docile and calm as the asinego [i.e. an obsolete word for donkey] **while our head is being thrust into the yoke. If in one mighty voice we do not protest this travesty on justice, we might as well surrender. The Supreme Court awaits our reaction. Be deliberate, yes, but not calm. Be determined, yes, but not impulsive. Be resolute, yes, but not violent. . . .**

Those who do not believe this may try through force of arms to accomplish it. If this happens, then it will take an army of one hundred million men to compel it. We have, through our forefathers, died before for our sacred principles. We can, if necessary, die again. You shall not show us how a white man "may go through the guts"[6] of a negro! You shall not mongrelize our children and grandchildren!

MRS. AUBIN NEWMAN, 1956[7]

Mrs. Aubin Newman, who lived in Natchez, wrote two letters to Judge J. Skelly Wright protesting a court-ordered desegregation decision handed down by the Fifth Circuit Court of Appeals. Judge Wright sat on the bench of the appeal court. In addition to the letters, she also supplied Judge Wright newspaper articles and cartoons depicting the evils of desegregation. Representative of other ordinary white people, Newman repeats much of the same argument made by Tom Brady in *Black Monday*. Her voice testifies to the depths to which the message of resistence seeped into white society and reflected irrational fears of desegregation.

When I read in the paper about you calling the Louisiana laws uncon-stitutional, and voided and nulled the laws of the soverign [*sic*] State of Louisiana which was under the constitutional 10th amendment I won-dered what on Gods earth was constitutional. I have wondered that ever since[.] [O]ur country has been taken for the worst ride ever in the history of this country by the off wing organization N.A.A.C.P. since I know and many other Americans know that some of the big men in the N.A.A.C.P. have in the past had affiliations with commu-nist gang, and the American Labor Unions are affi[l]iated with N.A.A.C.P. as well. Since the U.S. Supreme court ignored the 10th amendment of the States Soverignty, which was adopted, as a Constitutional law to try and force intergration on southern States, encroaching upon States Soverigntry to null and void laws of soverign States, being influenced by N.A.A.C.P. to force intergation, we believe they first should have made a thorough investigation of N.A.A.C.P. affi[l]iations before they feel right to ignore constitutional laws, and force intergration as the N.A.A.C.P. wants. . . . If the Supreme Court further ignores the 10th Amendment constitutional law, to force the law of intergration, therefore taking all meaning of States Rights and Soverigntry, would that not also, put all States under one rule, that of the Supreme Court, would that be dictatorship? I believe that to be what the Russians want, our country to be ruled under Dictatorship, and if they can use their influence on the negro race, especially the N.A.A.C.P. since the N.A.A.C.P. has never been investigated, wouldn't the Russians get first what they want? I imagine they are well aware of the N.A.A.C.P. influence on so many people in this country, who shut their eyes and refuse to see what is going on in this country, because they have put the negros ahead of the fact that our Constitutional laws . . . has always been the backbone of this nation, considering the people in this country are the States and the States are the union, and their forefathers adopted the Constitution and amendments to be adhered to.

Yes, Mr. Judge Wright, we will fight for segregation with every law at our command, as free people of this nation, not only for Constitutional Government, and segregation, but to try and keep our country from being sold down the river to communist dogs, and N.A.A.C.P. The N.A.A.C.P. tried to destroy the State of Miss. when their leader in Miss. Dr. T. R. M. Howard, the Ky. Negro, who got rich in Mound Bayou Miss. brought negro race agitators N.A.A.C.P. from northern States, to de[s]cend on the State of Mississippi like Vultures, with the sole aim of having lies and propaganda in biased northern newspapers so long[.] I imagine you read about it, since we have been able to expose that propaganda and lies as such, to the sati[s]faction of our Government[. T]he same negro leader who tried to destroy our State with lies and propaganda, was accused by F.B.I. Mr. J. Edgar Hoover, of making false and irresponsible charges against the F.B.I. [T]hat negro has not had so much propaganda & lies, in paper about Miss. since, but the weird minds of the N.A.A.C.P. is still working since they were responsible for propaganda leaflets being handed out to white students at U. of Alabama picturing interracial marriages when the students yelled: communist stuff, lets burn it and burn it they did right on the campus steps.

Judge Wright, I have been trying to expose to the people in Washington for a long time, the tactics the N.A.A.C.P. uses in trying to force integration, but I suppose they also have been under their influence so long, they cannot realize until its to[o] late what they are trying to do to this country, maybe it will be too late when they finally find out that many of them are influenced by communist[s], and God in Heaven will be the only one, who can help us then. . . .

If you have a family, pray to almighty God to direct you in the right way, if not for other peoples sake, for their sake, because this thing is bigger, than people realize, it does not just take in segregation or intergration and how well we know it.

Vice-Pres. [Richard M.] Nixon hinted that it was political reasons of the Chief Justice, that caused him to ignore the 10th Amendment to use the act of force on Southern States, for intergration, to encroach upon States Soverigntry and null and void State laws, but we know who and how many people in Washington have been influenced by N.A.A.C.P. to try and force intergration.

We do not respect N.A.A.C.P. as much as we do communist[s], at least you have learned what tactics the communist[s] use, but you never know what the N.A.A.C.P. will do next, how the Russians must be laughing today, since I imagine they know of how the harmony and peace of southern States of both races have been uprooted by the N.A.A.C.P. which will eventually lead to the educational program of the south being set back 100 years, as well as the great progress of the south.

I noticed you three Federal Judges were native sons of the great Soverign State of Louisiana. It must have been a terrible blow to each one of you to be forced by the Chief Justice to null and void the laws of that great soverign State, and to your parents as well. I heard it over the radio the night it happened and did not sleep much that night, because I realized what it meant to you. I could not have done it, even if the chief shot me at sunrise, because of my beliefs, in the moral, high standards of segregation and because of my respect for my pilgrim ancestors, whose names have gone down in History as others, in founding this great nation, some of them pioneers of Louisiana in the early 1700s. May God direct you three men. He is the highest power on this earth, because the earth and it[s] people belong to God.

Many parents in the south (white) would keep their children out of school before they would have them exposed to Sy[p]hilis, Gonnoreah, & the other disease, that is so prevelent among negroes (check statistics from Washington on that, I already have) and if the Government, tried to force the children to go to schools, I imagine we would hear of many mass murders and suicides, because so many people rather see their children dead than live a lifetime of shame and degredation, which intergration would cause[. T]hink, what it has caused in so many States, horrible crimes, the city of Chicago recently declared their city a reign of terror, other cities like it, have teen age gangs in schools[,] mixed races, committing the worst crimes in the history of this nation. Many white people moving south to escape such degredation.

Please let the other two Judges, native sons of La. read this letter, I lost my paper with their names. I want them to know they have my deepest, and most sincere sympathy, as well as you.

WILLIAM FAULKNER[8]

In a letter published in the Memphis *Commercial Appeal*, Mississippi's most famous author offered a pragmatic response to the Brown decision. Faulkner suggested that considering the poor condition of white-only school facilities and the poor quality of education for whites, the thought of continuing to support a dual-race school system was foolish. Mocking those who advocated segregation, Faulkner asked, "How foolish in simple dollars and cents, let alone in wasted men and women, can we afford to be?"

We Mississippians already know that our present schools are not good enough. Our young men and women themselves prove that to us every year by the fact that, when the best of them want the best of education which they are entitled to and are competent for, not only in the humanities but in the professions and crafts—law and medicine and engineering—too, they have to go out of the state to get it. And quite often, too often, they don't come back.

So our present schools are not even good enough for white people; our present state reservoir of education is not of high enough quality to assuage the thirst of even our white young men and women. In which case, how can it possibly assuage the thirst and need of the Negro, who obviously is thirstier, needs it worse, else the Federal Government would not have had to pass a law compelling Mississippi (among others, of course) to make the best of our education available to him.

That is, our present schools are not even good enough for white folks. So what do we do? Make them good enough, improve to the best possible? No. We beat the bushes, rake and scrape to raise additional taxes to establish another system at best only equal to that one which is already not good enough, which therefore won't be good enough for Negroes either; we will have two identical systems neither of which is good enough for anybody. The question is not how foolish can people get, because apparently there is no limit to that. The question is, how foolish in simple dollars and cents, let alone in wasted men and women, can we afford to be?

T. R. M. HOWARD, 1954[9]

In the early 1940s, Dr. T. R. M. Howard moved to Mound Bayou, Mississippi where he was the chief surgeon at the Knights and Daughters of Tabor Hospital. Howard, one of the few black physicians in Mississippi, used his position to establish his own medical clinic, purchase a plantation, and begin the Magnolia Mutual Life Insurance Company. In 1951, he founded the Regional Council of Negro Leadership, a local civil rights organization that aimed to increase voter registration, to eliminate segregation, and to stop police brutality against blacks. Six weeks after the Supreme Court handed down its Brown decision, Howard and other black businessmen and educators appeared before the governor's Legal Advisory Board. His remarks at the meeting of the board suggest great optimism for a vastly different Mississippi. Yet, within a short time of delivering his speech, Howard believed his activism made him a target of potential violence. He moved to Chicago.

. . . I wish to express my personal thanks to the Governor for calling in a group of Negroes to discuss one of the most vital issues of our age. A question as vital as the question which is before us today, cannot be settled by decree, or by a Committee of one group going behind closed doors—bringing the solution to the problem to the other group on a "take it or leave it" proposition.

This grave problem can and will be settled in our great state by men of good will of both races, sitting down at the conference table with mutual respect for each other[']s God-given American rights and work out the problem. There has never been any problem too great for Mississippians to solve and we are going to solve this problem together.

We, the Negro citizens of Mississippi realize that this segregation issue strikes at every issue for which the South has stood every since there has been a South. The thinking Negro knows that no people give up their vital traditions without a struggle.

During the 164 year history of our Supreme Court, there have been two momentous decisions which have dealt with race relations in these United States of America. The first was Taney's Dred Scott Decision in 1857, and the second was the unanimous decision of the Supreme Court outlawing segregation in the public schools of the United States of America on Monday, May 17th 1954.

A noted Journalist, Mr. Kenneth Toler, writing in the Sunday, July 18th 1954, [Memphis] *Commercial Appeal*, states and I quote, "in 1890 the purpose was to work out a plan for segregation of the races, the 1954 meeting has that same objective." The Negores who have come here today have not come to help work out any trick or plan to circumvent the decision of the Supreme Court outlawing segregation in the public schools. We believe that the decision is a just and humane decision and our beloved South should have known that it was the only decision that could have been given in the light of America's position in the world today. By a unanimous vote of 200 Negro leaders from all over the state at a mass meeting in Jackson Sunday July 25th and by an overwhelming vote of the Negro leaders last night, July 29th, we voted to not endorse any program of legal or voluntary segregation.

We have come to help chart the way for mutual understanding so that the public school in Mississippi may be saved within the spirit and framework of the Supreme Court's decision. We fully realize the tremendous responsibility that is ours in attempting to make any suggestions for the solution of so grave a social problem as segregation. In making any suggestion for the operation of our public schools in Mississippi, we believe that the leaders of both racial groups must be willing to confer and deliberate with each other, always on a high level of mutual discussion and always devoid of suspicion, fear or intimidation.

In this connection, we believe that the Governor should accept a 25 man Negro Committee, the names of which should be submitted by the Negro leaders here assembled, to work jointly and together with a 25 white member Committee, to work out the details of our future public school program in Mississippi.

We realize that the Supreme Court has only said that segregation is unconstitutional. It has not said yet when and how it is to end. We are not going to try to get in front of the Supreme Court on the "when and how."

Governor, we believe that the pressure for the recent Supreme Court decision was brought about largely because of the so-called Separate but Equal School theory. You have had some kind of an Equal school law since the Constitutional Convention of 1890. But we did not think about it until we begin to feel the sharp lash of the Supreme Court. You know, as well as we know that we have had the Separate all right, but in very few cases have we had the Equal. Fundamentally, there is no such thing as separate but equal in a matter as vital as the education of our children. The Mississippi Negro Public School system has been so lacking in buildings and facilities until the Negro children have developed a complex which has caused him to want to go to the white school in his community, not for social reasons, but because the white school was the best school in his community. No wonder Chief Justice Warren said in his historic decision, "To separate children from others of similar age and qualifications, solely because of their race generates a felling of inferiority as to their status in the community that may affect their hearts and minds in a way unlikely ever to be undone."

We believe that it is practical and logical to build our schools in Communities where the people live, not on the basis of race but for the convenience of the children. We believe that buildings and equipment should not be labeled for white or colored but a school built to all standard specifications for the children of Mississippi. We can all agree to start this type of a building program immediately. We should have assurance, however, by appropriate legislative approval that this school building program will proceed on its basis of need and not because the Negroes have entered into any segregation agreement. We should like to have the assurance that competent bi-racial committees will serve on this school building program. Governor, you have a tremendous wealth of Negro "know how" in Mississippi that you have never called on to help work out any of our mutual problems.

We believe that it is morally and legally wrong for those who have sworn to uphold the laws of our land to talk about abolishing the public school system, in order to evade the laws of our land. For Mississippi to abolish her public school system would be an unthinkable catastrophe, especially for the white children of the state, because you have for them a good public school system. For the average Negro child today you certainly don't have much to offer and we will see it go before we will agree to agree to help you circumvent the Supreme Court decision of May 17th.

In the light of my foregoing statements, I wish to conclude with the following suggestions for the operation of a system of public schools for all the children in the State of Mississippi.

I. As the Supreme Court Decision has done away with the laws dealing with our schools in Mississippi, we petition the Mississippi

State Legislature to write a new school law for the state of Mississippi without mentioning race, creed or color. A law which in substance will say, "Mississippi shall provide a school system for all of her children."

We endorse the Governor's plan to call a special session of the State Legislature to consider among the other things, a new school law, and appropriating enough money to build new schools and buy new equipment to bring all of our schools up to an arbitrary standard, which can best be fixed by our experts in the field of education.

II. We seriously recommend that competent Negroes be appointed to all policy-making Boards affecting both races on a State and local level. The day is past and forever gone when one race can work out all the problems affecting another group and bring it to him as a "take it or leave it" proposition. We are asking a chance to help shape our own destiny. We have seen so many costly blunders made in Negro school buildings and in other matters affecting the Negro simply because the Negro was not consulted. You may think you understand our problem, but you have got to be a Negro in Mississippi, at least 24 hours in order to understand what it means to be a Negro in this state.

III. We recommend that an independent bi-racial commission be appointed to look into the three institutions of higher learning which are today serving the Negro people of the state—as to location of these schools, as to the need for three separate schools of this nature, as to faculty qualifications, as to enrollment, as to physical plant, as to equipment, as to operation appropriation, in absolute comparison at all levels with similar institutions of higher learning in the State of Mississippi. Here, as in the elementary and High Schools, we have had the separate but in no case the equal.

IV. We recommend that because of the tremendous cost to the State of the Elementary and High School building program and because it would cost added millions in buildings, equipment and faculty employment to bring any one of the three State Colleges which today serve Negroes up to the recognized level of doing graduate work and professional work, that the Higher Institutions of Learning in the State of Mississippi which are already doing graduate and professional work open their doors immediately and admit all students who qualify for graduate and professional work, regardless to race, creed or color.

I wish to remind you that this is being done in every state in the Union today except Florida, South Carolina, Georgia, Alabama, and Mississippi. The thinking Negroes in Mississippi would like for this to be done without taking the matter to the Supreme Court. You and I know what the answer will be if the issue goes to the Supreme Court.

A brilliant young man in my town made application to the law department of our State University over six months ago and until this day he has not received an answer as to whether he will be accepted or rejected. Right here in Jackson, white nurses and Negro nurses sit in the same classes together. They are doing it in Arkansas, Louisiana and Texas. It can be done without racial trouble at the University of Mississippi.

Your big fear, of course, is social equality. There is not a thinking Negro in Mississippi today that is bothered about social equality, but we are mighty concerned about equality of educational opportunity.

V. We recommend that instead of the term voluntary segregation that we use and follow the path of voluntary integration, after the Supreme Court says "when and how." No child would be forced to attend any particular school and on the other hand, no child would be denied the right to attend a particular school, solely because of race, creed or color. We are willing to leave the details of a final plan to a fifty man bi-racial committee.

With all the injustices that you have heaped upon the Negro in Mississippi, with all the inequality which have been ours in the field of public education—with all the suffering which has been ours at your hands simply because the great God of the Ages made us black, with all that you have done, we have never let you down. We helped you drive out the wild beast, we cleared the wilderness, we have tilled your soil and made it the richest soil on earth. We have gone to the ends of the earth to fight, bleed and die for the basic fruits of Democracy that even today we don't know anything about in Mississippi. We have never failed you or let you down. Through 250 years of slavery and 91 years of physical freedom, you have taught us that the Constitution of the United States of Americas was the greatest document on Earth. You have taught the Negro to uphold and obey the laws of the land. During your present administration, Governor White, you have ask[ed] the Negro of Mississippi to accept the responsibility of citizenship, so today, when the eyes of the Democratic forces of the world are focused upon Mississippi, let us not reduce the Constitution to a mere scrap of paper by asking Negroes to help you evade the law of the land. A Chain is no stronger than it's weakest link, if Mississippi is a weak link in the Chain of American Democracy—America is weak.

Several months ago I saw a painting in one of the Colored schools in the Delta which was done by a teen-age Negro plantation boy. It was the picture of an old Negro man sitting in a rocking chair. There were deep bitten wrinkles in his dark face. His kinky, wooley hair had turned to a snowey [*sic*] white and there was a faraway expression in his age-dimmed eyes and at the old man's side stood a wooley headed Negro boy who was looking up into the old man's face, with his little mouth opened and at the side of the picture these words were written, "Grandpa, what was slavery?"

Governor, every Negro before you today is looking forward to that day when right here in Mississippi, our grandchildren will look into our faces and say, "Grandpa, what was segregation and discrimination in our Democracy.["]

J. H. WHITE, 1954[10]

Dr. J. H. White, president of Mississippi Vocational College (now Mississippi Valley State University), attended a July 1, 1954 meeting with Governor White. Dr. White and the other conservative blacks encouraged the governor to create a Legal Advisory Committee and to invite

100 leading men to meet with the committee and the governor. Among
those invited to attend the July 13 meeting was Dr. Emmett J. Stringer to
whom the letter that follows is addressed. Stringer was a black dentist
from Columbus and recently-elected state president of the NAACP.
Dr. White, a leader of the conservative faction, preferred to see
black-only schools and colleges improved before segregation began.
Like some other black leaders, he feared for the fate of institutions
they had created in a desegregated world. His letter to Stringer asks
the dentist to retreat from his support for the position assumed by the
Legal Advisory Committee.

I am writing you this letter as one Negro who is interested in the State
of Mississippi to another Negro who is interested in the State of
Mississippi.

Never in the history of our State has a Negro had the opportunity of
helping 900,000 Negroes any more than you have at the present time.
When I first met you, which was a few weeks ago, I was impressed
by your calmness and your gentleman-like manner. I am, therefore,
taking upon myself to write you from my heart as I feel about the
problem facing us today in our State. I wish to solicit your Christian
thinking in this matter.

Here in Mississippi our problem must be solved for the good of
both races that we are no longer required by law to have segregated
school—as a matter of law. It is one thing, Dr. Stringer, in making the
adjustment it still is a matter of years ahead to be worked out, because
we do not wish to force our children in the White schools any more
than we wish for the White children to be forced into our schools.
Laws are good in proportion as they live in the hearts of people. You
will agree with me, I am sure, of what our people at this time need;
it is education. And I think 90% of the Negroes in our State want the
Negro colleges to have the buildings, equipment, and course offerings
that will prepare teachers to train their children. They want the elementary and high schools to have this and then urge that every Negro
child be given adequate facilities which carries with it good teachers,
salaries, buildings, facilities, and course offerings that will enable them

to enrich their talents which God has given them for their own benefit and for the benefit of their fellow man.

I personally feel that the meeting we had at Jackson retarded the
progress of the Negro instead of advancing the Negro. Governor
White did not say what any Negro should say. I think he wanted us
to bring in a program whereby both races could work together for the
good of all people. I think Dr. Howard's address was not only out of
place, but was rather a blow to the good-will of the people of the
State. You would not have done something like that because I feel that
with your convictions, you are a different kind of leader. I am writing
you this letter of appeal because I feel that we can make a different
approach to this problem and bring the two races back together
because we are really separate at this time. The Negroes are losing
ground daily by public opinions.

You received your undergraduate work at Alcorn College. This is
your State and I think you owe your best for the good of the State; and
you can only give this by recognizing the fact that what the NAACP
is asking it will be generations and years before it will be accomplished. I do not think you feel that it can be accomplished now.
Therefore, we would like for you to go along with us in asking for
adequate facilities and other things that our people need first and
when you lay that foundation you have made a great contribution and
many other problems will be solved in years to come.

The White people of Mississippi are not ready and the Negroes of
Mississippi are not ready for many things that are being asked, and
I feel that if any one person in the State of Mississippi can help at this
point, you will be that person. I hope that you will realize that we can
not change over night discrimination and irregularities. We must
work constantly with faith in each other that these things might come
about. Governor White has done his best to get the type of schools we
want because Negroes are not interested in going to White schools. I
feel that 95% has been stated is true. What they want are things they
deserve and I feel that you are wrong in attempting to push little

Negro children in places where they are not wanted and where they are unhappy, and where they are not inspired. I hope you will think this over and I hope you will decide that afterall you get more done through peace and understanding than you can through trouble and misunderstanding.

I have talked with Dr. Howard at length. He is an individualist and he sees no good in the State that has allowed him to pull up by his own bootstraps. I am not with your program because I feel that it is not for the best for our people; and I feel that if you would stop and think awhile you will see yourself that you can give leadership to our people that they may have the things they deserve without [the] misunderstanding that is now prevailing throughout the State of Mississippi.

Down through the years, men have denied themselves for brotherly love. Moses received the Ten Commandments on Mount Sinai at the conclusion of his fast. Elijah talked with God on Mount Horeb at the conclusion of his period of prayer and fasting. Jesus began his great spiritual ministry at the close of his fast in the wilderness. My friend, Dr. Stringer, as we face a problem where understanding, intelligence are needed, may we learn to deny our selfish impulses and be obedient to impulses of brotherly love.

I hope you will pray and think on these things because I am your friend.

N. R. BURGER, 1956[11]

In 1909, N. R. Burger was born in Brookhaven, but he moved to Hattiesburg at a young age. He began his public school teaching career soon after graduating from Alcorn College in 1932. Realizing that he needed a master's degree to achieve a leadership role in the public school system and knowing too that no Mississippi school could meet his needs, Burger took a leave of absence from his job to complete his graduate education at Cornell University. In 1940, he became principal of Eureka High School in Hattiesburg, a position he held until his retirement in 1974.

Several years ago, the teachers in Mississippi were called upon to attach their signatures to a mimeographed form called the "Employee's Statement Under Subversive Activities Act 1950." In essence, this form with signatures attached, constituted an oath of loyalty to the constitutional form of government of the United States and of the State of Mississippi.

The Negro teachers did not hesitate one moment to sign these for at the time there seemed not to have been any question of their loyalty to the Constitution of the United States, nor to any law, local or otherwise, appertaining thereunto.

Inasmuch as there was unanimity on the part of the Negro teacher in signing these oaths, this mass of sworn statements served as expressions of devotion to this democracy and the constitution which undergirds it.

On May 17, 1954, the United States Supreme Court issued a decree outlawing segregation of the races in the public schools of this country. The Negro teachers of Mississippi, steadfast in their loyalty to the Constitution and the supreme law of the land, went on record during the state convention in March of 1955 as favoring the decree. During the state convention in March of 1954, the Negro teachers had expressed opinion in terms of favoring the then pending decree.

Of late, there have been suggestions from public speakers and, in some cases, editors of newspapers, that the Negro teacher should speak out for **forced** segregation, which is presently the law in Mississippi, so as to assure for themselves jobs.

The sentiments of Negro teachers, as I gather them, on such suggestions are these:

1. To advocate legal segregation for the sake of a job would not only be perjury in the face of the sworn statements already on file, but it would be an act of selling the principles of democracy, which no one should be called upon to do. For in such practices comes the precedent of making a commodity out of the rights of the individual to be sold or bought expediently. If the teacher is to sell—let's sell good will for the upgrading of humanity.

2. To advocate legal segregation for the sake of a job would be in violation of the teacher's professional integrity.

3. To advocate legal segregation for the sake of a position would crush the confidence of patrons whose children are being taught and would create the impression that the teacher holds his position higher than he does the welfare of the children he teaches.

4. To advocate legal segregation for the sake of the job on the part of those who have not yet done so would mean ostracism and loss of esteem with the child and the community as has happened to those who have done so.

5. To advocate legal segregation for the sake of a job would place the negro teacher in a dubious position to teach citizenship and its fundamental precepts to the students. It is the desire of every teacher to have students who stand and offer the Pledge of Allegiance to the flag of the United States of America, to see it not alone as a colorful banner, but as a symbol of the freedoms assured to all American citizens. These freedoms provide the opportunity for the individual to grow and develop in proportion to his ability to achieve economically, spiritually, morally and otherwise as long as he does not infringe on the rights of others. Certainly, it is not the desire of teachers to act or be cause to act in such a manner that students will come to look upon them (the teacher) with disdain.

At this stage of the present crisis the Negro teacher feels that he could easily be made the "goat" in the matter and his best position is the position of silence—a period to be used for constant preparation and professional growth which will enable him to accrue greater resources to do a better and more effective job of teaching children.

Chapter 13

FREEDOM SUMMER

Between the Supreme Court's 1954 Brown decision and the summer of 1964, advocates of black equality intensified their activities. The 1955 Montgomery, Alabama bus boycott, the 1957 desegregation of Central High School in Little Rock, Arkansas, the student sit-ins at a Woolworth's lunch counter in Greensboro, North Carolina in 1960, the 1963 Birmingham boycott, and in the same year, the March on Washington signaled the increased commitment of Americans to civil rights reform. In the same period, the Federal government passed legislation to end Jim Crow. The Civil Rights Act of 1957, the first civil rights law passed since Reconstruction, established a Civil Rights Division in the Justice Department, the purpose of which was to prevent interference with citizens's efforts to vote. The Civil Rights Act of 1960 allowed federal court referees to register black voters when a pattern of discrimination was discerned. Yet, the efforts of the Federal government to secure equal rights for African-Americans was notoriously ineffective.

During the period 1954 to 1963, black Mississippians concentrated their efforts to end racial discrimination by calling for equal access to education, public accommodations, and economic opportunity. Jackson police officers arrested freedom riders—black activists who attempted to force southern officials to recognize federally-mandated integration of interstate transportation. In 1960, African Americans in McComb requested that the Congress of Racial Equality organize and operate a voter registration campaign in their hometown. In 1962, after endless and futile machinations by Governor Ross Barnett, James Meredith enrolled at the University of Mississippi; a riot marked his appearance on campus. Throughout the early 1960s, students from Tougaloo College working with the National Association for the Advancement of Colored People, attempted to integrate lunch counters at downtown Jackson department stores. They also conducted a boycott of those stores, calling for equitable treatment of African-American customers and employees. In the summer of 1963, Medgar Evers, state Field Director of the N.A.A.C.P, was assassinated by Byron de La Beckwith.

By 1964, the nation regarded Mississippi as the last bastion of Jim Crow. Many advocates of civil rights reform assumed that if Mississippi could be transformed, the rest of the south would follow. Consequently, all eyes seemed to focus on the state. The summer of 1964, or Freedom Summer, was to be the pinnacle of civil rights agitation. As designed by the Congress of Federated Organizations (COFO)—an umbrella entity coordinating efforts at civil rights reform—the Freedom Summer Project pursued a two-pronged approach. Working with local organizers and activists, the project brought white student volunteers to Mississippi to help educate black youth and to register their parents to vote.

But, perhaps predictably, Freedom Summer began with violence. Three volunteers—two white northerners (Michael Schwerner and Andrew Goodman) and one African American from Mississippi (James Chaney)— disappeared while in Neshoba County preparing black residents of central Mississippi to receive Freedom Summer volunteers. Their bodies were eventually located near Philadelphia. The murderers of Chaney, Goodman, and Schwerner included Klansmen and local law enforcement officials. Contrary to the wishes of those who committed the murders, the deaths of the three men, although to volunteers a frightening event and one that hung over Freedom Summer like a perpetual threat, did not squash the project. Indeed, the murders motivated volunteers to work harder to end discrimination. Summer volunteers worked with black school children in Freedom Schools, conducted voter registration drives, held mock elections to train new voters, and helped publicize the inauguration of the Mississippi Freedom Democratic

party, an alternative to the regular party that secured recognition at the
1964 Democratic national convention.

DAVE DENNIS[1]

In 1962, Dave Dennis, a native New Orleanian, became field secretary of
the Congress of Racial Equality in Mississippi. Working largely with
volunteers from outside Mississippi, Dennis struggled to build support for
CORE in Jackson. By 1964, when he delivered the eulogy for murdered
Civil Rights worker James Chaney, he was one of the most visible Civil
Rights leaders in the state.

Sorry, but I'm not here to do the traditional thing most of us do at
such a gathering. And that is to tell of what a great person the individual was and some of the great works that the person was involved
in and etc. I think we all know it because he walked these dusty streets
of Meridian and around here long before I came here. With you and
around you. Played with your kids and he talked to all of them. And
what I want to talk about is really what I learned to grieve about.
I don't grieve for Chaney because the fact is I feel he lived a fuller life
than many of us will ever live. I feel that he's got his freedom and we
are still fighting for it. (AMEN)

But what I want to talk about right now is the living dead that we
have right among our midst, not only in the state of Mississippi but
throughout the nation. Those are the people who don't care (THAT'S
RIGHT), those that do care but don't have the guts enough to stand
up for it (THAT'S RIGHT), and those people who are busy up in
Washington and in other places using my freedom and my life to play
politics with. (ALL RIGHT) That includes the president on down to
the governor of the state of Mississippi, you see. In my opinion, as I
stand here, I not only blame the people who pulled the trigger or did
the beating or dug the hole with the shovel (ALL RIGHT), or buried
the people, not buried, sorry . . . But I blame the people in Washington,

D.C., and on down to the state of Mississippi for what happened just as much as I blame those who pulled the trigger (AMEN) Because I feel that a hundred years ago, if the proper thing had been done by the federal government of this particular country and by the other people responsible or the irresponsible people, we wouldn't be here to mourn the death of a brave young man like James Chaney, you see. (AMEN, ALL RIGHT)

As I stand here a lot of things pass through my mind. I can remember the Emmett Till case (YES), what happened to him (ALL RIGHT) and what happened to the people who killed him (ALL RIGHT). They're walking the streets right now and the brother of one is a police officer here in a place called Ruleville, Mississippi. (THAT'S RIGHT) I remember back down here, right below us here, a man by the name of Mack [Charles] Parker[2] and exactly what happened to him and what happened to the people who beat, (UMM, UMM), killed him (UMM), and drug him down the streets and threw him in the river (THAT'S RIGHT). I know that those people were caught but they were never brought to trial. (OH NO) I can remember back in Birmingham of the four young kids (RIGHT) who were bombed in the church (RIGHT) and had just went to service and I know what has happened to the people who killed them—nothing. (THAT'S RIGHT) Remember the little thirteen-year-old kid who was riding a bicycle and who was shot in the back? (THAT'S RIGHT). And the youth who shot him, who was a white guy from Birmingham, got off with three months. (ALL RIGHT, SHAME) I can remember all of that right now. Or I can remember the Medgar Evers case in [Byron de la] Beckwith. (YES) The person who was governor of the state at that particular time going up and shaking his hand when the jury said that it could not come to a verdict. (YES) I can remember all of that. (YES) And I can remember down in the Southwest area where you had six Negroes who'd been killed, and I can remember the Lees and all these particular people who know what has happened to those who have been killing them. I know what is happening to the people that are bombing the churches, who've been bombing the homes, who are doing the beatings around this entire state and country. (YES, ALL RIGHT)

Well, I'm getting sick and tired. (THAT'S RIGHT) I'm sick and tired of going to memorials, I'm sick and tired of going to funerals. (YES) I've got a bitter vengeance in my heart tonight. (SO HAVE I) And I'm sick and tired and I can't help but feel bitter, you see, deep down inside, and I'm not going to stand here and ask anybody here not to be angry tonight. (YES)

Yeah, we have love in our hearts, and we've had it for years and years in this country. (ALL RIGHT) We've died on the battlefield to protect the people in this country. (THAT'S RIGHT) We've gone out in World War I and in 1942 millions of us died too, you see. (YES) Meanwhile, you understand, there are people in this country with no eyes, without a leg, without an arm, to defend this country and to come back and do what? To live as slaves you see, and I'm sick and tired of that (I AM TOO) Yeah, I'm probably supposed to stand here . . . (YES) Got a lot more I want to say. (YES, GO ON)

You see, we're all tired (YES) You see, I know what's gonna happen. I feel it deep in my heart. When they find the people who killed these guys in Neshoba County, (ALL RIGHT) you've got to come back to the state of Mississippi and have a jury of their cousins, their aunts and their uncles. (ALL RIGHT) And I know what they're going to say— not guilty. Because no one saw them pull the trigger. I'm tired of that. (YES, GOD HELP US. I AM TOO; I'M SICK OF IT!)

See another thing that makes me even tireder though, and that is the fact that we as people here in this state and the country are allowing this to continue to happen. (THAT'S RIGHT) Even us as black folk. So I look at the young kids here—that's something else that I grieve about. For little Ben Chaney here and the other ones like him around in this audience and out on the streets. I grieve because sometimes they make me feel that, maybe, they have to go through the same thing, you see. (YEAH) And they are gonna have to go through the same thing. (GOD HELP US) Unless we as individuals begin to stand up and demand our rights and a change in this dad-blasted country, (RIGHT) you see. (THAT'S RIGHT) We have to stand up and demand it because tomorrow, baby, it could be your child. (YES, THAT'S RIGHT)

And one thing that I'm worried about is just exactly what are we going to do as people as a result of what happened, for what this guy died for and the other people died for. (RIGHT) We're going to come to this memorial here, say, "Oh, what a shame," go back home and pray to the Lord as we've done for years. (THAT's RIGHT) We go back to work in some white folks' kitchen tomorrow (ALL RIGHT) and forget about the whole God-blasted thing, you see (RIGHT, SPEAK). (Applause from congregation)

Don't applaud! Don't applaud! Don't get your frustration out by clapping your hands. Each and every one of us as individuals is going to have to take it upon ourself to become leaders in our community. (THAT'S RIGHT) Block by block, house by house, city by city, county by county, state by state, throughout this entire country. Taking our black brothers by the hand, (THAT'S RIGHT) one at a time, stepping across with our feet through the mighty oceans to the mighty country of Africa. Holding our hands up high, telling them that if they're not ready for us, "Too bad, baby, 'cause we're coming anyway." (THAT'S RIGHT). . . .

We can't take it any longer and be wiped off of the face of the earth. I look at the people of gray hair down here, the tiredness in the face and think about the millions of bolls of cotton you picked, the millions of actions it took to chop it for $10.00 a week, for $25.00 a week, or whatever you could get to eat (THAT'S RIGHT. AMEN. SICK AND TIRED OF IT.) I watch the people here who go out there and wash dishes and you cook for them. For the whites in the community and those same ones you cook for, wash and iron for, who come right out and say, "I can't sit down and eat beside a nigger," or anything like that. I'm tired of that, you see. (YES) I'm tired of him talking about how much he hates me (YES, THAT'S RIGHT), and he can't stand for me to go to school with children and all of that. (HERE YOU GO) But yet, when he wants someone to babysit for them, he gets my black mammy to hold that baby. And as long as he can do that, (ALL RIGHT) he can sit down beside me, (YES) he can watch me go up there and register to vote, and he can watch me take some type of public office in this state, and he can sit down as I rule over him just like he's ruled over me for years, you see. (ALL RIGHT)

This is our country, too. We didn't ask to come here when they brought us over here (AMEN, RIGHT), and I hear the old statement over and over again about me to go back to Africa. Well, I'm ready to go back to Africa, baby, when all the Jews, the Poles, the Russians, the Germans and they all go back to their country where they came from too, you see (RIGHT, SPEAK) And they have to remember that they took this land from the Indians. (YES, AMEN) And just as much as it's theirs, it's ours too now. (ALL RIGHT) We've got to stand up!

The best thing that we can do for Mr. Chaney, for Mickey Schwerner, (YES) for Andrew Goodman is stand up and demand our rights. (ALL RIGHT) All these people here who are not registered voters should be in line Monday morning from one corner of this county to the next, demanding, don't ask, if I can become a registered voter. Demand! Say, "Baby, I'm here." (THAT'S RIGHT, ONE MAN ONE VOTE, RIGHT)

People, you've got relatives in places like Neshoba County, talk to them. They're at a disadvantage. They only have 12 percent of the population that's black over there. So that man thinks he's going to run over us over there. But we're going in there, baby. (ALL RIGHT) We're going to organize in there, (ALL RIGHT) and we're going to get those people registered to vote and organized. I don't care if we are just 12 percent. Because that 12 percent is part of that almost 50 percent of this whole entire state, you see. (AMEN)

Don't just look at me and the people here and go back and say that you've been to a nice service, (AMEN) a lot of people came, there were a lot of hot-blasted newsmen around, anything like that. But your work is just beginning. (THAT'S RIGHT) I'm going to tell you deep down in my heart what I feel like right now. (TELL IT) If you do go back home and sit down and take it, God damn your soul! (THAT IS THE TRUTH)

(Some audience applause)

Stand up! (STAND UP!) Your neighbors down there were too afraid to come to this memorial, take them to another memorial. (AMEN) Take them up and take them down there. Make them register to vote and you register to vote. I doubt if one fourth of this house is registered. Go down there and do it (YES) Don't bow down anymore. (THAT'S RIGHT) Hold your heads up! (THAT'S RIGHT, RIGHT, ALL RIGHT, AMEN, AMEN)

SANDRA ADICKES[3]

Sandra Adickes, a New York school teacher, traveled to Hattiesburg to teach in one of the Freedom Schools operated by CORE. Adickes had taught the previous year in Prince Edward County, Virginia where the white community closed public schools rather than desegregate. The portion of the interview that appears below was conducted by Stephanie Millet.

Millet: . . . Let me back up just a little bit, and ask you if you think there was anything in particular in your upbringing or your background that contributed to your being predisposed towards this [civil rights volunteer] work.

Adickes: Yeah, I was asked that question, oh, a number of years ago. You know. Where do your politics originate? And when I thought, I thought, "Well, it's not Marxism; it's Methodism." And it was religion. And that was true of quite a few people. I mean, yes, black people came from the churches, but white women, and there were a number of ministers' daughters who were active in the civil rights movement. . . . And having been brought up in this faith, and having found this faith significant, one could not bear the contradictions. If this is what you believe, then this is what you must do. And particularly in the Methodist Church at that time, the Methodist Church was segregated. That's the basis for that famous line, "The most segregated time in America is Sunday at 11 a.m." I think Martin Luther King said that. And, these women and I found that contradiction unbearable. Social justice was an important tenet in Methodism from the very beginning. Not that every Methodist believes that. . . . So, it was my religious upbringing that had a great deal to do with my commitment to this. . . . I came down with about six other teachers who were going to Hattiesburg. We left Memphis and we stopped in Philadelphia. Oh. I remember, it was the fourth of July, and I remember on the way down, I could see no backyard barbecues. I mean, there was just no—. It was like an ordinary day. This was not like a holiday at all, and then the same was true when we got to Philadelphia, and I knew, well, "Ah. This is the city." There were the signs still, "colored bathrooms," "white bathrooms," and so forth, "by order of the police of Philadelphia." And I knew that this was the place, this was the city, or around here, that they had disappeared. And I thought, "Where? How? And by whom?" Where had they been taken? And how had they been killed? And by whom? So, that was on my mind when we were in Philadelphia. And then, when we finally arrived in Hattiesburg and, you know, just looking at this city now, it's just not like the city I remember. Because it was a really kind of dowdy, tacky town. We came in to a really crummy, rundown Greyhound Bus terminal, and our instructions were to call the COFO office as soon as we got there, and we did, and they came and got us. And then we were driven to this fourth of July picnic. Vernon Dahmer was sponsoring it, and I guess, it was on his property. And when I first saw Vernon Dahmer, I thought he was white.[4] He and I both have German ancestry so that accounts for his light skin, but I thought, "Oh, what a courageous man!" (Laughter.) "A local citizen, a white citizen who is sponsoring a fourth of July picnic." Well, then of course, later

I learned the facts of his life. And it was lovely. And we were meeting people, and I remember just having a very good time. And I remember encountering one of the best things about Mississippi, as far as I'm concerned: the pink and purple twilights here are just stunning. And as the sun was going down, Victoria Gray Adams[5] started dispersing us all to her relatives. We were going to stay there. She said, "We've got to get out of here." Darkness meant danger. So, she had us all assigned and we were transported to our hosts' homes before darkness fell. And I was dispersed to— . . . Mrs. Addie Mae Jackson. And I was dispersed to her home. So, I went to her home, and I was the only one of the teachers who went there. She had a small home. She was raising her dead daughter's children, her granddaughter. Her grandson wasn't living with her at the time, but her granddaughter was there, and I think her granddaughter is still a teacher in Hattiesburg. . . .

Millet: So, you hit the ground running there on July 6. What was that day like? Tell me about that day.

Adickes: Well, it was very exciting. You know, we were looking—. This is something we had worked hard for. So, when the kids started, and I mean just started pouring into school, it was just very, very exciting. And we were kind of disorganized. You know, it took a while to get our routines going, but the first day—. I mean, we'd all begin—. We usually began the days, as we did the first day, just, you know, in a group. In a large group. And, I think there were three of us in the school. Three instructors, and we would each give a presentation or a talk to each other, and then disperse in smaller groups. Usually, I know I taught English and somebody else was a history teacher, and somebody else was a math teacher, and we usually dispersed, you know, just according to subject area, and we would go to classrooms. We would start in the basement of the church, then we would go to classrooms. And then when it became too hot, as it quickly did, we would go outside, and we'd sit in groups under trees. And I remember doing, in my groups, we did a lot of reading and a lot of writing. . . . Most of the students who came were high school age. And certainly the ones

I dealt with were high school age. I don't remember having a great deal or many younger kids. They were there. They were clearly there, but I didn't deal with them. I dealt with the high school students, and maybe that's why, because high school students were what I was teaching at the time. Maybe that's why the kids still remember—. Kids! (Laughter.) Former students still remember those days. So, it was good, I mean the kinds of discussions. And I notice when I'm looking at the pictures, I know I had males in the classes, but it was the girls who really, and this has been my experience all my teaching life, it was the girls who really took the opportunity and ran with it. And got as much as they could from it.

Millet: . . . [M]aybe now, in retrospect you might perceive differences—between the freedom school that you had in Hattiesburg during Freedom Summer of '64, and the so-called public schools that African American students had usually attended?

Adickes: Well, they wrote about that in that journal, too, in that newspaper they put out. They were very outspoken about the differences. They were furious at the inequity, as I said, about the books, about the fact that they couldn't use the public library. That's why we chose. That they had a little room downtown where they could go. I never saw it, but they talked about this little room where all the cast-off books were kept, and those were the only—.

Millet: The black library.

Adickes: Yeah, the black library. And they were particularly angry with their teachers. I remember one day, I think it was the principal of their school.

Millet: And was he white or African American?

Adickes: Black. No, they were black. They had a separate school system. And with more compassion, one understands, you know. What else could they do except tow the line for the white establishment? The principal walked down somewhere near the school, near where we were having our classes, and the kids saw him, and he did not speak to them. He did not greet them. And after he passed, I mean, they hated him. They hated that man. They hated him for not being their advocate, for achieving whatever he achieved at their, as far as they were concerned, at their expense. So, we had that. There was that sense of: "Here, we know what a school is, finally. We have teachers who respect us, who want to hear what we have to say, who care about us, who want something for us in this life." Oh, yeah, but they took that back. Having tasted what school was, they were, I'm sure—. I mean, I'd be very interested to know. I never thought of this before. I'd be very interested to know what the academic year [laughter] '64, '65 was like for those teachers in that school that they went to. Because it did change. It changed their aspirations. I'm sure if you measured college attendance before Freedom Summer and college attendance after it, there would be such a leap. And now it's a norm. You go to college. You go to college after high school, and now their kids have. They've gone to college, and their kids have gone to college. It's transformed the way of life for them. . . .

Millet: Well, so your students wanted to close their freedom school experience with an action that implemented the Civil Rights Act. . . .

Adickes: So, then we decided we wanted to have lunch. We went downtown, first to Woolworth's. It was completely packed. And then we went into Kress's, and the rest I think you know about that.

Millet: Yes. . . . Well, so, you guys went into Kress's, and the waitress said, "I have to serve Negroes, but I don't have to serve white people who sit with them." So, your students decided that they would—.

Adickes: "Well, if you're not going to feed Sandy, we're not—. If Sandy can't eat, we won't eat." So then we left.

Millet: And immediately you were arrested for vagrancy.

Adickes: Right.

Millet: So, what happened? Can you describe exactly what took place from the time you got in that police car until you were bonded out?

Adickes: Well, I was worried about the kids. I was worried. Kids! [Laughter.] . . . I was worried about them, you know, but I needn't have. They were perfectly capable of getting wherever they wanted to go on their own. And I was taken to this awful jail. . . . However, arrangements had been made for this. I had posted—. We all had left some money available for bail, and I knew that very shortly the National Lawyers' Guild would come and bail me out. And that is, in fact, what happened. I was bailed out in an hour or so. . . .

Millet: So, did you fear for your life at any time? Or even your physical safety?

Adickes: No. Not then.

Millet: Not in the hands of the police?

Adickes: No, I wasn't that fearful when I was arrested because it was so public. And, I mean, white people, you know. They weren't going to mess with white people. That's when—. That did happen in the police car. I had a pair of cheap sunglasses on, wraparound sunglasses, and when I got in the car, one of the officers got in back with me. You know, I was so dangerous, he had to be there to restrain me in case I would do something desperate! And while we were riding to the jail, he said, "You in the Liberace sunglasses. Are you fuckin' them niggers?"

Millet: Liberace sunglasses?

Adickes: Yeah, Liberace, he said that. I guess Liberace, the musician, wore wraparound sunglasses like that. But those were his exact words.

Millet: How did you respond?

Adickes: I think I said, "No one has ever spoken to me like that down here. I don't see why you should." Or something like that. I mean, it was like, I was "white lady." I had mentally put on little white gloves and was putting him in his place. So, I guess it was just, you know, the crudeness of it, just brought out that kind of payoff: "I'm not afraid of you. You're a jerk!" That kind of response. And, there were times, I mean we had heard that they were coming into the community at night. That's when I said, you know, we stayed up all night, a shotgun at the door because we thought they were going to attack us then. And, my feeling was, you know, I'm doing exactly what I want to do. I believe in what I'm doing. I'm just not going to be afraid. I was not afraid. I was not afraid. I mean, I knew that things might be dangerous, and I certainly didn't do anything out of the ordinary or try to draw attention to myself, but I certainly believed in what I was doing, and I certainly cared about the people I was among. So I just wasn't fearful. . . . I really didn't have that kind of arrogant thought: "My white skin protects me." I was aware, I do remember once, riding with Mrs. [Victoria Gray] Jackson in her car and realizing I was putting her in danger, so I got down on the seat so I couldn't be seen. I was really concerned about not bringing harm to other people. I really wasn't that concerned for myself. I mean, I was afraid before I came down here, but I mean I wasn't—. When you deal with the reality, you know, it's a different situation, so I knew, you know, that night where we all huddled together, you know, that something might happen, but the other thing was that I knew that if people attacked folks in Palmer's Crossing, they were going to get hurt, too, because people—.

Millet: Although the SNCC [Student Nonviolent Coordinating Committee] workers were into the nonviolent technique—.

Adickes: Right. Nonviolence was tactical rather than ideological. I mean that was the way I was concerned about it, too. You know, what can you do with these people? There's no chance you can outweapon them. . . .

Millet: Although there was a component of the African American community who did sit up at night with their shotguns.

Adickes: Oh, yeah. And Palmer's Crossing was that kind of community.

Millet: That was the population?

Adickes: If white folks had come into that community, they would have used those guns. I had no doubt about it. And, as far as I was concerned, that was fine.

FREEDOM SCHOOLS

Students at one of the Hattiesburg Freedom Schools published the following Declaration of Independence. They worked collectively on the project to compile a list of grievances and solutions on which they could agree.

A Declaration of Independence[6]

In this course of human events, it has become necessary for the Negro people to break away from the customs which have made it very difficult for the Negro to get his God-given rights. We, as citizens of Mississippi, do hereby state that all people should have the right to petition, to assemble, and to use public places. We also have the right to life, liberty, and to seek happiness.

The government has no right to make or to change laws without the consent of the people. No government has the right to take the law into its own hands. All people as citizens have the right to impeach the government when their rights are being taken away.

All voters elect persons to the government. Everyone must vote to elect the person of his choice; so we hereby state that all persons of twenty-one years of age, whether black, white, or yellow, have the right to elect the person of their choice; and if this person does not carry out the will of the people, they have the right to alter or abolish the government.

The Negro does not have the right to petition the government for a redress of these grievances:

For equal job opportunity.

For better schools and equipment.

For better recreation facilities.

For more public libraries.

For schools for the mentally ill.

For more and better senior colleges.

For better roads in Negro communities.

For training schools in the State of Mississippi.

For more Negro policemen.

For more guarantee of a fair circuit clerk.

For integration in colleges and schools.

The government has made it possible for the white man to have a mock trial in the case of a Negro's death.

The government has refused to make laws for the public good.

The government has used police brutality.

The government has imposed taxes upon us without representation.

The government has refused to give the Negroes the right to go into public places.

The government has marked our registration forms unfairly.

We, therefore, the Negroes of Mississippi, assembled, appeal to the government of the State, that no man is free until all men are free. We do hereby declare Independence from the unjust laws of Mississippi which conflict with the United States' Constitution.

CHILDREN'S DESCRIPTIONS OF JIM CROW

The following documents were written by students, who participated in Hattiesburg area Freedom Schools. Teachers encouraged students to express their emotions about the conditions they encountered daily. Most of the essays were published in one of the Freedom School newspapers, which the students distributed in their community.

Neretha Stewart[7]

I am free in some ways, and in another way I am like a hen. A hen is let out of the coop, but there is a fence around her. An fence that holds this hen back from the out side. This hen is let out every day, and every day the hen looks at this fence that shouldn't be there. This is how the Negroes are brought to America not of their will, put to work in the fields, beat, cursed and treated like a dog. This should stop. This fence should be broken down. Why, not let the hen out of the coop and out of the Gate.

Larry B.[8]

There are lots of things I don't like about Hattiesburg. One thing is the bus drivers, which have already been brought to light to the eyes of the people. Bus drivers . . . are terrible. I have never had any of the incidents happen to me because when I was young I learned we were supposed to sit in the back part of the bus. I'm not going to sit in the back any more!

The one thing I don't like is these Jim Crow restaurants. What I mean by that is these places where they allow no one but white skinned people to eat and not people with black skins. Since the bill passed I eat where I want to.

The question that puzzles me is: Why couldn't we eat in these places before the Civil Rights Bill was passed? I know because we have black skin, but what has that to do with it. The black skinned people have fought in the war, become great scientists, and are qualified for the same jobs. All together we belong to America as much as the whites do. We were all created equal. Neither race is superior to the other.

Mattie Jean Wilson[9]

Well, it was this bus driver. I was on the first straight seat on the bus, and he told me to move back. I said, "I will not. I paid a dime and two pennies for a transfer and I'm not moving." He said, "You know white people must get on this bus." I said, "You know colored people must get on this bus, too."

Mrs. Mable L. V.[10]

I think this is the hardest place to try to live in. I have several reasons for saying this. The white people are saying, let white be white. If they should go in places where Negroes are eating, they advise other white people to pay for whatever they ordered and walk out and leave it! I think the Negroes should take a stand. If you are working in a place and they refuse to serve Negroes, the colored workers there should walk out and let whites do the work.

Now we have integrated Kress's and Woolworth's. We should move on a little further. We should go in other places because the whites are being hard on Kress's and Woolworth's. We should go on to drug stores and other places. If they refuse to serve us, we should sit a little while, then walk out before they call the police for disturbing the peace. After we leave we should go back another day and try again.

BENTON D.[11]

> Students and volunteers also aided the efforts of the neophyte Mississippi Freedom Democratic Party. In the account below, a student explains how he approached older black residents reluctant to register to vote.

On July 17th, I was out canvassing with Denise Jackson, one of the teachers at Mt. Zion Freedom School. We were trying to get the people to fill out Freedom Registration forms because there was going to be a convention the following day. The people gave us a hard time but we convinced some of them to fill out the forms. The people that wouldn't fill out forms said they didn't want to have anything to do with it. One lady said she didn't believe anything was going to change in Mississippi. A lot of people said the same thing.

Then there are the people who won't fill out forms because they are afraid of losing their jobs. But what's holding back the people who don't have to work? Why aren't the people who are retired registering? Are they afraid? If so, of what or whom? Are they afraid of their freedom? Or the responsibilities they must assume in trying to obtain their freedom?

One lady said, "Why don't you let God take care of all this? He can do anything." I said, "you aren't the only person who thinks so. But what are we supposed to do? Sit around all the time and wait for God to do everything when we can do some things for ourselves?"

When I said that it really got her. But I didn't stop there. I was determined to get her to fill out an F.R. form. So I continued to talk to her about things . . .

I saw that she was responding to my conversation so I didn't stop there. I was determined. I wanted that lady's eyes opened wide so that she could see all the troublesome problems confronting the Negro in Mississippi. I wanted her eyes opened wide so that she could see the things she could do.

I rendured another selection by a Negro poet named Melvin Tolsan [i.e. Tolson].[12] It goes like this

> *They tell us to forget*
> *Democracy is spurned,*
> *They tell us to forget*
> *The Bill of Rights is burned.*
> *Three hundred years we slaved*
> *We slave and suffer yet,*
> *Though flesh and bone rebel,*
> *They tell us to forget!*
>
> *Oh, how can we forget*
> *Our human rights denied?*
> *Oh, how can we forget*
> *Our manhood crucified?*
> *When justice is profaned*
> *And plea with curse is met,*
> *When freedom's gate is barred,*
> *Oh, how can we forget?*

It did the trick. I felt so glad and happy because I had opened up another world. I had torn down the wall.

FANNIE LOU HAMER[13]

By the mid-1960s, Fannie Lou Hamer became the voice of the Civil
Rights Movement in Mississippi. Her commitment to ending discrimination
and her powerful singing voice made her a colorful and compelling
spokesperson. She was a driving force in the Mississippi Freedom
Democratic Party and sought a seat in the House of Representatives on the
MFDP ticket. Her testimony before the Democratic Party's credentials
committee was the highwater mark of the MFDP's effort to secure seats at
the party's Atlantic City, New Jersey convention.

Mr. Chairman, and the Credentials Committee, my name is
Mrs. Fannie Lou Hamer, and I live at 626 East Lafayette Street,
Ruleville, Mississippi, Sunflower County, the home of Senator James
O. Eastland, and Senator [John C.] Stennis.

It was the 31st of August in 1962 that eighteen of us traveled
twenty-six miles to the county courthouse in Indianola to try to
register to become first-class citizens. We was met in Indianola by
Mississippi men, highway patrolmens, and they only allowed two of us
in to take the literacy test at the time. After we had taken this test
and started back to Ruleville, we was held up by the City Police
and the State Highway Patrolmen and carried back to Indianola,
where the bus driver was charged that day with driving a bus the
wrong color.

After we paid the fine among us, we continued on to Ruleville, and
Reverend Jeff Sunny carried me four miles in the rural area where I
had worked as a timekeeper and sharecropper for eighteen years. I was
met there by my children, who told me the plantation owner was
angry because I had gone down to try to register. After they told me,
my husband came, and said the plantation owner was raising cain
because I had tried to register, and before he quit talking the plantation owner came, and said "Fannie Lou, do you know—did Pap tell
you what I said?"

I said, "Yes, sir."

He said, "I mean that," he said. "If you don't go down and withdraw your registration, you will have to leave," said, "Then if you go down and withdraw," he said. "You will—you might have to go because we are not ready for that in Mississippi."

And I addressed him and told him and said, "I didn't try to register for you. I tried to register for myself." I had to leave that same night.

On the 10th of September, 1962, sixteen bullets was fired into the home of Mr. And Mrs. Robert Tucker for me. That same night two girls were shot in Ruleville, Mississippi. Also Mr. Joe McDonald's house was shot in.

And in June, the 9th, 1963, I had attended a voter-registration workshop, was returning back to Mississippi. Ten of us was traveling by the Continental Trailway bus. When we got Winona, Mississippi, which is Montgomery County, four of the people got off to use the washroom, and two of the people—to use the restaurant—two of the people wanted to use the washroom. The four people that had gone in to use the restaurant was ordered out. During this time I was on the bus. But when I looked through the window and saw they had rushed out, I got off of the bus to see what had happened, and one of the ladies said, "It was a state highway patrolman and a chief of police ordered us out."

I got back on the bus and one of the persons had used the washroom got back on the bus, too. As soon as I was seated on the bus, I saw when they began to get the four people in a highway patrolman's car. I stepped off the bus to see what was happening and somebody screamed from the car that the four workers was in and said, "Get that one there," and when I went to get in the car, when the man told me I was under arrest, he kicked me.

I was carried to the county jail, and put in the booking room. They left some of the people in the booking room and began to place us in cells. I was placed in a cell with a young woman called Miss Euvester Simpson. After I was placed in the cell I began to hear sounds of licks and screams. I could hear the sounds of licks and horrible screams, and I could hear somebody say, "Can you say, yes, sir, nigger? Can you say yes, sir?"

And they would say other horrible names. She would say, "Yes, I can say yes, sir."

"So say it."

She says, "I don't know you well enough."

They beat her, I don't know how long, and after a while she began to pray, and asked God to have mercy on those people.

And it wasn't too long before three white men came to my cell. One of these men was a State Highway Patrolman and he asked me where I was from, and I told him Ruleville. He said, "we are going to check this." And they left my cell and it wasn't too long before they came back. He said, "You are from Ruleville all right," and he used a curse word, and he said, "We are going to make you wish you was dead."

I was carried out of that cell into another cell where they had two Negro prisoners. The State Highway Patrolman ordered the first Negro to take the blackjack. The first Negro prisoner ordered me, by orders from the State Highway Patrolman for me, to lay down on a bunk bed on my face, and I laid on my face. The first Negro began to beat, and I was beat by the first Negro until he was exhausted, and I was holding my hands behind me at that time on my left side because I suffered from polio when I was six years old. After the first Negro had beat until he was exhausted, the State Highway Patrolman ordered the second Negro to take the blackjack.

The second Negro began to beat and I began to work my feet, and the State Highway Patrolman ordered the first Negro who had beat to set on my feet to keep me from working my feet. I began to scream and one white man got up and began to beat me in my head and tell me to hush. One white man—my dress had worked up high, he walked over and pulled my dress down—and he pulled my dress back, back up.

I was in jail when Medgar Evers was murdered.

All of this is on account we want to register, to become first-class citizens, and if the Freedom Democratic Party is not seated now, I question America, is this America, the land of the free and the home of the brave where we have to sleep with our telephones off the hooks because our lives be threatened daily because we want to live as decent human beings, in America?

Chapter 14

ECONOMIC DEVELOPMENT

In 1964, after having successfully campaigned as the right man to head the massive resistance movement from the governor's mansion, Governor Paul B. Johnson, Jr. delivered an inaugural address that shocked many Mississippians—black and white. He argued that the days of resisting civil rights reform were over and that Mississippi would focus its energy on building a better standard of living for all citizens. The timing of his inaugural address coincided with the start of Federal programs designed to reward Mississippi financially for desegregating its schools. His address also preceded Freedom Summer, the Civil Rights Act of 1964, and the Voting Rights Act of 1965, which collectively caused a revolution in Mississippi. By the close of his term in office, black Mississippians were voting in large numbers and placing African Americans in political offices. In 1969, a few months after Johnson left the governor's office, the Federal courts ordered Mississippi schools to integrate immediately. At long last, the modern Civil Rights Movement had destroyed Jim Crow. While Johnson's contribution to the Civil Rights Movement was minimal, and arguably negative, his emphasis on economic progress rather than a defense of old notions of the racial ordering of society accurately predicted the path that Mississippi would take over the next decades.

Johnson's address symbolized the start of a new day in Mississippi history. Once the state and white Mississippians ceased overtly to resist civil rights reform, the economic development that Johnson imagined possible took place over the next three decades. Industrial development had begun in earnest in the late nineteenth century and received a boost in the 1930s with the passage of the Balance Agriculture With Industry (BAWI) legislation that made it possible for local governments to offer prospective new businesses perks and advantages funded by government-backed loans. In 1939, Ingalls Shipyard in Pascagoula was the first enterprise to benefit from BAWI legislation. By 1960, sufficient industry had located in Mississippi to suggest a radical change had occurred: the 1960 census reported that for the first time more Mississippians worked in industry than on the farm. In keeping with the broader trends that affected the Sunbelt between 1970 and 2000, Mississippi saw an ever-increasing number of large-scale industries open or grow in the state. Petrochemical plants, furniture manufacturing facilities, paper mills, casinos, and most recently, the location of a Nissan automobile factory outside of Jackson indicated the changed nature of Mississippi's economy and ultimately of Mississippi itself.

In part, national trends accounted for Mississippi's economic development. The shift of industry out of the Ohio River Valley and into the south and southwest was determined by the growth of population in the south, and Mississippi benefitted from the relocation of industry. Mississippians also continued to rely on agriculture as a key ingredient in the economy, and while cotton and other traditional crops were less important to the economy, aquaculture, particularly catfish farms and processing plants, helped keep rural Mississippi a vibrant part of the economy. Other rural agriculture-based industries, like timber cutting, also contributed to Mississippi's mature development. Yet, perhaps the most dramatic change in the state's economy has owed to the advent of casino gambling. Gambling casinos along the Gulf Coast, in Tunica County, Natchez, Vicksburg, and Philadelphia annually pump millions of dollars into the state economies. But the energetic campaigns waged by the state and local entities to attract and develop industry have met with mixed results. In the documents that follow, the effort of the state to bring industry to Mississippi is illustrated, so too are some of the successes of modern industry suggested. But the documents also point to the difficult fights that have at times resulted from efforts at economic development, and in the case of catfish processing plant workers and the Choctaw nation, point out that the complicated legacy of Mississippi's past continues at times to shape even the most progressive efforts to bring Mississippi into the mainstream of American life.

PAUL B. JOHNSON, JR., 1964[1]

Paul B. Johnson, Jr., the son of a former governor, served as lieutenant governor under Ross Barnett before winning the office himself in 1963. His term in office coincided with the implementation of many Federal civil rights reforms. Like most white Mississippians of his generation, Johnson was no advocate of greater freedom for African Americans. He, however, was a pragmatist, who understood that strenuous resistance to civil rights reforms would not be fruitful.

The general welfare of all the people of Mississippi is the broad concern of your sate government . . . the government, the lieutenant governor, the Legislature and all the various departments and agencies.

The period, 1940 to 1960, has seen our state make great strides in industrial development. From 1960 to 1964 our progress was unusually great. This progress of the last four years can largely be attributed to three factors:

1). An enlightened, dedicated and hardworking Legislature,

2). A spirit of unity and singleness of purpose on the part of Mississippi's governmental, civic, business and educational leadership, and

3). A new spirit, a new drive, a new energy on the part of the working people of our state.

Yet, while we have made some truly significant advances, in a larger sense we are merely at the dawn of a great new era of opportunity for our people. As we move this state forward to an even greater and higher plateau of economic progress, the first crying need of our people is in the field of research.

The cornerstone of the program which I shall present to the 1964 session of the Legislature is a comprehensive and coordinated plan for basic and applied research closely tied to the universities and colleges of this state. . . . Only through research can we in Mississippi channel effectively our human and natural resources into the mainstream of Twentieth Century agricultural, industrial and commercial development. How great or how limited will be the opportunities open to your children? How adequate will be the services properly provi-ded the people by their local and state governments? How much greater will be the contribution Mississippi will make to the productivity and strength of our nation and the free world? All of these things and many more, are determined by the degree of Mississippi's success or failure in the broad field of activity referred to as "economic development."

Knowledgeable Mississippians are well acquainted with this term, and are vitally interested in the activities it describes, for we have just experienced four years of dramatic economic expansion. In 1960, by overwhelming majorities, a progressive legislature armed our citizens with many new development tools. Governor Barnett has provided the leadership. A growing number of public and private development organizations, and many individual citizens, have labored diligently with increasing effectiveness.

Yes, our state's progress since 1960 has indeed been remarkable. But, as of this hour, it becomes the success of yesterday. I am here to talk with you about tomorrow. . . .

One of Mississippi's most widely recognized needs . . . one of the few remaining gaps in our outstanding economic development program . . . is the need to utilize research more effectively in our economic development work.

The Legislature, in 1962, recognized this need but, very wisely, concluded that a competent analysis of our research need—and sound recommendations for means to meet this need—should be in hand before any portion of Mississippi's limited financial resources was invested in additional research facilities and staff.

An organization of international reputation, Stanford Research Institute, was employed to make a study and to suggest a course of action for Mississippi. Stanford's great experience in building research and development programs for business and industry, as well as for states, federal agencies and foreign nations, was put to work for Mississippi. The institute's considerable prestige among national leaders in industry, finance and government undoubtedly will be an asset in gaining acceptance for Mississippi's new research effort.

A document containing Stanford's analysis and recommendations now is in the hands of every legislator. In my opinion, this document holds the power to lift Mississippi's economy like no other proposal I have ever seen or heard.

I would single out for emphasis here the very great importance of the Stanford concept of a Mississippi Research and Development Center. It is unlike anything in existence at this time in America. Stanford's economic development specialists say it "would be a pioneering effort in this country." I say it will be one more "first" for Mississippi, underlining our national leadership in state-level economic development programs.

The Mississippi Research and Development Center, with its electronic computer, its technical library, its extension services and its housing for development agencies, will be closely allied with our institutions of higher learning and with our state agencies; yet, it will not be under the control of any single institution or agency.

The Center's prime objectives are to conduct applied research for economic development and to coordinate the research programs of state agencies and our educational institutions so as to minimize wasteful duplication of effort and, thereby, to make more effective use of our existing research capabilities. . . .

Another widely recognized need lies in the field of vocational and technical training. In the past twelve months, considerable progress has been made toward establishing vocational and technical training programs; yet, the reality is that we have scarcely begun to face up to the challenge of this great need.

. . . Our young people must have available to them the training which will orient them toward industrial employment. We must enable them to acquire the technical skills and the specialized knowledge which will open to them the high-wage jobs in new fields of endeavor being spawned by the modern technological revolution.

In addition, Mississippi must arm its industrial development effort with the ability to recruit labor for incoming new industry and to custom-train these workers for the jobs created by the new plants. This aspect of the training program is needed both for the upgrading of skills and earning power of our existing labor force, and as an added inducement to industry to select a Mississippi location. A number of states which compete with Mississippi for industrial plants and other factors of economic growth already have operating programs of this type, and we must meet their competition.

I will propose for the Legislature's consideration a specific plan for the strengthening and expansion of vocational and technical training in our public junior colleges, and this plan will be coordinated with Mississippi's industrial development program.

The Mississippi Agricultural and Industrial Board is the state's economic development agency. It administers the development program. It also functions as the state's promotional agency, advertising our tourist attractions nationally and presenting Mississippi's advantages to the national business community through advertising in business publications and direct contact with industrial prospects.

The famous A and I Board truly is the backbone and the muscle of Mississippi's action program. The dollars appropriated to the use of this agency probably are the most productive dollars spent by the State of Mississippi. My proposals for the further utilization of the A and I Board's capacity to serve our economic development aims, with special emphasis on industry in small towns, will include a strong recommendation for a substantial increase in its appropriation.

Further in the field of economic development, we will recommend appropriations for specific research projects designed to make possible a major breakthrough in the attraction of heavy industry to Mississippi and the physical and promotional development of our vast tourist travel potential. . . .

Not only must we increase our efforts to sell Mississippi to the nation as a place to visit; we must also develop physically the "product" we offer the traveling public—our state parks and other recreational facilities, including organized hunting and fishing camps; our Gulf Coast resort area; our historic sites; the pilgrimages. . . .

Agriculture and forestry have been, are now and, for the foreseeable future, will remain the largest elements in the Mississippi economy. It can be said that modern farming and scientific forestry constitute the biggest business in Mississippi. And it is estimated that 45 per cent of the new industries and expansions recorded in the last four years are related directly or indirectly to agriculture and forestry. . . .

Market research and product development can reap for Mississippi a much greater return from agriculture and forestry. A forest product or wood utilization laboratory is sorely needed at this state.

Many, many times in the past seven months I have outlined my plans for a marketing council to oversee the research and action program in this field. I will propose for legislative consideration the creation of the Mississippi marketing Council. Improved diagnostic service for beef and dairy cattle, poultry and small animals would now undergird and strengthen this ever-growing and prosperous segment of our agricultural development.

My friends, ours is a state in transition . . . a region changing, rapidly now, from an economy dominated by agriculture to one characterized by balance among agriculture, industry and commerce. I judge this change to be desirable, to be in the best interest of all our people. During my service as your governor, it is my ambition to facilitate desirable change, to promote and further a healthy balance in our economy. From these thoughts came the label my administration's constructive proposals bear . . . the A I C Program . . . a program for the balanced and interrelated development of agriculture, industry and commerce . . . a program which has for its ultimate aim a better material existence for every citizen. In my pursuit of this, I ask you prayers for my guidance . . . and your active support for our common success.

In Mississippi, we have endured three political campaigns of a particularly bitter character in the past seven or eight months. By virtue of our political system, the opposing camps are now one . . . for the next four years. I would point out to you that the Mississippi economy is not divisible by political party or faction, or even by race, color or creed. As of this hour, Paul Johnson is working for everybody with every resource at his command.

In every challenging hour of state and national life, a leadership of frankness and moving strength has met with that understanding and support of the people themselves, which is essential to great accomplishment. I shall present this type of leadership.

I will say to you that you and I are part of this world, whether we like it or not; what happens in it, through no fault of ours, affects us. Too, we are Americans as well as Mississippians. As a practical matter, we are at this moment "in the mainstream of national life." National policies have direct bearing on our economy, on our political freedom, on our daily living, whether we like it or not.

I am convinced in my own heart that you will give solid and unremitting support in these critical but challenging days of our state and national life.

I want our people to know that Paul Johnson is fully aware of the forces, the conflicts that fashion our environment. Hate, or prejudice, or ignorance will not lead Mississippi while I sit in the Governor's chair. I will oppose with every fiber of my being, and with every resource at my command, any man, any faction, any party, or any authority which I feel is morally wrong or constitutionally in error . . . and I will stand accountable for my action; but, if I must fight, it will not be a rear-guard defense of yesterday . . . it will be an all out assault for our share of tomorrow.

In such a spirit on your part and mine, we face our common problems with a great truth and assurance . . . laid down in Biblical times: "Except God build the city, they labor in vain who build it."

Thank you; God bless you all.

CATFISH, 1980[2]

In October 1980, the Mississippi Department of Agriculture and Commerce distributed the following press release describing catfish production in Mississippi. At the time, the industrial catfish business in the state was approaching maturity.

Mississippi is the leading catfish producing State, accounting for 58 percent of the total acreage in the 10 States surveyed.[3] Mississippi growers accounted for 67 percent of the total sales and 69 percent of foodsize total sales. . . .

Growers in ten selected States sold 43.4 million pounds (live weight) of catfish during the period January 1–July 31, 1980, according to the Crop Reporting Board. Total value of sales was $33.8 million. Foodsize catfish comprised 93 of total sales weight followed by the fry/fingerling size group with 6 percent and broodfish the remaining 1 percent.

Foodsize catfish *sales* totaled 40.3 million pounds during January 1–July 31, 1980, with an average live weight of 1.12 pounds. Total value of sales was $28.6 million, averaging 71 cents per pound. Processors were the main *sales outlet*, receiving 78 percent of the total live weight. Mississippi, the leading State in foodsize catfish sales, comprised 69 percent of total sales. Foodsize catfish *inventory* totaled 63.9 million pounds as of August 1, 1980. Mississippi had the largest inventory with 42.5 million pounds, followed by Alabama with 11.2 million pounds.

Fry/fingerling catfish *sales* totaled 2.72 million pounds during January 1–July 31, 1980 with an average live weight of .042 pounds.

Total value of sales was $4.84 million, averaging $1.78 per pound. The primary *sales outlets* for fry/fingerlings were to producers of catfish, totaling 63 percent of the live weight sold. Fry/fingerling sales was led by Mississippi with 1.20 million pounds. *Inventory* of fry/fingerlings as of August 1, 1980, was 11.9 million pounds or 424 million fish.

Producers were utilizing 56,200 acres of water surface on August 1, 1980, and reported intentions to expand their operations by 16,1000 acres during 1981. States planning on the largest expansions are Mississippi, Alabama and Arkansas. The primary source of water supply for raising catfish was from wells, at 73 percent, followed by "rain and/or watershed" at 15 percent.[4]

CATFISH WORKERS ON STRIKE, 1981[5]

Juxtaposed to the glowing comparative figures that made Mississippi a leader in catfish production and processing, the following account of catfish workers on strike points to the harsh realities of labor in the industry. The article also suggests that a "modern" agri-business like catfish processing may be less humane and profitable to workers than chopping cotton.

Sweat pours down Virgie Pitts' face as she paces in the scorching Delta heat. It's another 100-degree day here in the "Catfish Capital of the World."

But unlike other hot summer days of years past in Humphreys County, on this recent day there were five black women walking a picket line.

Virgie Pitts pauses, wipes her brow and begins to talk in a soft, hesitant voice. "I've never felt so good. One day we'll get what we deserve. If not for me, then for those that will come later."

Miss Pitts is one of 108 black, mostly women, employees at the Welfed Catfish Co.,'s processing plant who have been on strike since April 22. Before the strike, the plant had 144 non-supervisory workers—all of them black.

The issue is a familiar one in Mississippi. The company won't collectively bargain with the employee's union, despite an order to do so by the National Labor Relations Board.

To Miss Pitts, the issue seems simple. "We won an honest election. At least I always thought the majority wins. The bossman won't even sit down with us. It just doesn't seem fair."

The National Labor Relations Board, through its Memphis, Tenn., and Washington offices, agrees. . . .

In its decision of March 25 this year, the NLRB in Washington found that Welfed, by its refusal to bargain with the United Food Commercial Workers Union, had "interfered with, restrained and coerced . . . employees in the exercise of their rights." The ruling concluded that the company "is engaging in unfair labor practices" and ordered Welfed to bargain with the union. . . .

The dispute [between the union and the company] stems from a union certification election held June 27, 1980, at the Welfed plant. In the election, which was supervised by the NLRB, the Welfed employees voted 90 to 41 for collective bargaining representation by the United Food and Commercial Workers Union.

The employees had asked the union to help them organize because of frustration with Welfed's pay scale, lack of employee benefits and working conditions.

Their complaints included:

• Pay at the minimum wage regardless of job seniority. A few jobs pay 10 to 20 cents per hour more than the legal minimum.
• Not being paid for the hours spent waiting at the plant for fish to arrive for processing. Workers say they are told to clock out while there are no fish, which has been 1 to 3 hours a day.
• Receiving no fringe benefits. Employees didn't get sick pay, health insurance, a retirement plan, paid holidays or vacations from Welfed Catfish.
• Working conditions the employees feel were unsafe. They said it is a common occurrence for workers to suffer serious cuts. Several employees have lost parts of fingers or need skin grafts on their arms.

Most employees who work near the dry ice packing area say that the carbon dioxide smoke emitted by the thawing dry ice has affected their breathing on several occasions. Some of the older employees said that after working all day when the smoke was thick they have had trouble breathing at night.

Miss Pitts is one of the workers who have been injured on the job. She has a long, thick scar that covers most of her forearm. In June 1980, she was working a scraper when her arm was caught in a machine and ten inches of her skin was torn off.

"It happened so quick. I was skinning a fish. I looked down and the skin was off my arm. I don't remember anything else. They took me to the hospital and I was out of work for seven weeks. All I got was $214 in workman's compensation." Miss Pitts lets out a deep breath, then adds, "And this scar."

After discussing unionization informally among themselves, several employees got in touch with Local 1224 of the United Food and Commercial Workers Union. The local is based in Jackson and is responsible for the entire state. After meeting with representatives of the union, authorization cards were distributed among the employees.

To get authority to hold an NLRB certification election, the union had to get 44 of the 144 non-supervisory employees to sign cards. Within two days of initial distribution, 108 cards had been signed.

"Most everyone wanted a union," said Florida Jones, one of the employees who gathered signatures. "We don't get paid enough for one person to live. Some weeks we've taken home $50 or $60. How is someone supposed to support a family on that. If they didn't treat us like dirt, we wouldn't need a union." . . .

When Welfed informed the union on April 16 that it was going to continue to contest the NLRB order to bargain, the union set a strike date of April 22.

On the morning of April 22, the first day of the strike, 8 of the 144 workers in the bargaining group crossed the strikers' picket line and went to work.

Since the strike started, Welfed has hired non-union labor in an effort to maintain production levels. Welfed said it is operating at levels close to normal production. . . .

"These scabs (non-union workers) are taking twice as long to process the fish as our people would. It takes time to train them and most of them don't stay on the job long," Jones alleged. "And you know that fancy law firm (representing the company) is costing them a pretty penny."

By striking, the United Food and Commercial Workers union hopes to apply enough economic pressure on Welfed Catfish to force it to the bargaining table. . . .

After more than 15 weeks on the picket line, with no end in sight, frustration among the strikers is growing. Despite union assurances of eventual victory in the 5th Circuit Court of Appeals, many are feeling impatient.

"I don't know what kind of strike it is when the company is still operating," said Frank Moore, a 19-year old United Food and Commercial Workers Union member. "I wish there were some way of knowing if we were making progress."

Despite the hardships and frustration, striker Ruth Nalls, a mother of 8, viewed the strike as a positive experience.

"It's like a training school where we're learning to be good union members. The strike is showing us that we have to help each other and care for each other if we're ever to get anywhere." . . .

The striking employees are finding various ways to spend the extra time on their hands.

Betty Hobson has been fishing "most every day" during the strike. Ms. Hobson said she won't go back to work at Welfed until conditions change.

"I figure Welfed is doing me a favor. I'd rather be fishing, myself, than work inside their smelly factory."

Some strikers have temporary jobs. Others have searched for jobs and found none. Most of the work that is available to blacks in Humphreys County is in the cotton fields, as day laborers.

For the first time in 15 years, Miss Pitts is chopping cotton. The last time she did this work, she was 8 to 15 years old and making 20 to 30 cents an hour. Now there is a minimum wage of $3.35 per hour which applies to field workers and that is what she is being paid.

"I never thought I'd be chopping cotton again," said Miss Pitts, during a rest break in the fields. "Not that I mind it too much, I like to work. I'm making as much or more than I did at Welfed. Besides, I ain't never going back there unless we get a union."

"All we're doing is trying to better ourselves."

ADVERTISING MISSISSIPPI, 1987[6]

In 1987, Jerry McDonald, Executive Director of the Department of Economic Development, unveiled a $1 million advertising campaign funded by a Special Session of the legislature. The campaign, titled "Mississippi . . . More than a river," involved the design of four advertisements, three of which appear below. The advertisements appeared in airline magazines, national and regional business publications, travel magazines, and on airport displays in major cities from Dallas and Minneapolis to New York and Atlanta.

"We're on a Collision Course with History"

The following advertisement, and indeed two of the others, mention Mississippi's technological advancement. The emphasis on technology served two purposes in the 1987 advertising campaign. References to technological advancement were intended to appeal to high-tech industries and also re-enforce Mississippi's desire to become home to the Superconducting Super Collider that the Federal government was then proposing to finance.

One of nature's oldest assets makes Mississippi the perfect location for America's newest high-tech quantum leap.

The Superconducting Super Collider will be the world's most powerful atom smasher, a surgically precise tool for unlocking the most intimate secrets of matter itself.

Mississippi is a prime site for the SSC. For good reason. Our Selma chalk formation exceeds all geological requirements for construction of the super collider. But, while the right foundation is essential, what we've built here in Mississippi is equally important.

We're talking about a tradition of technological leadership.

Mississippi is home to NASA's National Space Technology Laboratory, the National Center for Physical Acoustics and the Institute for Technology Development, as well as our own Technology Transfer Center. Our universities are leading the way in biomedical research, polymer sciences, and microelectronics design.

Our commitment to technology and education makes Mississippi an obvious choice for the historic SSC program. Our significant geological superiority makes the choice a natural.

We're in the right place. With the right stuff.

We'd like to tell you more about our past, our future, and what we can do for you now.

"Our Idea of a Super Highway is all Wet"

One of the advertisements unveiled in the 1987 "Mississippi . . . More than a river" campaign touted to industries the benefits of the Tennessee–Tombigbee Waterway, which through a series of locks and damns connected the two rivers, effectively providing a "super highway" between the midwest and Mobile.

The Mississippi River has always been America's central highway of commerce. It's served the country so well as an outlet to the Gulf of Mexico and the world that we've built another.

The Tennessee–Tombigbee Waterway can't compare with Ol' Man River in size or in fame, but it's cut a new path to the sea for the people of America's heartland. The cost of transport to and from the country's core regions is lower now. And the Tenn–Tom is bringing millions upon millions of dollars of new trade and industry to Mississippi.

We have some other good ideas about transportation.

For example, we're spending $1.5 billion to improve and extend our highway system. We're constantly expanding our deep water and inland ports. Our rail and air transport facilities are busier than ever. And we're taking full advantage of a location that places major markets and a growing population in the tens of millions within a 500 mile radius.

The Mississippi River and the Gulf give us a natural edge in transportation. But our commitment to innovative projects like the Tenn–Tom—and American's new technology breath, the Superconducting Super Collider—shows that Mississippi's not just sitting at home waiting for the world to knock at our door.

We're opening the door, creating new opportunities, and stepping out into the future.

We'd like to tell you more about where we've been, where we're going, and what we can do for you now.

"Others May Teach Physiology, But We Wrote the Book"

The following advertisement, which also constituted part of the "Mississippi . . . More than a river" campaign, like the previous one, uses one text (in this case education reform) to drive home the point that Mississippi was ready to become home to the Superconducting Super Collider.

Arthur Guyton is a teacher who has students he's never seen.

One of American's leading physicians, Doctor Guyton wrote the standard text on physiology used in medical schools around the world. His own classroom is in Jackson, Mississippi, at the University of Mississippi Medical Center.

Doctor Guyton is just one of Mississippi's great educators. The fact, is our commitment to education is as strong as our determination to meet the future on more than equal terms.

Our Educational Reform Act of 1982 set new standards for students, teachers and administrators. We're already seeing the results at every level. And other states are following our lead. But that's nothing new. We established the nation's first network of junior colleges. And we're installing a supercomputer that will move our universities to the forefront of research.

Our new educational system gives Mississippians a significant advantage in the competition of ideas, information and innovation. That's one big reason why we're a prime candidate for America's next high-tech masterpiece—the Superconducting Super Collider.

It's also a big reason why more and more exceptional leaders, like Doctor Arthur Guyton, are finding the perfect climate for intellectual growth among the tall pines and rolling hills of Mississippi.

We'd like to tell you more about our achievements, our prospects, and what we can do for you now.

CASINO GAMBLING IN NESHOBA COUNTY[7]

In 1990, the Mississippi state legislature passed a bill allowing river boat gambling in Mississippi. The law was touted as a prize in the state campaign for economic development. After the first casino opened in August 1992, other casinos rapidly followed. The following editorial, published in the *Mississippian* (the student newspaper at the University of Mississippi) uses history to argue that the Choctaw should be allowed to operate a casino.

Today is the last day of a restraining order issued last month preventing casino gambling on Mississippi Choctaw land. The issue has been controversial, at times pitting Governor Fordice against the Choctaw chief, at times dividing the Choctaw themselves. Ultimately the decision must be a Choctaw one, however, especially since it will be primarily the Choctaw who suffer the consequences of either path.

Like most nations of the Southeast, the Choctaw are certainly no stranger to lengthy deliberation. The wisdom of this tradition has proved itself time and time again, while hasty individual action has too often led to disaster. This lesson has only become more apparent since the Choctaw discovered European societies . . .

First of all, neither the English nor the French seemed to understand, or to care, that the Choctaw had their own style of government. The Europeans expected to see clear positions of leadership and blind allegiance to authority, as in their own cultures. Leadership in the loose Choctaw confederacy, however, depended upon earning the respect and trust of one's village, perhaps a few surrounding villages, or (rarely) one of the large divisions of the Choctaw Nation. In order to remain in leadership, a Choctaw had to continually demonstrate skill in council, organization or warfare.

Such an informal arrangement was apparently beneath the French, who designated "medal chiefs" and dealt with them as if they were in charge, and beneath the English, who designated their own "medal chiefs." These men often had little actual influence among the Choctaw, which is in itself a recipe for confusion.

The problem was that some of the Choctaw wanted to trade with the English in the North, some with the French to the South . . . They each demanded exclusive contracts with the Choctaw as a whole. Furthermore, . . . European disregard for Choctaw conceptions of crime and punishment pushed the Choctaw to fight among themselves. . . .

As Choctaw experience with European imperialism nears its fifth century, the situation now facing them with regard to casino gambling is little different. Their original economy has been destroyed by European encroachments, leaving them with a grinding poverty found on all reservations to this day. Choctaw per capita income is slightly higher than that of African-Americans in Mississippi . . . only because of a 1960's campaign for "Choctaw Self-Determination."

"This effort paid off in 1979," observes [Eagle] Walking Turtle, "when, under the aegis of Chief Phillip Martin, the first tribal enterprise opened its doors." Others followed, but Choctaw income still hovers around half that of white Mississippians. It is for this reason that Chief Martin argues that casino gambling is needed. The attorney for the opposition, however, argues that "most of the benefits are illusions," because the management of this particular enterprise will be non-Choctaw. (A Las Vegas corporation wants to lend the Choctaw the money to build a casino in exchange for a seven-year management contract, but the Choctaw have reasons to be wary of such loaning: it was one of the primary means of coercion, along with threat of force, employed by the U.S. government to deprive them of their land.)

"Does it benefit the Choctaw people to get some more jobs sweeping floors and washing dishes," asks the opposition attorney, "while their children are exposed to gambling, corruption, prostitution . . . ?"

Certainly there is non-Choctaw convenience on both sides of the gambling question. If the Choctaw take the contract, it means profit for the Las Vegas corporation. If the Choctaw reject the contract, it means less competition for non-Choctaw river boat gambling. On top of all this, the federal government requires the Choctaw to obtain an agreement with Governor Fordice, who is anti-gambling and at first refused, before accepting the Las Vegas contract. This law is yet another affront to Choctaw self-determination, compounding the economic threat.

Fordice finally relented last year, but the internal argument has continued, resulting in the recent court order to delay the contract until Choctaw tribal member Brantley Willis can be heard. Today marks the end of this order.

From Las Vegas, Washington, or Jackson, external interests still try to worm their way into Choctaw lives. Nowadays the exploitation is more subtle, but the consequences are just [as] severe. The Choctaw are still fighting for their lives and dignity. The proper role for non-Choctaw is listening and learning.

SHEP MONTGOMERY, 1994[8]

Writing in the *Mississippi Business Journal*, Shep Montgomery points out that while casino gambling carried the weight of Mississippi's economic development in the early 1990s the boom was certain to burst at some point.

While Mississippi's record-breaking economic indicators showed the stellar effects of casino gambling during 1993, moderate performance in other sectors of the economy could be a precursor of what the state's economy would look like after the casino boom subsides.

For the past year, most of the national stories on Mississippi's growing economy have been glowing. The state was rated by U.S. News and World Report as the fastest-growing state to emerge from the 1990–1993 recession. In addition, the Fordice Administration recently was praised by the Wall Street Journal as one of three governors in the nation to receive A's for exercising superior fiscal responsibility.

By nearly all accounts, 1993 was a banner economic year for Mississippi, according to Southeast State Indicators, a quarterly forecast of economic conditions published in December 1993 . . . Last year, the state showed strong economic indicators and measures of competitiveness all around, including:

- employment gains ranking the fourth highest in the nation;
- a rebound in corporate income tax rates for the first time in five quarters;
- increases in hours worked, a fall in unemployment income, and the lowest insured unemployment rate in a decade;
- a reversal of a four-year slide in the state's finance, banking, and insurance industries;
- an 11 percent increase in construction.

All told, the growth in the gross state product expanded a strong 5.5. percent during 1993, well above estimates made during the same period . . .

News of personal income growth has been heralded by state economic development officials as a reliable indicator of what has actually occurred in the economy, since it measures the increase in the amount of money in the average Mississippian's pocket. . . .

Growth in personal income has been accompanied by a corresponding increase in retail activity in nearly every county of the state. . . .

Casino gambling accounted for the vast majority of employment gains that Mississippi experienced during 1993—gains which overshadowed improvements in the state's manufacturing sector.

That observation begs the question of whether Mississippi will be able to continue to maintain its upward spiral of economic performance—an era of performance not seen since the 1970s when factories began to move into the state from the North—and keep pace with other recovering states, economic forecasters say.

"If you take out gaming, there has definitely been an upturn in the state's economy, but it's not that much in advance of the rest of the country," [Mary Ann] Hill [an economic forecaster with the state Institution of Higher Learning's Center for Policy Research and Planning] said.

Some economists have warned that unless additional tax revenues generated by the booming casino gambling are plowed back into the economy to aid development or build infrastructure, that Mississippi could return to the annual 2 percent rates of economic growth that dominated during the 1980s.

For instance, durable manufacturing rolls remained unchanged throughout 1993, while furniture manufacturing, and nondurables showed weaknesses. . . .

State economic forecast estimates show that almost half of the decrease in unemployment during the last year has been due to the gaming industry, while manufacturing employment has stagnated. . . .

The future of manufacturing should be a continuation of national trends, specifically the creation of more low-skill, low-paying jobs. . . .

Some declines in manufacturing soon may be offset by rising wages prompted by a rising rate of inflation in the South that is outpacing increases in the other parts of the country. . . .

But even the much-heralded increase in personal income isn't likely to continue steadily because of consumer debt cycles that have repeated themselves during the past couple of years, some economic forecasters predict . . . .

For her own part, Hill is predicting that Mississippi won't lead the . . . national economic recovery and growth trends next year. . . .

Chapter 15

BATTLE OVER THE FLAG

Despite the economic, social, and political changes that have occurred between 1964 and today, Mississippi's reputation as a backward and benighted place has remained intact. Hollywood producers and writers, whose conceptions of Mississippi were often formed during the Civil Rights Movement, have perpetuated stereotypes of the state. Major movie releases, even those set in contemporary Mississippi, frequently portray the state as one occupied only by white racists and passive black victims; all are poorly educated and slow talkers. Too often, in Hollywood's imagination, Mississippi roads are graveled, and air conditioned facilities are few and far between. Popular culture has grasped features of Mississippi's past and refused to relinquish them. Unfortunately, as events in 2000 and 2001 plainly illustrated, Mississippians have done too little to alter the persisting image of the state as a reactionary backwater in the nation.

In early 2000, Governor Ronnie Musgrove asked the state legislature to remove the Confederate battle flag from the state flag. Fearful that doing so would provoke a firestorm of protest, the legislature and governor appointed a state flag commission to make a recommendation to the legislature about the state flag. The commission, headed by former Governor William Winter, traveled across the state holding public meetings at which citizens could voice their opinions about the state flag. Some Mississippians wanted the flag changed; others did not. Juxtaposing the rhetoric of proponents of a new flag and proponents of the 1894 flag brings to light the two Mississippis that emerged in the late twentieth century: one Mississippi refused to relinquish the ideas of previous generations; the other was ready to discard references to and symbols of the slavery and the Civil War. After heated public debate, the flag commission offered an alternative state flag, and the legislature voted to permit a popular referendum on the two designs. Results of the April 2001 referendum were one-sided, as 67 percent of citizens casting ballots chose the old flag design, which featured the Confederate battle flag. The debate over the flag, both before and after the referendum, reveals much about the image of Mississippi and identity of Mississippians from many points of view, including the points of view of blacks, whites, business owners, religious leaders, and non-residents.

MR. JONES, 2000[1]

At the October 19, 2000 public hearing conducted by the State Flag Commission in Tupelo, a middle-aged, white male identified as Mr. Jones made a passionate plea to remove the Confederate emblem from the state flag.

I recommend that Mississippi change the state flag to better represent the citizens of our state. [Scattered applause] The Confederate battle flag should no longer be displayed to represent Mississippi. Mississippi has advanced past the issues for which the stars and bars stood. Keeping a symbol of a war to dismantle the United States of America and perpetuate slavery is detrimental to our state [READ YOUR HISTORY] and to our people. [UNINTELLIGIBLE DISRUPTIONS FROM THE AUDIENCE]

WILLIAM WINTER: Let's give Mr. Jones the same courtesy we have given everyone else.

MR. JONES: I have not said a word while ya'll have spoken. We must realize that the flag is hurtful to some of our citizens; it is offensive to some of my Afro-American friends. [WHY ARE YOU SPEAKING UP FOR AFRO-AMERICAN PEOPLE?] It is therefore offensive to me. We must know *we* allowed the Confederate flag to become a symbol of hate. We stood by and let the K. K. K., White Citizens Council, and the Aryan nation use the flag to represent their beliefs. I'm ashamed to say I saw no meetings as this. I saw no letters to the editor. I saw no commission appointed to stop the desecration of the flag then. [DID YOU WRITE ANY?] We had our chance. We failed. Now, like it or not, 90 percent of the people in the United States who see the Confederate flag displayed will think that person is a racist. If . . . [catcalls interrupt]. We cannot wish to portray that [WHERE'D YOU GET THEM FIGURES?] for a state or a people. Thank you.

AN AFRICAN-AMERICAN FEMALE, 2000[2]

The State Flag Commission held a public hearing on November 13, 2000 in Jackson. A young black woman made the following comments.

During the Civil Rights Movement, the southern cross was overwhelmingly used to symbolize defiance of equal rights. Profanities were shouted as the Confederate cross was proudly waved when black children tried to integrate white schools. The Confederate cross was proudly waved as the statement "Segregation Now and Segregation Forever" echoed through the south. The truth must be faced. A flag can mean more than one thing. The same flag that represents heritage to one group can represent the institution of slavery and segregation to another. On this issue, Senator John McCain [of Arizona] said, "My ancestors fought for the Confederacy. But I don't believe their service needs to be commemorated in a way that offends people whose ancestors were once denied their freedom by mine." In conclusion, I would like to ask you to imagine you were an eight-year old girl in Crystal Springs, Mississippi in 1962. Your father, a Methodist minister, is one of the few black citizens to fight inequality, as he helps F.B.I. agents investigate the murder of a black man for looking at a white women. Your family is constantly harassed. There are obscene phone calls, burned crosses, and white men who drive by while waving the southern cross. Imagine the fear and hopelessness, that surrounds you as you wonder if your father will be the next to be murdered. Now, almost forty years later that eight year old girl, my mother, is a citizen of the state of Mississippi. Today, she sees a flag with the same confederate cross that haunted her before flying over the state capital. Is it pride that she feels? Or is it the same fear she felt so long ago? Does she feel that the flag truly represents her as a Mississippian or a time when she was inferior by law. Again, Mississippi is this the heritage you are proud of?

AFRICAN-AMERICAN FEMALE, 2000[3]

On November 9, 2000, a middle-aged, black woman addressed the State Flag Commission at its Gulfport public hearing. Like many others who advocated one position or another on the removal of the Confederate battle flag from the state flag, she couched her address in personal terms.

I grew up here on the Mississippi Gulf Coast. I was one of the kids who was the first children in integration. The flag was always there as a reminder that we were not wanted there—football games, pep rallies. Whenever anything went down that was bad it would have something to do with that flag. All of those are reasons enough for me not to want it; however, the most important reason for the state of Mississippi not to have the Confederate battle flag on the state flag is because it is the flag of the enemy of the United States of America. It would no more be justified to have a swastika on our state flag. It is the enemy of the United States of America. Until that symbol of the division of America is removed, we will not be one nation under God.

JIMMY REED, 2001[4]

Jimmy Reed was a resident of Oxford. In his letter to the editor of the Jackson *Clarion Ledger*, Mr. Reed denounced efforts to eliminate the Confederate battle flag from the state flag. His letter was written largely in response to the endorsement of a new state flag by the Mississippi Religious Leadership Conference.

The members of Mississippi Religious Leadership Conference who view the state flag as a symbol of racism are hypocrites.

Will they speak out against Kwanzaa now being celebrated? Kwanzaa celebrates heritage passed down from a continent where the worst forms of racism—slavery, genocide, female genital mutilation—are still being practiced.

Whatever connection the flag had with slavery in this country, if any, was broken forever at Appomattox. No true Southerner who cherishes this flag believes it connotes any notions of slavery.

If these ministers want to strike a blow in the name of human rights, they should blow their holier-than-thou hot air in a direction where it might do some good for the entire human race.

Their desire to see the flag changed will only satisfy a bunch of spoiled brats while widening the gap between those of us with strong emotional attachment to a symbol that has nothing whatsoever to do with racism in the 21st century and those same spoiled brats, who, given an inch, will take a mile.

WILLIAM K. SCARBOROUGH, 2001[5]

William K. Scarborough was a professor of history at the University of Southern Mississippi. Like other Mississippians who wished to preserve the old state flag, Scarborough relished the idea that the issue would be put to a popular vote, but he doubted that the attack on Confederate symbols would cease.

Now that the flag commission has made its recommendation [to allow Mississippians to vote on a state flag], the battle has been joined. Judging by your recent editorials and your series on the flag debate in South Carolina, you now view the contest as a moral crusade—one of right versus wrong, good versus evil, righteousness versus bigotry.

Those who support the current flag are labeled "extremists" and the new flag is seen as the certain path to peace, harmony and racial reconciliation. Presumably, a change in the state flag will eliminate poverty, crime, the disintegration of families, a substandard education and will usher in a veritable utopia for all Mississippians.

I submit to you that the true "extremists" are those who seek to equate the Confederacy with Nazi Germany, slavery with the Holocaust and the Confederate battle flag with the swastika and that the adoption of a new flag is not likely to promote racial reconciliation if a majority of the population is opposed to the change.

Despite your protestations that a referendum on the issue would get "divisive" (as if all elections were not potentially divisive), it now appears that the people will be permitted to vote on a state flag.

If that vote is for a new design, I will accept the verdict of the electorate. Will you do the same?

Or will you continue to act as the mouthpiece of the NAACP and continue to agitate for a change in the banner that has represented this state for 106 years?

We shall see whether you truly believe in democracy or whether you support it only when the vote turns out the way you want it to.

DAVID BOWEN, 2001[6]

David Bowen, a resident of Jackson and former Democratic Congressman, published the following essay in the Jackson *Clarion Ledger*. In the essay, he, like Jimmy Reed, challenges the arguments advanced by proponents of a new flag.

The great flag fight is now upon us. You may be like me, with friends on both sides and undecided at this point.

One thing is abundantly clear: The acrimony involved in a statewide referendum will do more harm to Mississippi than any flag would.

State legislators, understandably, will not spare us this ordeal by falling on their swords and adopting a new flag. If you want a legislative resolution, you will get the flag we have had since 1894.

The task of the flag commission would have been easier had they recommended a more attractive design. The blue-white-blue stripes and clump of stars in the union corner with a fat one in the middle does not pass muster on aesthetic or historic grounds. But perhaps the state Legislature will improve on it before the referendum.

As an alternative, why not the red, white and blue stripes of the present flag and a circle of stars in the corner, perhaps thirteen, as in our flag and in the Revolutionary U.S. flag?: Or what about the famous Magnolia Tree Flag of the Republic of Mississippi?

Either one would be better-grounded historically and would avoid the dreaded St. Andrew's Cross, which many of our fellow Mississippians say they find "racially divisive."

That design, more accurately the Beauregard Battle Flag, is certainly one of the world's most beautiful flags, but I fully understand why some of our black citizens do not care for it, namely, as they often point out, because some very nasty people like to wave it and display it on their pick-up trucks.

That argument for a new flag has one serious flaw. What if the KKK and other assorted nasties decide—just to embarrass us—to embrace the new flag and wave it at their rallies? Then we would be forced to abandon that flag and adopt yet another new one.

Another point made by the champions of a new flag is that we should all be prepared to make compromises for the good of the state.

That is a splendid idea. But the question it raises from the majority of our population who are being asked to give up a flag they love is, what will the other side sacrifice as their part of the compromise?

One truly excellent response would be for a group of black leaders to meet and declare they are willing to give up something which is not just a symbol of disunity, as they describe the flag, but the embodiment of racial disunity, discord and discrimination.

That is the morally and constitutionally bankrupt system of racial preferences euphemistically known as affirmative action.

As we are now often reminded, a symbol which so many Mississippians find offensive is incompatible with progress. And nothing is more offensive and inimical to racial reconciliation than a system which continues in new form the discredited racial discrimination of the past.

Such an enlightened gesture would draw tourists, conventions and new industries to our state.

There might well be other good-will concessions contributing to racial progress and supportive of the rich diversity of our state. Let us not place limits on good works.

We await these words of encouragement from the champions of a new flag.

PHIL HARDWICK, 2001[7]

Phil Hardwick is a contributing columnist to the *Mississippi Business Journal*. His article, which is cast as a dialogue between two old friends, advocates the removal of the Confederate banner from the state flag.

Once again we find Fred and Red at the Main Street coffee shop discussing issues of the day and other serious matters, such as whether the unseasonably warm weather will last through the weekend.

Fred: I see you've installed one of those banner flagpoles on your house.

Red: I've been meaning to do that a long time. Last Veterans Day I looked around, and all my neighbors had those little flag banners stinking out from their houses or sprouting from trees in their front yards. One neighbor has his son's high school banner, another has one with an acorn on it, and the lady across the street has a big yellow one with a tennis racket on it. I decided it was time for me to show off what I believed in.

Fred: So you went and bought an American flag kit?

Red: More or less. That big appliance store was giving them away with the purchase of a new big screen TV. I needed a new TV. Figured I might as well kill two birds with one stone.

Fred: But you aren't flying the American flag? You're flying the Mississippi flag?

Red: Now there you go Fred, showing your ignorance again. Pass some of that artificial sweetener this way, please sir.

Fred: You have managed to confuse me this morning, Red. I thought you said that Veterans Day brought out the American in you, so you went and got an American flag. Now you are flying a Mississippi flag.

Red: The weather has got your ears messed up. I didn't say that at all. I said that on Veterans Day I got to thinking about getting a flag. The appliance store gave me a choice—an American flag or what used to be the Mississippi flag. According to the Mississippi Supreme Court, Mississippi does not have a flag. So, let's just refer to it as the "Flag Formerly Known as the State Flag of Mississippi."

Fred: I haven't seen you this emotional about something in a long time.

Red: This flag thing did it. Not only am I flying the "flag formerly known as the State Flag of Mississippi" on my house, I am sporting a new bumper sticker on my pickup that says, "Preserve Mississippi's Heritage." It's time to take a stand on this issue.

Fred: Good for you. People should stand up for what they believe in.

Red: That's right. Do you want a bumper sticker? I've got a half dozen of them.

Fred: No thanks.

Red: Why not? Your grandfather fought at Vicksburg. You're a bona fide ancestor of a Confederate veteran. Aren't you proud of your heritage? And shouldn't people stand up for what they believe in, like you just said?

Fred: I'm very proud of my heritage and I love Mississippi. But I'm not going to put one of those bumper stickers on my vehicle. And I'm a descendent of a Confederate veteran, not an ancestor.

Red: Whatever.

Fred: This flag thing is really getting some people riled up, isn't it?

Red: Man, you are not kidding. People are tired of having things shoved down their throats. This is one time we can make a stand.

Fred: Some people might say that the old Mississippi flag was shoved down their throats.

Red: Well then they can just vote for a new one, if and when we have a vote that's going to cost $3 million. Ask the server to bring us some more coffee, will you?

Fred: I applaud you for standing up for what you believe in. You obviously have strong feelings about it.

Red: (standing up) Oh my gosh, look at the time. I told the wife I would bring home some butter. She's baking a cake for the church bazaar tonight. I better get going. Now, you are going to vote, aren't you?

Fred: Of course.

Red: Good. I'm glad we're finally having freedom of choice. Isn't that what everybody wanted—freedom of choice?

Fred: Um hmm.

Red: Well, tell everybody to vote for "The Flag Formerly Known as the State Flag of Mississippi." And tell them to call me if they need a bumper sticker.

Fred: I'm not voting for the "Flag Formerly Known as the State Flag of Mississippi."

Red: (sitting back down and leaning forward) My gosh, Fred. Don't say that so loud. Somebody might hear you. Are you feeling okay?

Fred: I feel fine. It's just that if more people vote for "The Flag Formerly Known as the State flag of Mississippi" then we will be worse off than we are now.

Red: What in the devil's name are you talking about? The best flag wins. Whichever one. And that will be it.

Fred: I'm afraid not, Red. If the old flag wins then I fear we will see people filing lawsuits, marching in the streets, telling others not to have their conventions in Mississippi, and talking on national television about how we can't get away from our racially-troubled past. Not only that, some people say that economic development will be hurt. How do you think some company is going to feel if they announce a new plant in Mississippi, then get a visit to their annual stockholders' meeting by some group wanting to boycott Mississippi?

Red: That's a scare tactic, and you know it, Fred. What we have here is pure and simple—some people want one flag and some people don't want it. An election by the people is the way to decide it, and the vote is final. Loser goes home.

Fred: So you think this is all about choice?

Red: Absolutely. Nothing more. Nothing less.

Fred: Sorry, Red. This isn't about choice.

Red: So, what's it about?

Fred: It's about peace.

WALLY NORTHWAY, 2000[8]

Wally Northway was a staff writer for the *Mississippi Business Journal*. Although sympathetic to the effort to removal the Confederate emblem from the state flag, he is not willing to surrender his love for the Civil War or relinquish his admiration for his relatives who fought for the Confederacy.

Recently there was a scathing piece in the newspapers by a syndicated columnist in which he, writing on the South Carolina flag controversy, essentially called Confederate soldiers murderous traitors who slaughtered thousands of Americans. The columnist, an African-American, made the analogy that flying an emblem containing the Confederate flag over South Carolina was like flying the Vietnamese flag over Washington, D.C.

The column was full of rather shoddy history work. It wasn't thought through very well. It was less fact and much more emotion. But that's understandable. The flag controversy is an emotional issue. We're emotional creatures. And, most importantly, symbols are based on emotion—they bring out feelings. In fact, symbols are feelings. Without passion, symbols are impotent.

I grew up in the 1960s, and began forming my views on race in the early 1970s. I was there when "Black Power" first emerged. In a movement that had many symbols, none to me was more powerful, nor intimidating, as the raised, clenched fists of the black community. Part of my discomfort was that I knew it excluded me—kind of like standing outside a party without an invitation. But there was something ominous about the clenched fist. It made me think of potential violence. It would have been naive of me then, even as a boy, to think that there was not at least one in the African-American community, who, when they raised their fist, meant it militantly and at least privately held the wish that white America would crumble—maybe die. I found that a teeny bit unnerving.

Yet, I had black friends, folks I knew and trusted, who used the symbol every day. They used it as a form of greeting, even to me. I felt comfortable enough to return the gesture, raising catcalls and laughs. There was no offense meant; there was none taken.

Why? Just the other day I was talking about the flag controversy with a friend when he made a profound point: We empower symbols. A symbol is just an object until made animate by our feelings and emotions. That would explain why the clenched fist was both uncomfortable and non-threatening to me at different times. It depended on who was displaying it. It depended on if I knew them. It depended on what I felt was in their heart. In the end, as interpreter of the symbol, it was I who was giving the black fist power or not. I created the symbol, not the black community. A raised fist meant nothing at all to me unless I applied some emotion and passion and transformed it into something real and disconcerting.

Obviously to the columnist and many other Americans, the Confederate flag stands for murder, treachery, inhumane treatment, dissolution, despair, fear, anger. I more than understand that. And I sympathize.

I wish the Confederate flag wasn't over South Carolina, Mississippi or any place. Moreover, I wish all symbols that offended anybody, anywhere, could forever be removed from sight and existence. That seems impossible. But maybe not.

If we were to all turn a blind heart to those potentially hurtful symbols, control our emotions and not paint with a broad brush those who, due to whatever motivation, continue to cling to that object-would-be-symbol, those emblems would disappear.

"I never have believed in the institution of slavery. This is truly a dark hour."

Those words were written by Walter Ranson during the winter of 1864 as the Civil War raged. Ranson was a Southerner. Indeed, he was a Confederate officer that served under Generals "Stonewall" Jackson and Robert E. Lee. And he was my great-great grandfather, and I'm proud of it. In his Civil War diary that covers half the war, he never made a racial slur, held a loathing for slavery and saw himself as a defender of his home, not humiliating servitude.

Is my forefather a heroic or regrettable figure (a.k.a., symbol)? That's up to interpretation. Is my response to that columnist's piece riddled with emotion because he made indirect reference to my great-great grandfather? Absolutely. I can't help it. And I would guess that columnist's emotions over the flag issue are just as strong and just as hard to control.

As far as the flag goes, I feel no affinity for the Confederate banner. I don't feel a rush of pride when I see it wave or plastered over the rear window of a pickup truck. It doesn't mean anything to me. Do what you want with the flag, I'll help lower it, but leave my great-great grandfather out of it.

I'm an avid reader of the Civil War. I find it fascinating. By the same token, I'll be the first to say that there has never been a darker, more senseless hour in our nation's history. Casualties amounted to hundreds of thousands—more than a million for sure if you include "traitorous" Confederate losses. And it proved absolutely nothing.

Yes, the emancipation of the slaves was achieved, but freed to what? From the shackles of slavery straight into a pit of hopelessness which took another 100 years to surmount, and only after more bloodshed and terror. Thus, the only thing the Confederate flag can ever mean to me is "meaninglessness."

Mississippi writer Shelby Foote once said that the United States was founded on compromise. The Civil War was the result of Americans not reaching compromise. The war divided Americans. And in some very regrettable ways, it still divides some of us.

The only flag that has ever meant anything at all to me is the good ol' Stars and Stripes. It's the only one to which I've ever pledged my allegiance. And it's the only one that stirs feelings—pride, devotion. To me, it is a symbol of individual freedom—for everybody—something the Confederate flag never will.

GREGORY KANE, 2001[9]

Gregory Kane is an African-American columnist at the *Baltimore Sun* and a Pulitzer Prize finalist. His post-election commentary is a biting indictment of Mississippi that captures the opinion of many non-Mississippians when they think of the state.

The American Legislative Exchange Council recently issued its annual "Report Card on American Education." By a delicious irony, the report was sent out about the time those geniuses in Mississippi voted overwhelmingly to keep a Confederate logo on the state flag.

The council, based in Washington, is the nation's largest bipartisan, individual-membership association of state legislators, with nearly 2,400 members. Its report ranks each state by academic achievement. Anyone care to guess where, of 50 states and the District of Columbia, Mississippi ranked?

Bingo! Dead last, coming in at No. 51. Yes, even the folks in Washington, thought to have the nation's worst public schools, ranked ahead of Mississippi. Mind you, D.C. came in at No. 50, an embarrassment that doesn't stop its residents from clamoring for statehood. . . .

It's fitting that Mississippians chose to keep the emblem. A symbol representing a country, the Confederate States of America, that felt a certain pride in keeping its population ignorant should be on the flag of the country's most ignorant state.

In fact, it might do well to look at how the rest of the states that formed the old Confederacy did in the report. None of those 11 states finished in the top 25. The highest was Virginia, ranked No. 27. Then came Texas at 35, Florida at 38, North Carolina at 40, Arkansas at 42 and then Nos. 45 through 49 were Tennessee, Alabama, Georgia, South Carolina and Louisiana, respectively.

When the Confederate States of Bubbadom were formed in 1861, educating the populace was clearly not at the top of the agenda.

Apparently, not much has changed in the ensuing 140 years. When Confederate flag wavers claim they're proudly celebrating the history of their ancestors by their act, folks in places such as Iowa (No. 1), Maryland (No. 24) and New Jersey (No. 25)—where the residents aren't too bright but still smarter than residents of the Bubba states— have to ask: pride in what?

The Confederacy was one of the most backward, repressive and ignorant countries that ever existed. Its most flagrant sin was the perpetuation of chattel slavery, which latter-day Confederate flag-wavers excuse by claiming that most whites in the South didn't own slaves.

They say it with pride, but that's nothing to be proud of. Most whites in the antebellum South were poor, illiterate and uneducated, as were most of the black slaves. The disparity in wealth was so great that few could own slaves. That made the South not a democracy but an oligarchy. It wasn't a noble experiment in participatory democracy and racial brotherhood, as today's Confederate flag-wavers claim. For the slaves, it was a police state. For free blacks and poor whites, it wasn't much better.

Still, those rubes in Mississippi—and their fellow Confederate flag-lovers elsewhere—will swear that the old South was a paradise, an idyllic place of happy nigras serving kindly massas mint juleps. Or, since they persist in living in denial about the South's horrid racial history, neo-Confederates will claim that the Confederacy's war against the Union was a heroic defense of states' rights. The states' rights to do what, exactly?

To keep large numbers of its citizens in illiteracy and ignorance, to name just one of the those dubious "rights." The Confederate battle flag is thus a fitting symbol for Mississippi, as well as its sister Southern states, judging by their poor-to-mediocre academic performances.

You would think that today's Mississippians, blacks and whites, would say, "To hell with the Confederate flag. Let's raise our educational level." Barring a mass migration of brainiacs to the state, that's not likely to happen in the near future.

Black and white Mississippians will continue to fight the old battles, not realizing that, if they win the old ones, they haven't won much and haven't even begun to fight the new one.

And the new one, for all Americans—black, white, Asian, Hispanic, Native American, Northerners and Southerners—is education.

Our students are woefully behind those of other industrialized nations in math and science. Visit Europe, and you'll find most students there learning at least two foreign languages. American students struggle with English. Ask the average Mississippian to describe God, and he'll pain a picture of a drawling, moonshine-swigging, good ol' boy whose native tongue is Americanese.

The National Association for the Advancement of Colored People and other black organizations should abandon the fight against the Confederate battle flag.

If its wavers want to live in a past marked by violence, ignorance and repression, let them. More progressive-thinking Americans have more important battles to fight.

TED RALL, 2001[10]

Ted Rall is a syndicated columnist and cartoonist who lives on the east coast. His work, including the essay that follows, is characterized by a high degree of sardonic and biting commentary.

There are three problems with democracy.

First and foremost, very few citizens consider their vote valuable enough to be worth dragging their butts out of their E–Z Boys on Election Day. Then, when they summon the energy to exercise their franchise, and it really does come down to single votes, the system breaks down. Case study: Florida. Worst of all? The system sometimes works.

On April 17, Mississippi voters voted 65 percent to 35 percent in favor of keeping their current state flag, which features—as many Southern state flags did until recently—the Confederate battle flag in its upper left-hand corner. Not since California's immigrant-bashing Proposition 187 has the case against letting the people decide ever been made more eloquently.

Predictably, the vote was split along racial lines. According to Reuters: "There was no racial breakdown of the vote but predominantly white precincts voted overwhelmingly—as much as 90 percent in some cases—for the old design." The state is about 61 percent white and 36 percent black. In Very Ol' Miss, the descendants of slaves have a long way to go before they're accorded basic respect from those whose ancestors trafficked in human flesh.

Typical of contemporary politics, neither side in the flag debate ponied up honest reasons for its stance. The pro-Confederate flag side cited "Southern heritage" and "history," but those are precisely the best reasons for getting rid of the thing. Southern apologists are correct when they note that the Civil War wasn't fought over slavery alone, but emancipation was by far the happiest result of Sherman's march. And regardless of the honor of those who fought in gray, during the last 136 years the stars and bars have served as an anything-but-subtle icon of the Klan, racism and segregation. That flag is the flag of Bull Connor, George Wallace and David Duke. Those who wish that the South would rise again are far more interested in putting blacks back into chains—or at least in the back of the bus—than independence from an oppressive federal government.

"Heritage?" Southerners ought to be ashamed of their past.

Supporters of a new, Confederate-free flag also missed the mark in their public statements. A flier published by a pro-business group read: "It's not right that our kids can't find good jobs close to home because companies won't locate in our state, but it's a fact. . . . They have the wrong idea about Mississippi. A State flag that includes the Confederate flag just adds to those false opinions."

For one thing, the ballot results prove that those opinions aren't false. For another, IBM and Ford cozied up to Adolf Hitler; why, white voters reasoned, would they avoid Mississippi because of a little old flag? If corporate America is staying away, ethics and racial sensitivity have nothing to do with it.

The truth is harsh and painfully obvious. The only reason you stick a Confederate decal on your car or truck is to scream a big "f___ you" to passing blacks. The only reason you vote to fly that same flag over public buildings is because you think that "f___ you" ought to be the official state motto. The April 17 referendum told black Mississippians that they are hated and reviled by their white neighbors.

I'm a privileged white male Ivy League graduate living in Manhattan, but it doesn't require a huge empathic leap to fathom the day-to-day horror of being black in an ass-backward dump like Mississippi. Not only does your job suck, your boss fantasizes that you're all gussied up in shackles. The best that can be said about Mississippi's white voters is that they care more about their depraved "heritage" than your everyday reality.

MICHAEL KELLEY, 2002[11]

As the following two letters illustrate, even after the election, Mississippians continued to battle over the flag. Michael Kelley, who signed his letter to the editor of the *Clarion-Ledger*, Brevet Colonel, CSA, was a resident of Pascagoula and the commander of the 37th Texas Calvary. His letter appeared as a rejoinder to those who believed that the victory of the 1894 flag would continue to cast Mississippi in a negative light.

The U.S. flag has far more connection with negative symbolism than the battle flag or the Mississippi flag.

It flew over New England slave ships that brought Africans to America; it flew over efforts to commit genocide against the native peoples; it flew over Union troops while they raped, robbed and murdered black Southerners; it flew with Union General Turchin in Athens, Ala., where he earned his conviction for war crimes by a Union court martial; and it flew over Union officers who hunted own and tortured black Southerners to get them to volunteer for the U.S. Colored Troops.

The continuation of the state flag was chosen in democratic referendum by a majority of the people. Unless I recall my civics classes incorrectly, we base our government on the democratic process and it would seem the people did unify to make their choice known.

"Let us stand together. Although we differ in color, we should not differ in sentiment," said LT Gen. Nathan Bedford Forrest, CSA, July, 1875.

TOMMY J. MUIRHEAD, 2002[12]

Tommy Muirhead of Flora wrote the following letter to the editor of the *Clarion-Ledger* in response to claims by Mel Evans, who had previously contended on the editorial page that the Confederate emblem was a symbol of slavery.

[Mel Evans] needs to know the true facts about my flag, which I fly proudly on my property.

The South had it's [sic] own president, senate, congress, constitution, currency and military.

The South wanted to be its own country. It was about secession.

No Confederate flags ever flew on any slave ships. The Confederate flag had nothing to do with slavery.

General Robert E. Lee was the greatest general that ever lived. He didn't believe in slavery at all.

I don't care how hard you try you can't change history.

Find out the real history and learn to live with it.

NOTES

CHAPTER 1

1. *True Relation of the Hardships Suffered By Governor Don Hernando De Soto and Certain Portuguese Gentlemen in the Discovery of the Province of Florida. Now Newly Set Forth by a Gentleman of Elvas* in *The De Soto Chronicles: The Expedition of Hernando De Soto to North America in 1539–1543*, edited by Lawrence A. Clayton, Vernon James Knight, Jr., and Edward C. Moore. Vol. 1 of 2 (Tuscaloosa and London: University of Alabama Press, 1993), 104–13.
2. Chicaca was an Indian village, likely located near Cotton Gin Port, that included nearly 200 residencies.
3. Mavilla was a large Indian village located north of modern-day Mobile, Alabama. Soto and his men had recently fled Mavilla after massacring Indians there.
4. "Cacique," the word Spaniards used to describe indigenous West Indian and North American chiefs, derives from the Haitian word for "lord."
5. Sauechuma was a nearby village that was a rival of Chicaca.
6. Juan Ortiz was the translator for the Soto mission. He had spent more than a decade in the southeast before the Soto mission began.
7. *Iberville's Gulf Journals*, translated and edited by Richebourg Gaillard McWilliams (University, Alabama: University of Alabama Press, 1981), 42–50.
8. As a measure of distance, "league" is an imprecise word, though when used by mariners, historians believe it is the equivalent of approximately three nautical miles.
9. Biscayans were large boats designed to be rowed or poled. Like life boats on modern vessels, they were stored aboard sailing vessels. When shallow water prevented a sailing vessel from reaching shore, sailors manned biscayans to do so.
10. Vermilion was a bright red or scarlet colored fabric, in this case likely made of wool.

11. Francophone settlers in Canada and Louisiana called the Native American pipe a "calumet." Often calumets had a long carved stem decorated with feathers. Native Americans regarded the calumet as a sign of peace and friendship.

12. Sagamite was a porridge made of coarse hominy.

13. D'Iberville used "Annochy" for the Biloxi Indians; the Moctoby were a small band of Native Americans associated with the Biloxi and Pascagoula Indians living on the Pascagoula River.

14. By 1699, the Mougoulascha had recently moved to near modern-day Baton Rouge, Louisiana, where they lived among the Bayougoula. Traditionally, however, they had lived in the area of Iberville Parish, Louisiana and were then generally called the Quinipissa.

15. The Quascha lived near the mouth of the Arkansas River; the Yagueneschyto were a band of the Chitimacha living near the confluence of Mississippi River delta and the Atchafalaya Basin.

16. The Byloccy, Moctoby, and Pascagoula Indians lived along the Pascagoula River. The Ouma (Houma) originally lived in central Mississippi, but by 1699, they had moved to the area near the Mississippi River around the 38th parallel, which is the contemporary border between Mississippi and Louisiana. "Thecloel" is an early French name for the Natchez Indians. The Bayacchyto lived along Bayou Chico in what is now Louisiana.

17. A felucca is a single masted, flat bottomed sailing vessel best suited for navigation on rivers, narrow inlets, and protected bays.

18. *The Journal of Sauvole: Historical Journal of the Establishment of the French in Louisiana by M. De Sauvole*, translated and edited by Jay Higginbotham (Mobile: Colonial Books, 1969).

19. Halberds were fierce weapons. They were part spear and part battle-axe mounted on a pole five to seven feet in length.

20. Actually, the English ship captain was William Lewis Bond.

21. Chicachas is a village name associated with an Indian group living above modern-day Memphis.

22. In the early 1700s, the Tonicas or Tunicas resided along the Yazoo River, but soon afterwards, they removed to the area in modern-day Louisiana near the confluence of the Red and Mississippi rivers.

23. The Chactas were originally from modern-day north Alabama and Georgia but moved to the east bank of the Mississippi River near Memphis.

24. Henri de Tonty was the companion of the French explorer La Salle, who had in the mid-1780s originally claimed the Lower Mississippi Valley for Louis XIV.

25. The Apalaches lived between the Apalachicola and Aucila Rivers in modern-day Florida.

26. The river of the Colapissas (or as usually seen the Acolapissas) was the Pearl.

CHAPTER 2

1. Régis du Roullet to Périer, March 16, 1731 in *Mississippi Provincial Archives, French Dominion: Collected, Edited, and Translated by Dunbar Rowland and A. G. Sanders,* rev. ed., Patricia Galloway, editor (Baton Rouge, Louisiana State University Press, 1984), 66–71.
2. The Cushtushas were an Indian nation near New Orleans. Yowani was a Choctaw village near modern-day Shubuta, Clarke County, Mississippi.
3. The Chakchiuma lived along the Yazzo, Yalobusha, and Tallahatchie rivers.
4. Périer to Maurepas, December 10, 1731 in *Mississippi Provincial Archives, French Dominion,* 101–105.
5. The Coroas or Koroas lived in the Red River basin of Louisiana.
6. Diron d'Artaguette to Maurepas, September 1, 1734 in *Mississippi Provincial Archives, French Dominion,* 134–37.
7. Noyan to Maurepas, January 4, 1739 in *Mississippi Provincial Archives, French Dominion,* 162–65.
8. Chickasaw Chiefs to Vaudreuil, August 27, 1743 in *ibid.,* 212.
9. Vaudreuil to Maurepas, December 28, 1744 in *ibid.,* 230–31.

CHAPTER 3

1. Casandra Carter to Jane Everett, November 25, 1811, typescript in editor's possession.
2. Matthew Carter, Jr. to Griffin Mizell, March 1, 1813, in editor's possession.
3. The rumors of war to which Carter refers are those related to the War of 1812 and the conflict between southeastern Indians and white settlers in the Mississippi Territory.
4. Matthew Carter, Jr. and Ann Carter to Griffin Mizell, September 8, 1822, in editor's possession. The letter is postmarked Jackson County. Mizell lived in Telfair County, Georgia.
5. Matthew Carter, Jr. to Griffin Mizell, October 16, 1825, in editor's possession.
6. Matthew Carter, Jr. to Griffin Mizell, November 16, 1828, in editor's possession.
7. Matthew Carter, Jr. to Griffin Mizell, June 7, 1829, in editor's possession.
8. Benjamin Lafayette Smith "Autobiography," Mississippi Department of Archives and History, Jackson, Mississippi.
9. Joseph Benjamin Lightsey Diaries, Mississippi Department of Archives and History, Jackson, Mississippi.
10. The words "gininiseing," "iligatering," and "colbin mitginhugin" are the character's understanding of words that appeared in the agricultural journal.

The only one that can be reasonably interpreted is "iligatering," which was likely intended to be "irrigating."

11. Amanda Worthington to Albert Worthington, October 12, 1857, Worthington Family Papers, Mississippi Department of Archives and History, Jackson, Mississippi.

12. Amanda Worthington to Albert D. Worthington, October 27, [1857], Worthington Family Papers, Mississippi Department of Archives and History, Jackson, Mississippi.

13. Amanda Worthington to Albert D. Worthington, January 17, 1858, Worthington Family Papers, Mississippi Department of Archives and History, Jackson, Mississippi.

14. Franklin L. Riley, "Diary of a Mississippi Planter, January 1, 1840," *Publications of the Mississippi Historical Society* 10 (1909), 312–39.

CHAPTER 4

1. A. Hutchinson, *Code of Mississippi: Being an Analytical Compilation of the Public and General Statutes of the Territory and State* ... (Jackson: Price and Fall, 1848), 513 15, 517, 519–21.

2. Jan Hillegas and Ken Lawrence, editors, *The American Slave: A Composite Autobiography*, Supplement, Series I, volume 10, *Mississippi Narratives*, *Part 5* (Westport, Conn.: Greenwood Press, 1977), 1935–39.

3. Jan Hillegas and Ken Lawrence, editors, *The American Slave: A Composite Autobiography*, Supplement, Series I, volume 6, *Mississippi Narratives, Part 1* (Westport, Conn.: Greenwood Press, 1977), 122–25.

4. Jan Hillegas and Ken Lawrence, editors, *The American Slave: A Composite Autobiography*, Supplement, Series I, volume 6, *Mississippi Narratives, Part 1* (Westport, Conn.: Greenwood Press, 1977), 239–40, 243–46, 248–49.

5. Jan Hillegas and Ken Lawrence, editors, *The American Slave: A Composite Autobiography*, Supplement, Series I, volume 6, *Mississippi Narratives, Part 1* (Westport, Conn.: Greenwood Press, 1977), 255, 264–66.

6. Thomas Shackleford, *Proceedings of the Citizens of Madison County, Mississippi, At Livingston in July 1835, In Relation to the Trial and Punishment of Several Individuals Implicated in a Contemplated Insurrection in this State* (Jackson: Mayson and Smoot, 1836), 8–11.

7. James M. Wesson to John Francis Hamtrack Claiborne, August 11, 1858, J. F. H. Claiborne Papers, Southern Historical Collection, Edward Wilson Round Library, University of North Carolina, Chapel Hill, North Carolina. The Claiborne Papers have been microfilmed, and a copy is available at the Mississippi Department of Archives and History.

CHAPTER 5

1. Harry Dickinson to William Sharkey, September 3, 1859, McGavock Family Papers, Tennessee State Library and Archives, Nashville, Tennessee (microfilm). The original letter is located in the McGavock Family Papers in the Southern Historical Collection, University of North Carolina, Chapel Hill, North Carolina.

2. *Letter of Lucius Q. C. Lamar, In Reply to Hon. P. F. Liddell, of Carrollton, Mississippi* (n.p.: 1860). The letter is dated December 10, 1860.

3. "An Address Setting Forth the Declaration of the Immediate Causes Which Induce and Justify the Secession of Mississippi From the Federal Union and the Ordinance of Secession" and "An Ordinance to Dissolve the Union Between the State of Mississippi and Other States United with her Under the Compact Entitled 'The Constitution of the United States of America' " appear as separately numbered appendices at the end of *Journal of the State Convention and Ordinances and Resolutions Adopted in January, 1861, With an Appendix* (Jackson: E. Barksdale), 3–7.

4. *Congressional Globe*, 1861, 487.

5. See, William Need to John J. McRae, February 8, 1861, John J. McRae Papers, Mississippi Department of Archives and History, Jackson, Mississippi.

6. William Need's association with the Democratic Natchez *Free Trader*, a newspaper that began publication in 1835, is not certain.

7. Giuseppe Garibaldi is broadly regarded as the father of modern Italy. In 1860, his military campaign to unite all of Italy reached its apex when he overthrew the Kingdom of Naples and captured Sicily. As a politician committed to Italian nationalism, Garibaldi cherished the individual right to self-determination, a fact that made him a icon among secessionists.

8. "Dismal Swamp tragedies" refers to Nat Turner's slave rebellion in August 1831. The rebellion began in Southhampton County, Virginia and reached into the Dismal Swamp, an immense swamp that spills over into North Carolina. The rebellion resulted in the deaths of about 50 whites and the execution of the slaves suspected of participating, including Turner. For many white southerners, the Turner rebellion served as evidence of the intentions of all slaves.

9. Sir Peter and Lady Teazle were characters in Richard Brinsley Sheridan's 1777 comedy, *The School for Scandal*, an often-anthologized play that is still staged today.

CHAPTER 6

1. Matthew A. Dunn to Virginia Dunn, September 5, 1863, Matthew A. Dunn and Family Papers, Mississippi Department of Archives and History, Jackson, Mississippi.

2. Matthew A. Dunn to Virginia Dunn, October 13, 1863, Matthew A. Dunn and Family Papers, Mississippi Department of Archives and History, Jackson, Mississippi.

3. Matthew A. Dunn to Virginia Dunn, November 7, 1863, Matthew A. Dunn and Family Papers, Mississippi Department of Archives and History, Jackson, Mississippi.

4. Matthew A. Dunn to Virginia Dunn, August 1, 1864, Matthew A. Dunn and Family Papers, Mississippi Department of Archives and History, Jackson, Mississippi.

5. Matthew A. Dunn to Virginia Dunn, August 22, 1864, Matthew A. Dunn and Family Papers, Mississippi Department of Archives and History, Jackson, Mississippi.

6. Jeremiah S. Gage to Mrs. P. W. Gage, July 3, 1863, Gage Family Collection, Department of Archives and Special Collections, University of Mississippi, Oxford, Mississippi.

7. George Washington Cable, ed., "A Woman's Diary of the Siege of Vicksburg" *Century Magazine* vol 30, 1885.

8. Cordelia Lewis Scales to Loulie W. Irby, October 1862, Cordelia Lewis Scales Letters, Southern Historical Collection, Edward Round Wilson Library, University of North Carolina, Chapel Hill, North Carolina.

9. Scales had been deathly ill with "congestion." Her physician thought she might have "a brain fever" and ordered her hair cut short so that he might more effectively place ice packs on her head.

10. Cordelia Lewis Scales to Loulie W. Irby, January 27, 1863, Cordelia Lewis Scales Letters, Southern Historical Collection, Edward Round Wilson Library, University of North Carolina, Chapel Hill, North Carolina. The January 27 one is dated "Destruction Hollow," reflecting the changed conditions on her Oakland Plantation.

11. Martha Cragan to Governor Charles Clark, November 28, 1863, Governor's Papers, RG 27, Mississippi Department of Archives and History, Jackson, Mississippi.

12. Cotton cards were handheld paddles used to separate cotton fiber in preparation for spinning.

13. Governor Charles Clark to Martha Cragan, December 6, 1863, Governor's Papers, RG 27, Mississippi Department of Archives and History, Jackson, Mississippi.

CHAPTER 7

1. Contract between W. R. Bath and Ned Littlepage, January 5, 1866, Records of the Assistant Commissioner for the State of Mississippi, Bureau of Refugees,

Freedmen, and Abandoned Lands, National Archives, Washington, D. C. (Microfilm reel 49.)

2. Julia Dixon to Harry St. John Dixon, January 25th, [1869], Harry St. John Dixon Papers, Mississippi Department of Archives and History, Jackson, Mississippi.

3. Julia Dixon to Harry St. John Dixon, November 5, 1869, Harry St. John Dixon Papers, Mississippi Department of Archives and History, Jackson, Mississippi.

4. Julia Dixon to Harry St. John Dixon, January 29, [1870], Harry St. John Dixon Papers, Mississippi Department of Archives and History, Jackson, Mississippi.

5. *Testimony Taken by the Joint Select Committee to Inquire into the Condition of the Affairs in the Late Insurrectionary States: Mississippi*, vol 1 of 2 (Washington, D.C.: Government Printing Office, 1872), 272–74.

6. Isaac Bourne to President Ulysses S. Grant, September 1, 1874 Source— Chronological File, Northern and Southern Districts of Mississippi, General Records of the Department of Justice, Record Group 60, National Archives, Washington, D.C. (Microfilm roll 1).

7. Henry B. Whitfield to E. Pierrepont, November 6, 1875, Source— Chronological File, Northern and Southern Districts of Mississippi, General Records of the Department of Justice, Record Group 60, National Archives, Washington, D.C. (Microfilm roll 1).

8. Colfax County is now called Webster County.

9. William Frazee to Judge R. A. Hill, July 8, 1876, in Source—Chronological File, Northern and Southern Districts of Mississippi, General Records of the Department of Justice, Record Group 60, National Archives, Washington, D.C. (Microfilm roll 2).

10. Anonymous to I. Tarbell, August 25, 1876, Source—Chronological File, Northern and Southern Districts of Mississippi, General Records of the Department of Justice, Record Group 60, National Archives, Washington, D.C. (Microfilm roll 2).

11. James Zachariah George, a lawyer from Carrollton, was the chair of the state Democratic party during the latter days of Reconstruction. In the early 1880s, he became a United States Senator.

12. The Grant Parish, Louisiana cases, were decided by the U.S. Supreme Court in 1875. The cases are officially-known as *United States v. Cruikshank et al.* The cases stemmed from a number of convictions under the Enforcement Act of 1870. The Supreme Court ruled that the previous convictions should be overturned, claiming that charges against the offenders lacked specificity.

13. "A Negro" to Governor John M. Stone, September 26, 1878, John M. Stone Papers, Mississippi Department of Archives and History, Jackson, Mississippi. The letter was written from Baltimore, Maryland.

14. When citing the deaths of thousands of Mississippians, the author refers to the results of the yellow fever epidemic of 1878 and 1879.

15. The Chisholm referred to was William Wallace Chisholm, a Republican politician and minor officer holder in Kemper County. In 1877, local citizens accused Chisholm of murdering a long-time rival, and Chisholm secured himself and his family in jail. A mob tore into the jail, murdering Chisholm and two children. Charles Caldwell was a Republican and state senator. In 1875, a group of whites murdered him on the streets of Clinton to rob the Republican party of a strong African-American voice.

16. "A Negro" to Stone, undated, John M. Stone Papers, Mississippi Department of Archives and History, Jackson, Mississippi. The letter was written from Washington, D.C.

17. Winfield S. Featherstone of Holly Springs, the individual most likely referred to in the letter, had achieved the rank of general during the Civil War. Yet, it is not certain to which of Mississippi's many Featherstones the author refers. The author implies that Featherstone was dead, but in 1879, ex-General Featherstone was, in fact, still alive.

18. Reuben Reynolds was a leader of the Democratic party in Monroe County.

19. James G. Blaine, a Senator from Maine, was a leading contender for the Republican nomination for president in 1880, but he did not receive the nomination. In 1884, his party nominated him, but Grover Cleveland defeated him in the general election.

CHAPTER 8

1. Minute Book, Holmes County Grange #7, Patrons of Husbandry, Mississippi State Grange Papers, Mississippi Department of Archives and History.

2. "Circular Letter to members of the Farmers Alliance of Mississippi," n.d., in Baskin Family Papers, Mississippi State University, Starkville, Mississippi. The letter was signed by J. H. Beeman, J. R. Moore, S. R. Lamb—all members of the executive committee.

3. Frank Burkitt to Walter B. Barker, July 21, 1892, John M. Stone Papers, Mississippi Department of Archives and History.

4. "Prohibition the Remedy," Meridian, *Mississippi White Ribbon*, June 30, 1890.

5. "Hookworm Disease: Don't Pollute the Soil," in *Report of the Board of Health of Mississippi From September 30, 1909 to June 30, 1911* (Nashville: Press of Brandon Printing Company, 1911), 119–143.

6. *Mississippi Boy Convicts* (Jackson: Hederman Brothers Printers, 1911).

7. Rene Bache, "Shrimps and Babies," *The Technical World Magazine* 16 (January 1912): 497–504.

8. Lewis Hines was an acclaimed, muckraking photojournalist.

CHAPTER 9

1. Frank H. Foote to Charles K. Regan, July 30, 1890, Charles K. Regan Papers, Mississippi Department of Archives and History.
2. Carthage *Carthaginian*, September 5, 1890.
3. Jackson *Clarion-Ledger*, September 11, 1890.
4. Carthage *Carthaginian*, September 19, 1890.
5. *Journal of the Proceedings of The Constitutional Convention, of the State of Mississippi, Begun at the City of Jackson on August 12, 1890, and Concluded November 1, 1890* (*Jackson: E. L. Martin, 1890*) 618–620.
6. Nellie Nugent Somerville, *Moral Leadership: The True Basis of Woman Suffrage* (Greenville, Miss.: *Democratic Times* Printers, n.d.). A copy can be found in the microfilmed Nellie Nugent Somerville Papers, Mississippi Department of Archives and History.

CHAPTER 10

1. Charles Banks to Booker T. Washington, July 9, 1914, in *The Booker T. Washington Papers, 1914–1915*, vol. 13 of 14, Louis R. Harlan and Raymond W. Smock, editors (Urbana and Chicago: University of Illinois Press, 1984), 84–85.
2. Perry Wilbon Howard was a lawyer in Jackson. He was the leading African American in the Republican party in Mississippi and, in fact, served as special assistant to the U.S. Attorney General throughout much of the 1920s. Afterwards, he practiced law in Washington, D.C.
3. Emmett J. Scott, "Letters of Negro Migrants of 1916–1918," *Journal of Negro History* 4 (July 1919): 290–340; idem, "Additional Letters of Negro Migrants of 1916–1918," *Journal of Negro History* 4 (October 1919): 312–465.
4. The letter, written to R. S. Abbott, editor of the *Chicago Defender*, is dated September 22, 1917.
5. The letter is dated May 12, 1917.
6. The letter is dated May 16, 1917.
7. P. K. Meschack (Ellisville, Mississippi) to Governor John M. Stone, August 24, [18]95, Record Group 27, Mississippi Department of Archives and History.
8. "Text Books in Mississippi," *Opportunity: Journal of Negro Life* 18 (April 1940): 99–100.
9. Jackson *Daily Clarion-Ledger*, April 14, 1937.
10. Presumably, the Chairman Summers referred to is the Republican John William Summers, a six-term U.S. representative from Washington. Yet, Summers served between 1919 and 1933, running unsuccessfully to recover his seat in 1934 and 1936.

11. Harris Dickson, "Phrases of the People," in *American Stuff: An Anthology of Prose & Verse by Members of the Federal Writers' Project* (New York: The Viking Press, 1937), 149–52.

12. Richard Wright, "The Ethics of Living Jim Crow: An Autobiographical Sketch," in *American Stuff: An Anthology of Prose and Verse by Members of the Federal Writers' Project* (New York: The Viking Press, 1937), 41–46, 48–50.

CHAPTER 11

1. G. T. Grove to Franklin D. Roosevelt, September 20, 1932, quoted in William T. Schmidt, editor, "Letters to Their President: Mississippians to Franklin D. Roosevelt, 1923–1933." *Journal of Mississippi History* 40 (Fall 1978), 231–52.

2. J. F. Craig to Franklin D. Roosevelt, February 2, 1933, in ibid.

3. G. E. Rivers to Franklin D. Roosevelt, December 22, 1932, in ibid.

4. Will Danis to Franklin D. Roosevelt, November 11, 1932, in ibid.

5. Untitled resolution dated September 5, 1931, signed W. T. Childress (chair), B. D. Moss (secretary) in Theodore G. Bilbo Papers, McCain Library and Archives, University of Southern Mississippi, Hattiesburg, Mississippi.

6. "Effect of the Cotton-Cut," in Holly Springs *The South Reporter*, January 6, 1933.

7. R. L. Musgrove to Henry A. Wallace (Secretary of Agriculture), April 22, 1935, William M. Colmer Papers, Box 1, University of Southern Mississippi.

8. G. B. Mayberry to H. L. Mitchell, November 23, 1939, Southern Tenant Farmers Union Papers, Microfilm reel 13.

9. Hyacinth Yerger to William M. Colmer, March 2, 1934, in William M. Colmer Papers, Box 19, University of Southern Mississippi.

10. Lorena A. Hickok to Harry Hopkins, June 11, 1934, Harry Hopkins Papers, Roosevelt Presidential Library, Hyde Park.

11. F. M. Tatum to William M. Colmer, April 19, 1938, Box 334, Colmer Papers, University of Southern Mississippi.

12. R. H. Crosby to William M. Colmer, June 8th, 1938, Colmer Papers, University of Southern Mississippi.

13. Employees of Tatum Lumber Company to William M. Colmer, April 8, 1938, Colmer Papers, University of Southern Mississippi.

14. Resolutions of the Gulfport Central Labor Union, American Federation of Labor, of a meeting of the Central Labor Unions of Vicksburg, Jackson, Meridian, Hattiesburg, Laurel, Biloxi, Bay St. Louis, Gulfport, held Gulfport Saturday, May 14. Signed Robert L. Reed, Secty. Central Labor Union, Gulfport, Colmer Papers, University of Southern Mississippi.

15. E. I. Bateman to William M. Colmer, May 25, 1938, Colmer Papers, University of Southern Mississippi.

16. Richard Cox was the president of Gulf Park College, a private women's college located in Long Beach. The college grounds were later acquired by the state of Mississippi, which established a campus of the University of Southern Mississippi at the location.

CHAPTER 12

1. Tom P. Brady, *Black Monday* (Brookhaven, Miss. Published by the Citizens' Councils of America, Jackson, 1955), 59–65, 88–89.
2. Brady's original footnote attributes the quote to a speech by Abraham Lincoln delivered at Springfield, Illinois, on June 16, 1858.
3. Brady attributes the quote to O. O. Emmerich, editor of the McComb, *Enterprise Journal.*
4. Brady attributes the quote to the *Constitution of the Union of Soviet Socialist Republics.*
5. The Scottsboro case, the trial for rape to which several African-American youths were cruelly and criminally subjected, occurred in 1936. After the so-called Scottsboro boys allowed the Communist Party in the United States to supply them legal counsel, proponents of massive resistence pointed to the work of communists on behalf of the defendants as evidence of communist involvement in the Civil Rights Movement.
6. Brady attributes the quote to William Shakespeare, *Hamlet*, IV:3.
7. Mrs. Aubin Newman to J. Skelly Wright, February 16, 1956, Papers of Judge J. Skelly Wright, Box 12, file 1, Library of Congress.
8. "Letter of the Week," in the NAACP Papers, Part 3c, Microfilm Reel 1.
9. Speech of T. R. Howard in "Transcript of Meeting of Legal Educational Advisory Committee and Negro Leaders, July 30, 1954," unpaginated, George Washington Owens Papers, Mississippi Department of Archives and History.
10. J. H. White to E. J. Stringer, D.D.S., August 25, 1954, NAACP Papers, Series II, Box A-227, Library of Congress.
11. N. R. Burger, "The President's Corner," *Mississippi Education Journal* 33 (February 1956), 97.

CHAPTER 13

1. From *Freedom is a Constant Struggle: An Anthology of the Mississippi Civil Rights Movement.* (Montgomery, AL: Black Belt Press), 360–63.
2. Mack Charles Parker was taken from the jail at Poplarville, having been accused of raping a white women, in 1959 and lynched.

3. Sandra Adickes Oral History, volume 731, Center for Oral History and Cultural Heritage, University of Southern Mississippi.

4. Vernon Dahmer was a successful farmer and business owner in Forrest County. He was also a prominent member of the NAACP and a leader in the effort to get blacks registered to vote. In 1966, Sam Bowers and other white supremacists fire bombed the Dahmer home, causing Mr. Dahmer to suffer fatal injuries.

5. Then known as Victoria Gray Jackson, Mrs. Jackson was a national board member of the Southern Christian Leadership Conference and one of the founders of the Mississippi Freedom Democratic Party (MFDP). In the summer of 1964, she ran on the MFDP ticket for the U.S. Senate seat held by John C. Stennis.

6. "Declaration of Independence, Palmer's Crossing, Hattiesburg, Mississippi, St. John Methodist Church," *Freedom News*, July 25, 1964, unpaginated.

7. Untitled essay by Neretha Stewart in the Ellin Freedom Summer Collection, McCain Library and Archives, University of Southern Mississippi, Hattiesburg, Mississippi.

8. Larry B., "What I Don't Like About Hattiesburg," *Student Voice of True Light*, July 20, 1964, unpaginated. Available in the Ellin Freedom Summer Collection, USM.

9. Mattie Jean Wilson, "When I was Going on Hardy Street," *Student Voice of True Light*, July 20, 1964, unpaginated. Available in the Ellin Freedom Summer Collection, USM.

10. Mrs. Mable L. V. "What I Think About Hattiesburg," *Student Voice of True Light*, July 25, 1964, unpaginated. Available in the Ellin Freedom Summer Collection, USM.

11. Benton D., "When the Wall Falls," *Student Voice of True Light*, undated, unpaginated. Available in the Matthew Zwerling Freedom Summer Collection, Box 11, USM.

12. Melvin B. Tolson taught at Wiley College in Marshall, Texas between 1924 and 1947. He took a leave of absence from his job to pursue a master's degree in 1930–1931 at Columbia University. While in New York, he began writing poetry and completed a thesis that required he interview artists associated with the Harlem Renaissance. Between 1947 and his death in 1966, he taught at Langston University in Langston, Oklahoma, serving as mayor between 1954 and 1960. The poem quoted here can not be identified, but likely, considering the style, was an early work.

13. From Credentials Committee Transcript, Papers of Joseph L. Raugh, Library of Congress, quoted in Kay Mills, *This Little Light of Mine: The Life of Fannie Lou Hamer* (New York: Plume, 1994), 119–21.

CHAPTER 14

1. "Inaugural Address," typescript in the Paul B. Johnson Papers, University of Southern Mississippi, Hattiesburg, Mississippi.

2. From "Catfish 1980," a press release dated October 20 and issued by the Mississippi Crop & Livestock Reporting Service.

3. The ten surveyed states were: Alabama, Arkansas, California, Georgia, Idaho, Louisiana, Mississippi, Missouri, Pennsylvania, and Texas.

4. Mississippi growers utilized 32,620 acres of water surface, and they planned to expand their operations by 11,480 acres during 1981. The primary water supply for growers was wells; well water accounted for 95 percent of the water in ponds.

5. Jim Estrin, " Pickets in the land of catfish," Jackson, *Clarion Ledger*, August 16, 1981.

6. The four advertisements and related documents can be located in the "Economic Development" vertical file in the McCain Library and Archives, University of Southern Mississippi.

7. Ricky Baldwin, "The Mississippi Choctaw are still caught in the middle," University, *Daily Mississippian*, November 9, 1993.

8. Shep Montgomery, "State's economy still rolling on casino gambling wave: But can the economy still boom amid sagging manufacturing?" *Mississippi Business Journal* (March 14, 1994).

CHAPTER 15

1. "Flag Special" on *First Friday* (Jackson: Mississippi ETV, 2000), videorecording.

2. Ibid.

3. Ibid.

4. Jackson, *Clarion-Ledger*, January 3, 2001, 8A, "Religious Group full of 'hypocrites.' "

5. Jackson, *Clarion-Ledger*, January 4, 2001, 8A, "Will 'C-L' accept flag vote outcome?"

6. Jackson, *Clarion-Ledger*, January 6, 2001, 15A, "Flag war needs compromise on both sides."

7. Phil Hardwick, "From the Ground Up Look out! Red and Fred tackle the volatile flag issue," *Mississippi Business Journal* 23 (January 15–January 21, 2001).

8. Wally Northway, "One Writer's Perspective: Emotions can cloud judgement on 'symbolic' issues," *Mississippi Business Journal* 22 (February 7–February 13, 2000).

9. Gregory Kane, "Mississippi is Deserving of Its Worst Schools Rank," *Baltimore Sun*, April 25, 2001.

10. Ted Rall, "One Mississippi, Two Mississippis: State Voters Make the Argument Against Democracy," Common Dreams News Center, wsyiwyg://2http://www.commondreams.org/views01/0419-01.htm.
11. Jackson, *Clarion-Ledger*, May 7, 2002, "U.S. flag connected with far more negative symbolism."
12. Ibid, "Learn the facts of Confederate flag."

INDEX

Printed in the United States
98823LV00001B/73-99/A